HARDEN'S

London
Restaurants
2000

© Harden's Guides, 1999

ISBN 1-873721-28-5 (paperback)
ISBN 1-873721-32-3 (bonded leather)

British Library Cataloguing-in-Publication data: a catalogue record for this book is available from the British Library.

Printed and bound in Finland by Werner Söderström Corporation

Research and editorial assistant: Antonia Russell

Harden's Guides
14 Buckingham Street
London WC2N 6DF

Distributed in the United States of America by Seven Hills Book Distributors, 1531 Tremont Street, Cincinnati, OH45214

CONTENTS

Ratings & prices

RATINGS & PRICES

Ratings

Our rating system is unlike those found in other guides (most of which tell you nothing more helpful than that expensive restaurants are, as a general rule, better than cheap ones).

What we do is to compare each restaurant's performance with other restaurants in the same price-bracket.

This system has the advantage that it helps you find – whatever your budget for any particular meal – where you will get the best "bang for your buck".

The following qualities are assessed:

> **F** — Food
> **S** — Service
> **A** — Ambience

The rating indicates that, *in comparison with other restaurants in the same price-bracket*, performance is …

> **❶** — Exceptional
> **❷** — Very good
> **❸** — Good
> ④ — Mediocre
> ⑤ — Disappointing

Prices

The price shown for each restaurant is the cost for one (1) person of an average three-course *dinner* with half a bottle of house wine and coffee, any cover charge, service and VAT. Lunch is often cheaper. With BYO restaurants, we have assumed that two people share a £5 bottle of off-licence wine.

Telephone number – until Easter 2000, the 'new-style' numbers shown in this book will work only if dialled in their entirety, including the '020'.

Map reference – shown immediately after the telephone number. (Major coffee shop chains are not shown on the maps.)

Last orders time – the first entry in the small print (Sunday may be up to 90 minutes earlier).

Opening hours – unless otherwise stated, restaurants are open for lunch and dinner seven days a week.

Credit and debit cards – unless otherwise stated, Mastercard, Visa, Amex and Switch are accepted.

Dress – where appropriate, the management's preferences concerning patrons' dress are given.

Smoking – cigarette smoking restrictions are noted. Pipe or cigar smokers should always check ahead.

Special menus – if we know of a particularly good value set menu we note this (eg "set weekday L"), together with its formula price (FP) calculated exactly as in 'Prices' above. Details change, so always check ahead.

FROM THE EDITORS

This is the ninth edition of our annual guide, designed to help you find the right London restaurant for any particular occasion and then, as briefly as possible, to tell you everything you need to know about it.

The Survey

Once again this year, the guide has been compiled with the benefit of a much-enlarged survey. This year over 4,000 people participated (some 18 per cent more than last year). We are very grateful to all who did so, and also to those who have helped expand the range of the survey by introducing friends and colleagues.

Reporters eat out, on average, 3.4 times a week. Thus the survey reflects the experiences of some 700,000 meals eaten in the preceding 12 months.

Whose views?

We have ourselves visited every restaurant or chain listed in this book – always anonymously and at our own expense. But, for the most part, we use these personal experiences only to help us to interpret and explain the results of the survey – we do not seek to superimpose our personal views. Rather, we seek from our informed starting-point to analyse and comment on the views and ratings from our 'reporters'. In the rare cases we feel that we can add something by noting our dissent from the general view, we do so in the text. The numerical ratings reflect the survey results.

The survey, however, can provide no useful information on the 'hot' summer openings (upon which we receive little or no commentary), and it is of only limited assistance where there has been a recent major chef or ownership change. In these cases, our own opinions are, of necessity, more to the fore, and, in these cases only, any numerical rating reflects our personal opinions.

We believe that it is this pragmatic combination of the views of thousands of people with the impressions from our own personal visits which enables the production of an up-to-date guide of unequalled reliability.

Please help us to make the next edition even more accurate. If you register for the free updates, you will be invited, in the summer of 2000, to take part in our next survey. **If you take part in the survey, you will, on publication, receive a complimentary copy of Harden's London Restaurants 2001.**

Richard Harden   **Peter Harden**

SURVEY – MOST MENTIONED

These are the restaurants which were most frequently mentioned by reporters. (Last year's position is given in brackets.) An asterisk* indicates a first appearance in the list of a recently opened or re-launched restaurant.

1	The Ivy (2)
2	Oxo Tower (1)
3	Mirabelle*
4	Bank (4)
5	Le Caprice (12)
6=	Livebait (14)
6=	Bluebird (3)
8	Quaglino's (6)
9	Le Pont de la Tour (5)
10	The Square (18)

11	Blue Elephant (11)
12	The River Café (13)
13	Nobu (23)
14	Belgo (17)
15	Bibendum (15)
16	Vong (20)
17	The Criterion (9)
18	Zafferano (26)
19	Mezzo (8)
20	Le Palais du Jardin (10)

21=	Gordon Ramsay*
21=	The Sugar Club (38)
23	Coq d'Argent*
24	Chez Bruce (-)
25	Le Gavroche (25)
26	City Rhodes (19)
27=	Chutney Mary (35)
27=	Axis*
29	La Poule au Pot (-)
30	La Tante Claire (22)

31=	Andrew Edmunds (32)
31=	Titanic*
33	The Avenue (36)
34	Café Spice Namaste (27)
35	Rules (-)
36	L'Oranger (16)
37	Savoy Grill (-)
38	fish!*
39	1 Lombard Street*
40	Kensington Place (28)

SURVEY – NOMINATIONS

Ranked by the number of reporters' votes for:

Top gastronomic experience

1 Gordon Ramsay*
2 The Ivy (2)
3 Mirabelle*
4 The Square (4)
5 Le Gavroche (6)
6 Chez Bruce (-)
7 Nobu (-)
8 The River Café (8)
9 Zafferano (-)
10 Club Gascon*

Favourite

1 The Ivy (1)
2 Le Caprice (2)
3 Chez Bruce (8)
4 The River Café (7)
5 Nobu (-)
6 Mirabelle (-)
7 Zafferano (6)
8 Le Palais du Jardin (4)
9 The Square (-)
10 Clarkes (-)

Best for business

1 City Rhodes (1)
2 Bank (4)
3 Savoy Grill (5)
4 Oxo Tower (3)
5 1 Lombard Street*
6 Le Pont de la Tour (2)
7 The Ivy (7)
8 Square (6)
9 Coq d'Argent*
10 Axis*

Best for romance

1 La Poule au Pot (1)
2 Andrew Edmunds (2)
3 The Ivy (6)
4 Julie's (7)
5 Oxo Tower (3)
6 Launceston Place (5)
7 The Blue Elephant (4)
8 Odette's (-)
9 Le Caprice (10)
10 The Criterion (8)

Best breakfast/brunch

1. Pâtisserie Valerie
2. Bank
3. Simpsons-in-the-Strand
4. Savoy River Restaurant
5. La Brasserie
6. Claridges Restaurant
7. Le Caprice
8. Fox & Anchor
9. Chelsea Bun Diner
10. Montana

Best bar/pub food

1. The Eagle
2. Churchill
3. Anglesea Arms
4. The Engineer
5. The Havelock Tavern
6. Chelsea Ram
7. The Ladbroke Arms
8. The Enterprise
9. The Cross Keys
10. Windsor Castle

Most disappointing cooking

1. Oxo Tower
2. Bluebird
3. Mezzo
4. Titanic
5. Quaglino's
6. La Tante Claire
7. Pharmacy
8. The River Café
9. The Criterion
10. Mirabelle

Most overpriced restaurant

1. Oxo Tower
2. Oak Room Marco Pierre White
3. The River Café
4. Mezzo
5. Bluebird
6. Le Pont de la Tour
7. Quaglino's
8. Le Coq d'Argent
9. Bibendum
10. La Tante Claire

SURVEY – HIGHEST RATINGS

FOOD   SERVICE

£60+

FOOD	SERVICE
1 Gordon Ramsay	1 Le Gavroche
2 The Square	2 Connaught
3 Le Gavroche	3 Gordon Ramsay
4 Tatsuso	4 Savoy Grill
5 Capital Hotel	5 Capital Hotel

£50-£59

FOOD	SERVICE
1 Nobu	1 Dorchester Grill
2 Pied à Terre	2 Aubergine
3 Aubergine	3 The Lanesborough
4 City Rhodes	4 Pied à Terre
5 The Birdcage	5 Le Soufflé

£35-£49

FOOD	SERVICE
1 Chez Bruce	1 Oslo Court
2 Clarke's	2 Le Caprice
3 Chezmax	3 Chezmax
4 Assaggi	4 The Ivy
5 Zafferano	5 Assaggi

£25-£34

FOOD	SERVICE
1 Chez Liline	1 Caraffini
2 Fung Shing	2 Soulard
3 Pizza Metro	3 Sotheby's Café
4 Monsieur Max	4 Springbok Café
5 Mandarin Kitchen	5 Quincy's

£24 or less

FOOD	SERVICE
1 Lahore Kebab House	1 Tandoori Lane
2 Ranoush	2 Mandalay
3 Faulkner's	3 Anglo Asian Tandoori
4 Shree Krishna	4 Khan's of Kensington
5 Kastoori	5 The Old School Thai

AMBIENCE

1 The Ritz
2 Blakes Hotel
3 Windows on the World
4 Savoy River Restaurant
5 Connaught

1 The Birdcage
2 The Lanesborough
3 Dorchester Grill
4 Aubergine
5 The Waldorf Meridien

1 La Poule au Pot
2 Brasserie 24
3 The Ivy
4 Blue Elephant
5 Momo

1 Sarastro
2 Bah Humbug
3 Maggie Jones's
4 Andrew Edmunds
5 Langan's Bistro

1 Gordon's Wine Bar
2 Bar Italia
3 The Westbourne
4 Café 209
5 Souk

OVERALL

1 Gordon Ramsay
2 Le Gavroche
3 Connaught
4 The Square
5 Capital Hotel

1 Aubergine
2 Dorchester Grill
3 The Birdcage
4 Nobu
5 Pied à Terre

1 The Ivy
2 Le Caprice
3 Chez Bruce
4 Oslo Court
5 Chezmax

1 Caraffini
2 The Gate
3 Soulard
4 The White Onion
5 The Green Olive

1 Café 209
2 Anglo Asian Tandoori
3 The Atlas
4 Tandoori Lane
5 Yum Yum

SURVEY – BEST BY CUISINE

These are the restaurants which received the best average food ratings.

We have divided the most represented restaurant cuisines into two price-brackets, while of the less represented cuisines just the best three are shown.

For further information about restaurants which are particularly notable for food, the lists on page 188 indicate, using an asterisk (*), restaurants with an exceptional or very good rating for food.

Modern British

£35 and over
1 Chez Bruce
2 Clarke's
3 City Rhodes
4 The Glasshouse
5 755

Under £35
1 Mesclun
2 The Havelock Tavern
3 The Anglesea Arms
4 The Mason's Arms
5 The Apprentice

French

£35 and over
1 Gordon Ramsay
2 Pied à Terre
3 Aubergine
4 Chezmax
5 The Square

Under £35
1 Monsieur Max
2 Club Gascon
3 The White Onion
4 Les Associés
5 Bleeding Heart

Italian/Mediterranean

£35 and over
1 Assaggi
2 Zafferano
3 Tentazioni
4 Grissini
5 Cibo

Under £35
1 Del Buongustaio
2 The Green Olive
3 Luigi's Delicatessen
4 Aglio e Olio
5 Made in Italy

Indian

£35 and over
1 Zaika
2 Vama
3 Tamarind
4 Salloos
5 Star of India

Under £35
1 Lahore Kebab House
2 Shree Krishna
3 Kastoori
4 Battersea Rickshaw
5 Rasa

Chinese

£35 and over
1 Ken Lo's Memories
2 Mao Tai
3 Dorchester, Oriental
4 Zen
5 Mr Wing

Under £35
1 Fung Shing
2 Royal China
3 Mandarin Kitchen
4 Mr Kong
5 Hunan

Japanese

£35 and over
1 Shogun
2 Tatsuso
3 Matsuri
4 Miyama
5 Suntory

Under £35
1 Inaho
2 Café Japan
3 Kulu Kulu
4 Ikkyu
5 Itsu

British, Traditional
1 Connaught
2 Dorchester Grill
3 Wiltons

Vegetarian
1 The Gate
2 Blah! Blah! Blah!
3 Food for Thought

Burgers, etc
1 Ed's Easy Diner
2 Wolfe's
3 Hard Rock Café

Pizza
1 Pizza Metro
2 Pizzeria Castello
3 Eco

East/West
1 Nobu
2 The Birdcage
3 Vong

Thai
1 Chiang Mai
2 Latymers
3 Esarn Kheaw

Fish & Chips
1 Faulkner's
2 Toff's
3 Brady's

Fish & Seafood
1 Chez Liline
2 Lobster Pot
3 Back to Basics

Greek
1 Vrisaki
2 Halepi
3 Lemonia

Spanish
1 Cambio de Tercio
2 Gaudi
3 Lomo

Turkish
1 Gallipoli
2 Iznik
3 Sarcan

Lebanese
1 Ranoush
2 Maroush
3 Al Hamra

TOP SPECIAL DEALS

The following menus allow you to eat in the restaurants concerned at a significant discount compared to evening à la carte prices.

The prices used are calculated in accordance with our usual formula (ie three courses with house wine, coffee and tip).

Special menus are by their nature susceptible to change – please call ahead to check that they are still available.

Weekday lunch

£55+ Oak Room MPW

£40+ Gordon Ramsay
La Tante Claire

£35+ Capital Hotel
1837 at Brown's Hotel
Floriana
Halcyon Hotel
The Landmark Hotel
Suntory

£30+ Aubergine
The Halkin
Ikeda
L'Incontro
Nobu
Putney Bridge
Zen Central

£25+ Al Bustan
Che
Chez Moi
Chutney Mary
Defune
Dorchester, Oriental
Gaudi
Livebait
Montpeliano
Mr Chow
Offshore
Roussillon
Salloos
San Martino
Turner's

£20+ 3 Monkeys
Artigiano
Bengal Clipper
The Brackenbury
Bradley's
Buchan's
Café du Jardin
Chiswick
Del Buongustaio
English Garden
Goolies
Icon
Jindivick
Kensington Place
Leonardo's

Lou Pescadou
Montana
Motcombs
Orsino
Oxo Tower
La Poule au Pot
Rain
Rasa Samudra
Red Fort
The Room
Sonny's
Stratford's
Le Suquet
Villa Bianca
Wódka
Zen
Zen Garden

£15+ Big Easy
Boudin Blanc
Café Lazeez
& Café City Lazeez
Cantinetta Venegazzú
Carnevale
The Cross Keys
Cuba Libre
Daphne
La Dordogne
English House
Globe Restaurant
Harbour City
Inaho
Kavanagh's
Newton's
Odette's
Pasha
Le P'tit Normand
Le Sacré-Coeur
Singapore Garden
Sofra
Sushi Wong
Le Versailles
Wilson's

£10+ Angel of the North
Ben's Thai
Bu San
East One
Galicia
The Good Cook
Khan's of Kensington

Khyber Pass
Lemonia
Mandalay
The Polish Club
Thai Square
Toff's
Vegia Zena
Weng Wah House

£5+ Diwana Bhel-Poori
House
Sarcan

Pre/post theatre (and early evening)

£40+ Dorchester Grill

£35+ Capital Hotel

£30+ Bentley's
Simpsons-in-the-Strand
Teatro
The Waldorf Meridien

£25+ The Avenue
Bank
Bluebird
Che
Christopher's
Circus
The County Hall
Launceston Place
Livebait
Luigi's
Mezzo
Savoy Grill
Veeraswamy

£20+ Archduke Wine Bar
Bertorelli's
Café des Amis du Vin
Café du Jardin
Charco's
Chiswick
Footstool
Luna Nuova
Manzi's
Mezzonine
Orsino
Orso
Oxo Tower
Red Fort
The Room
Stephen Bull
Stratford's
The Tenth

£15+ La Bouchée
Carnevale
L'Estaminet
Hujo's
Kavanagh's

Navajo Joe
Plummers
Seashell
Sushi Wong
Townhouse Brasserie

£10+ Hornimans
Mon Plaisir

Sunday lunch

£45+ The Ritz

£40+ Dorchester Grill

£35+ Capital Hotel
Putney Bridge
Wiltons

£30+ Coq d'Argent
Mirabelle

£25+ Al Bustan
Bluebird
Chutney Mary
The County Hall
English Garden
The Ivy
Mezzo
La Porte des Indes
Sonny's

£20+ Les Associés
Browns
Buchan's
Café du Jardin
Café Lazeez
Goolies
Kensington Place
Leonardo's
192
La Poule au Pot
Stratford's
Village Bistro
Zen
Ziani

£15+ Bengal Clipper
Mims
Newton's
Odette's
Orso

£10+ Babur Brasserie
Malabar

How the major groups measure up

SR	A-Z	Belgo	Harvey Nichols	Grp Chez Gérard	MPW	Conran
		Ivy Caprice				
	Aubergine Zafferano					
					Mirabelle	
20						
						P dl T B&G
		Sheekey's				
	Ken Lo SW1					
	Oranger	Pasha	Prism			
40	**GROUP**					
	Ken Lo W8			B. St Q'tin		
		GROUP	5th Fl Café	Scotts		
			GROUP		Criterion	
		Daphne's				
60			5th Fl Rest.			
			Oxo Tower	Café Fish		Sartoria Blue Print
				GROUP **GROUP**		Orrery
				Oak Room		
						But Whf
	Spiga			Ch. Gérard Bertorelli's Livebait Richoux Soho Soho		
		Collection Bam-Bou				P dl T
80						**GROUP**
						Coq d'Arg
	Spighetta				Quo Vadis	Bluebird Quaglino's
		Belgo			Big Chef	
						C del Ponte
						Zinc Mezzo
100					Titanic	Mezzonine

THE CHAIN GANG

Myth has it that restaurants are owned and run by jolly individuals in big white hats. However, the contemporary London reality could not be more different – of the 40 top restaurants listed on page 9, only about a tenth conform to the slightest extent to this stereotype. Nowadays, the ownership of most major restaurants (and, progressively, smaller ones too) would be more accurately characterised by men in grey suits. Consolidation of the industry means ever more places are becoming parts of larger combines.

The qualities of the respective groups are therefore of increasing importance to restaurant-goers. This is our second annual review, from the customer's point of view, of the industry's real 'movers and shakers'. We cover the top 12 most talked-about 'quality' groups (which have at least three restaurants apiece).

This year – as well as calculating each group's average Food, Service and Ambience ratings from the results of our survey of over 4,000 reporters – we have also derived an overall Satisfaction Rating (SR). This SR gives equal weight to Food, Service and Ambience, and the same weight to each brand in a group (regardless of size). The resulting ranking is expressed as a 'percentile '– 1 being the best possible figure and 100 the worst.

The members of the respective groups used for the calculations are referred to in the write-ups, or – for the six most important groups – the table opposite. Groups are ranked in descending order of SR.

F S A

1. Nigel Platts-Martin (SR 13)   ❶❷❷

By a considerable margin, London's best group. All of his establishments – the *Square, Chez Bruce* and, now, the *Glasshouse* – are distinguished by cooking of the very first rank. The group is still small and the challenge is to maintain quality as it expands.

2. Red Pepper Group (SR 25)   ❷❷❸

The *Red Pepper* (which gives its name to the group) is, in fact, the weakest member of this otherwise consistently good-to-very-good group. It also includes two of the best local restaurants in town, the *White Onion* and *Green Olive*, as well as the commendable *Purple Sage*.

3. Kensington Place Group (SR 31)   ❸❷❷

The KP group – owner of *Kensington Place*, *Launceston Place* and the *Brackenbury* – is a good-overall, if slightly complacent, performer. It was acquired in mid-1999 by the group which runs the Avenue and Circus (whose standards are lower).

4. A-Z Restaurants (SR 40) ❷❸❸

A-Z's rating is dragged down by some unremarkable
middle-market performers (*Spighetta*, *Spiga* and
Ken Lo's W8). However, this should not be allowed to
distract too much attention from the fact that it runs
possibly London's best Italian (*Zafferano*), one of its best
French restaurants (*Aubergine*), a high-quality oriental
(*Ken Lo's SW1*) and the re-emerging *Oranger*.

5. Savoy Group (SR 42) ❸❷❷

With so many larger restaurants paying so little attention
to service or comfort, the solid virtues of this group of
de luxe hotel restaurants are becoming more apparent.
Cooking tends to be the weak link.
Group members: *Connaught, Savoy River Room*, *Savoy Grill*,
Claridge's, Simpson's-in-the-Strand

6. Belgo Group (SR 48) ❸❸❷

Belgo Group brings together a number of extremely
disparate sub-groups under a single corporate umbrella.
The moules/frites emporia from which the group
takes its name are poor and greedily priced – sustained,
apparently, by slick marketing. Mogens Tholstrup's
restaurants – *Bam-Bou*, *Daphne's*, *Pasha SW7* and
The Collection – are similar, in a more upmarket way.
His great knack is to make his restaurants 'in'-places
without apparently worrying too much about details
like food or service. By standing this logic on its head,
the division run by Jeremy Corbin and Christopher King
– the wonderful *Ivy/Caprice* (and now *Sheekey's*) group –
would, if it had remained a stand-alone, still rate as the
best in London.

7. Harvey Nichols (SR 52) ❸❸❷

It used to be easy to say that Harvey Nichols places, (the
Oxo Tower and the *Fifth Floor*) tended to be 'ambience-led'
which was a polite way of saying that food and service
weren't up to much. They've confounded this nice,
simple analysis by opening *Prism* – a good all-rounder
that's actually strongest in the food department!

8. Bank Group (SR 58) ❸❸④

Owned by fishmongers Cutty's, this fast-expanding group
is most notable for its newest member, *fish!*, whose clean,
no-nonsense, middle-market chain-prototype is already
widely regarded for its food and service – perhaps the
fact that atmosphere's the weakest link in the formula is
part of the attraction! *Bank,* the best of the mega-
brasseries, is also set to multiply, even if its standards are
drifting rather. The Dulwich outpost, *Lawn,* performs
creditably enough.

9= Groupe Chez Gérard (SR 68)   ③③②

Groupe Chez Gérard should really be called Curate's Egg Restaurants – most properties have their own individual permutations of strengths and weaknesses, with only *Scott's* a consistently good performer across the board. In other cases good(ish) food is let down by poor(ish) ambience (*Livebait,* for example) or vice-versa (*Soho Soho*). The eponymous steak-houses are fairly so-so across the board, with food the weakest link.

9= Marco Pierre White (SR 68)   ③④③

Considering the ballyhoo MPW generates, he is associated with a lot of surprisingly lacklustre ventures. His stellar new baby, *Mirabelle*, is the only indisputable bright spot. The past year has seen the closure of the *Café Royal Grill*, a (presumably forced) revamp of *Quo Vadis*, the launch of the culinarily disastrous *Titanic*, falling standards at the *Big Chef* and continuing failure to address the dismal service at the *Criterion*. Reporters remain largely immune to the attractions that so bedazzle the Michelin men at his flagship, the *Oak Room*.

11. Conran Restaurants (SR 79)   ④④③

London's best-known group seems all set to become a collection of upmarket tourist traps, exploiting its high (and carefully promoted) name-recognition to charge very high prices for products of a very poor standard. A harsh summary? Look at the group's dismal consumer satisfaction profile (shown on the chart on page 18) – all but one of its restaurants are in the bottom two-fifths of the league, and some are so poorly rated they can't really sink much further! Note also that half the top ten restaurants most often nominated 'overpriced' are members of the group (p11). Most telling of all, however, are the views – expressed in vehement terms, and to an extent quite unmatched elsewhere – of the many reporters who now perceive the group to be incompetent, greedy and arrogant.

12. Gruppo – Oliver Peyton (SR 90)   ④④④

Mr Peyton runs a pair of bar/nightclubs – *Atlantic Bar & Grill* and *Mash* – which masquerade as restaurants. Judged as the former, they have a certain appeal (if one which seems to be fading). Judged as the latter, they are simply a disaster. *Coast* has long been the odd man out – a restaurant first, and a 'scene' second – but it too is now in decline.

THE RESTAURANT SCENE

As we approach the Millennium...

London's restaurants are in the rudest of health. This year we list a record 102 new restaurants (ten up on last year, and some three times the number in our first, 1992 guide). Even this figure understates the true level of activity, though, ignoring as it does the expansion of existing chains, and also the fact that we have felt it right to cover only a representative sample of the many new chain-prototypes. Closures, at 43 this year, were down from 48 last year (and 58 two years ago).

The buzz at most levels of the market has been notably absent at the very top. Gordon Ramsay emerges as the capital's undoubted culinary king, almost by default. In recent years, he vied with Pierre Koffmann (at La Tante Claire) as reporters' gastronomic champion, but the latter's disastrous move to Knightsbridge has robbed the capital of a great restaurant. In general, 'real' people seem ever less interested in Michelin-pleasing temples of gastronomy. For the first time, neither Chez Nico nor the Oak Room MPW made reporters' Gastronomic top 10!

Each year we list what appear to us to be the ten most significant openings of the previous 12 months. This year, our selection is as follows:

Asia de Cuba	The Park
fish!	Pétrus
Giraffe	Prism
The Glasshouse	The Real Greek
Grano	Zaika

This coming winter will undoubtedly see quite a lot of central activity (with China House, home and Isola three big names to look out for), but, as the above selection suggests, what has been apparent over the last 12 months is that much of the activity has been in the less traditionally 'obvious' areas. With the West End, in particular, arguably beginning to approach saturation, this is likely to be the pattern for the immediate future.

The '90s have seen a sea change in London's restaurant scene and it now has a pace which would have been unthinkable when we wrote our first guide. From being horribly backward, this is now one of the world's most interesting eating-out cities. After such a surge of growth, it is tempting to think the market must now be mature. We believe that this is far from being the case. Many of the more notable developments of these boom years have pre-supposed a gaucheness and ignorance on the part of customers which, if it ever existed, lasted only briefly. Addressing the real need – the provision of varied, quality dining at reasonable prices in all moderately affluent parts of the capital – is a process which has only just begun.

OPENINGS

The Admiral Codrington
Aglio e Olio
Al Duca
L'Amandier
Angel of the North
Aroma II
Artigiano
Asia de Cuba
The Atlas
Ayoush
Babe Ruth's NW3
Bam-Bou
Barra
Basilico
The Black Truffle
Brompton Bay
Buona Sera W1
Café Lazeez W1
Café City Lazeez
La Candela
Canyon
China House
China Jazz
Chunk
The Crown
Deco
Denim
Dibbens
The Duke of Cambridge
Fairuz
FireBird
fish!
Friends
Frith Street
Gili Gulu
Giraffe
The Good Cook
Grano
Ha Ha
Halepi NW3
Hot John's
Idaho
Indigo N1
Isola
Itsu
Lanes
Latitude
Laughing Gravy
Lawn
The Little Square
Lomo
Lundum's
Maremma

Metrogusto
Mohsen
Moorgate Oriental
The Mortimer
mychi
Noho NW3
Offshore
Olio & Farina
Pacific Oriental
La Pampa
The Park SW1
The Park NW6
Passione
Pepe Nero
La Perla SW6
Pétrus
Philip Owens at the ICA
The Poet
Popeseye SW15
Porchetta Pizzeria
Prism
prospectGrill
Pukkabar
Quilon
Rasa Samudra
The Real Greek
Riso
Santa Fe
Sauce
Shimla Pinks
Shoeless Joe's WC2
6 Clarendon Rd
Smiths of Smithfield
Soup Opera
Soup Works
Tajine
Tas
Terrace
Thai Square
The Thatched House
3 Monkeys
Tiger Tiger
Time
Titanic
Toast
The Vale
Yima
Zaika
Zander

CLOSINGS

Albero & Grana
Anonimato
Au Jardin des Gourmets
Beauchamp's
Bistrot 2 Riverside
Boyd's
Café des Arts
Café O
Café Royal Grill Room
Café Sofra (all sites)
Chavot
Cy
dell'Ugo
Fashion Café
Football Football
Hamine
Hothouse Bar & Grill
Interlude
Justin de Blank
Kartouche
Kalamaras, Mega
Mange 2
Masako
Museum Street Café
No 1 Cigar Club
Pasta di Milano (all sites)
La Perla SW3
The Room
San Frediano (again)
Les Saveurs
Secret Garden
Sheekey's EC4
Silks & Spice NW8
Simply Nico SW10
Smokey Joe's
Smollensky's W1
Snows by the Pond
Sri India
33
Thomas Goode
Vegetarian Cottage
Woz (briefly Bistrorganic)
Zujuma's

DIRECTORY

Comments in "double quotation-marks" were made by
reporters.

Establishments which we judge to be particularly notable
have their NAME IN CAPITALS.

a.k.a. WC1 £ 33 ❸❷❷

18 West Central St (020) 7836 0110 4–1C

"Surprisingly good" modern British cooking is served at this "sophisticated" and "loud" Covent Garden-fringe "warehouse", where you "eat above a lively bar". / 11.30 pm, Fri & Sat 1 am, Sun 9.30 pm; closed Mon & Sat L.

Abbaye EC1 £ 26 ❹❹❸

55 Charterhouse St (020) 7253 1612 9–2A

It's "better than Belgo" (which is not, in truth, hugely difficult), and this large Belgian outfit in Smithfield offers "good mussels" and "the best beer selection". / 10.30 pm; closed Sat & Sun; no smoking area.

The Abingdon W8 £ 34 ❸❸❸

54 Abingdon Rd (020) 7937 3339 5–2A

The "intimate" booths are the top spots at this "relaxed", "neighbourhood" bar/restaurant in a quiet Kensington street; it delivers "consistently good food and service". / 11 pm; set Dinner £24(FP).

L'Accento Italiano W2 £ 29 ❸❷❸

16 Garway Rd (020) 7243 2201 6–1B

"Simple dishes, well cooked" and a "friendly" welcome maintain a loyal local following for this "good-value" Bayswater Italian; it's "not one of those places stuck in the '70s". / 10.30 pm; smart casual.

Adams Café W12 £ 24 ❸❷❹

77 Askew Rd (020) 8743 0572 7–1B

Shepherd's Bush couscous house whose "unusual food and pleasant service" make it a "good local eatery" (it's licenced, but you can also BYO); it also has its fans "as a daytime workers' café". / 11 pm; D only.

Admiral Codrington SW3 £ 30 ❸❸❷

17 Mossop St (020) 7581 0005 5–2C

The "delightfully light and airy" new restaurant at the rear of 'The Cod' – a once infamously Sloaney Chelsea boozer – attracts a crowd that's more 'Prada' than 'Barbour'; its "shortish menu" of brasserie staples is "well-executed". / 11.15 pm.

Afghan Kitchen N1 £ 14 ❷❹❸

35 Islington Gn (020) 7359 8019 8–3D

"A tiny place with big portions", this "unassuming" Afghani café in Islington is "a great deal"; "slow service is the only drawback". / 11 pm; closed Mon & Sun; no credit cards.

Aglio e Olio SW10 £ 24 ❷❸❸

194 Fulham Rd (020) 7351 0070 5–3B

"Delicious, basic Italian food" that's "good value" (by the standards of Chelsea's 'Beach') has already made this "noisy" newcomer a popular stand-by. / 11.30 pm.

Al Bustan SW1 £40 ❸❷④
27 Motcomb St (020) 7235 8277 2–4A
"Usually good", not unattractive Belgravia Lebanese, which deserves a wider following. / 11 pm; set weekday L £26(FP).

Al Duca SW1 £32 ❷❸❸
4-5 Duke Of York St (020) 7839 3090 3–3D
Muted, minimalist St James's modern Italian, which opened just as we went to press; a day-one visit found variable cooking (with some highlights), but the modest prices disarm criticism and owner Claudio Pulze's record suggests it's more likely to get better than worse. / 10.45pm; closed Sat L & Sun.

Al Hamra W1 £39 ❷④④
31-33 Shepherd Mkt (020) 7493 1954 3–4B
"Top-notch", if pricey, cooking is the highlight at this long-established Lebanese, characterfully located in Shepherd Market (with great outside tables in summer); "unless you speak Arabic, you may be treated like a tourist". / 11.30 pm; no Switch.

Al San Vincenzo W2 £43 ❷❷④
30 Connaught St (020) 7262 9623 6–1D
The Borgonzolo family's "tiny", "quiet" Bayswater venture is still venerated by its fans for its "very personal" service and some of the most "interesting" Italian cooking in town; this year, however, there were a number of "disappointing" overall experiences. / 10 pm; closed Sat L & Sun; no Amex & no Switch.

Al Sultan W1 £35 ❷❷④
51-52 Hertford St (020) 7408 1155 3–4B
Lesser-known Lebanese, on the fringe of Shepherd Market, whose small fan club rates it "one of the best"; rather characterless décor, however, dampens enthusiasm. / 11.30 pm.

Al's EC1 £22 ④④❸
11-13 Exmouth Mkt (020) 7837 4821 8–4D
"Decent" snacks – "great all-day breakfasts", in particular – are still praised at this Clerkenwell diner, but it has lost its place as local hang-out of choice. / 11 pm.

Alastair Little W1 £47 ❸❸④
49 Frith St (020) 7734 5183 4–2A
Small and Spartan Soho spot – once celebrated for its modern British cooking – which is, at last, staging a recovery; some "can't really fault it", nowadays, but many still find it "uninspired". / 11 pm; closed Sat L & Sun.

Alastair Little, Lancaster Road W11 £35 ❸❸④
136a Lancaster Rd (020) 7243 2220 6–1A
"Interesting" cooking is again winning greater acclaim at the "cramped" and slightly "sterile" Ladbroke Grove outpost of this once path-breaking modern British chef. / 11 pm; closed Sun.

Alba EC1   **£ 29**   ❷④④

107 Whitecross St   (020) 7588 1798   9–1B
*"A great local Italian for the Barbican", offering "real pizzas"
and other "deft, classic Italian dishes"; the stark style can
seem rather "chilly".* / 11 pm; closed Sat & Sun.

Alfred WC2   **£ 30**   ❷❸④

245 Shaftesbury Ave   (020) 7240 2566   4–1C
*"Spartan" and "noisy", it may be, but the "real surprise" at
this "affable" Theatrelander – decked out like a '50s kitchen –
is the strength of its "good all-round" British menu; there's also
an interesting selection of drinks.* / 11 pm, Sat 11.30 pm; closed Sun.

All Bar One   **£ 27**   ④④④

289-293 Regent St, W1   (020) 7467 9901   3–1C
3-4 Hanover St, W1   (020) 7518 9931   3–2C
36-38 Dean St, W1   (020) 7479 7921   4–2A
5-6 Picton Pl, W1   (020) 7487 0161   3–1A
7-9 Paddington St, W1   (020) 7487 0071   2–1A
108 New Oxford St, WC1   (020) 7307 7980   4–1A
19 Henrietta St, WC2   (020) 7557 7941   4–3C
48 Leicester Sq, WC2   (020) 7747 9921   4–4A
58 Kingsway, WC2   (020) 7269 5171   2–1D
84 Cambridge Circus, WC2   (020) 7379 8311   4–2B
311-313 Fulham Rd, SW10   (020) 7349 1751   5–3B
587-591 Fulham Rd, SW6   (020) 7471 0611   5–4A
152 Gloucester Rd, SW7   (020) 7244 5861   5–2B
126-128 Notting HI Gt, W11   (020) 7313 9362   6–2B
74-76 Westbourne Grove, W2   (020) 7313 9432   6–1B
197-199 Chiswick High Rd, W4   (020) 8987 8211   7–2A
1 Liverpool Rd, N1   (020) 7843 0021   8–3D
1-3 Hampstead Ln, N6   (020) 8342 7861   8–1B
79-81 Heath St, NW3   (020) 7433 0491   8–1A
60 St John's Wood High St, NW8   (020) 7483 9931   8–3A
1 Chicheley St, SE1   (020) 7921 9471   2–3D
30 London Bridge St, SE1   (020) 7940 9981   9–4C
32-38 Northcote Rd, SW11   (020) 7801 9951   10–2C
7-9 Battersea Sq, SW11   (020) 7326 9831   10–1C
527-529 Old York Rd, SW18   (020) 8875 7941   10–2B
42 Mackenzie Walk, E14   (020) 7513 0911   1–3D
91-93 Charterhouse St, EC1   (020) 7553 9391   9–1B
18-20 Appold St, EC2   (020) 7247 6841   9–1C
63 Threadneedle St, EC2   (020) 7614 9931   9–2C
16 Byward St, EC3   (020) 7533 0301   9–3D
3 Cannon St, EC4   (020) 7220 9031   9–3C
44-46 Ludgate HI, EC4   (020) 7653 9901   9–2A
*"Cheerful" service contributes to the success of this
mushrooming chain of "loud" and "fun" bars; even those who
think they're "naff" admit they're "reliable", and "portions are
huge".* / Mon-Thu 10 pm, Fri-Sun 9 pm; Hanover St, Kingsway, City and E14
branches close part of weekend; no booking.

Alma SW18 £23 ④⑤❷
499 Old York Rd (020) 8870 2537 10–2B
*Wandsworth hostelry, popular for its "great pub atmosphere"
– "especially on rugby days" – and "honest" grub.* / 10.30 pm;
closed Sun D.

Alounak £20 ❶❸❸
10 Russell Gdns, W14 (020) 7603 1130 7–1D
44 Westbourne Grove, W2 (020) 7229 0416 6–1B
*"Great kebabs and BYO economy" provide "excellent value for
money" at this "authentic" Persian duo, near Olympia and in
Bayswater.* / Midnight; no Amex.

Alphabet W1 £29 ❷④❶
61-63 Beak St (020) 7439 2190 3–2D
*"Groovy" Soho bar, where a "seriously happening"
twentysomething crowd gathers; the "imaginative" grub wins
approval.* / 10.30 pm; closed Sat L & Sun; no Amex; no booking.

Amandier W2 £43 ❸❸④
26 Sussex Pl (020) 7723 8395 6–1D
*"Interesting French cuisine", from the team formerly at La
Ciboulette (RIP), is making fewer waves from these obscure
new Bayswater premises (which are not helped by deadeningly
suburban décor); the basement Bistro Daniel offers a
fewer-frills approach.* / 10.30 pm; closed Sat L & Sun.

Anarkali W6 £25 ❷❸④
303-305 King St (020) 8748 1760 7–2B
*The décor is "standard Brit-Indian", but the "reliable,
high-quality food" (particularly the specials) puts this
quarter-centenarian Hammersmith curry house a cut above
the norm.* / Midnight.

Andrew Edmunds W1 £30 ❸❷❶
46 Lexington St (020) 7437 5708 3–2D
*"Once introduced, you return many times as an old friend" to
this "fun", "squashed", "no-fuss" "charmer", in a candlelit
Soho townhouse; the modern British cooking is "usually good
value", and the amazing wine list a "great draw".* / 10.45 pm.

Angel of the North N1 £23 ❸❸❸
353 Upper St (020) 7704 8323 8–3D
*It has an "odd atmosphere" – "neither a café or a restaurant"
– but some tip this "cramped" Islington spot, with its "unusual
mix" of dishes, as a "surprisingly good" newcomer.* / 11 pm;
no Amex; set weekday L £15(FP).

The Anglesea Arms W6 £26 ❶⑤❸
35 Wingate Rd (020) 8749 1291 7–1B
*"Great ingredients, imaginatively prepared" guarantee that
"seats are in short supply" at this "buzzy", Brackenbury
Village gastropub; it's "smoky", though, and service is "still so
slow" – "you'll be drunk before you get your dinner".* / 10.45 pm;
no Amex; no booking.

Anglo Asian Tandoori N16   £ 19   ②②②
60-62 Stoke Newington Ch St   (020) 7254 9298   1–1C
Low-lit Stoke Newington Indian whose "courteous" service, "well prepared" traditional cooking and "reasonable" prices make it a top local choice. / 11.45 pm, Fri & Sat 12.30 am; no Switch.

Anna's Place N1   £ 31   ④❸④
90 Mildmay Pk   (020) 7249 9379   1–1C
Anna's departure is starting to tell at this long-established Islington townhouse – the special charm has gone, and the "weary" Scandinavian cooking is getting "expensive for what it is". / 10.45 pm; D only; closed Sun; no credit cards.

Antipasto & Pasta SW11   £ 26   ❸②❸
511 Battersea Park Rd   (020) 7223 9765   10–1C
"You can hardly go wrong on half-price nights" (every Mon, Thu and Sun) at this "no-nonsense" Battersea spot; it serves "good, solid Italian food at reasonable prices". / 11.30 pm; no Amex.

The Apprentice SE1   £ 27   ❷⑤⑤
31 Shad Thames   (020) 7234 0254   9–4D
"Well-presented food" at "great-value" prices attracts many willing 'guinea pigs' to the dining room of this South Bank catering school; that "service varies widely" is all part of the fun, but you must "bring your own atmosphere". / 8.30 pm; closed Sat & Sun; no smoking area.

Aquarium E1   £ 31   ❸④❸
Ivory Hs, St Katharine-by-the-Tower   (020) 7480 6116   1–2D
"The food's a bit hit-and-miss, but when it hits it's great", at this "fun" and "modern" fish place, which has "nice views of St Katharine's Dock"; service is "patchy". / 11 pm; closed Mon D & Sun.

Arancia SE16   £ 24   ❷❸④
52 Southwark Park Rd   (020) 7394 1751   1–3D
"Cramped" but cosy Italian – a beacon in barren Bermondsey – whose short menu delivers "fresh" and "very reasonably priced" cooking. / 11 pm; closed Sun; no Amex; set always available £14(FP).

Arcadia W8   £ 36   ④④❸
35 Kensington High St   (020) 7937 4294   5–1A
"A friendly owner and two parrots" are among the attractions of this "small and quaint-ish" modern British outfit, just off Kensington High Street; some feel its culinary standards are "15 years out of date". / 11 pm; closed Sat L.

Archduke Wine Bar SE1   £ 32   ⑤④④
Concert Hall Approach, South Bank   (020) 7928 9370   2–3D
Eminent suitability "ahead of a performance on the South Bank" allows this wine bar – set into the arches of Hungerford Railway Bridge – to get away with cooking which "makes you weep". / 11 pm; closed Sat L & Sun; no smoking area; pre-th. £22(FP).

Arkansas Café E1   £ 19   ③③④

Unit 12, Old Spitalfield Mkt   (020) 7377 6999   9–1D
"Rough and ready" but "a delight for lovers of good meat well cooked" – patron 'Bubba' oversees this "basic" market café BBQ, which serves decent burgers, ribs, and the like. / L only; closed Sat; no Amex.

Aroma II W1   £ 28   ④③④

118-120 Shaftesbury Ave   (020) 7437 0377   4–3A
The basis for press enthusiasm about this new Theatreland Chinese eluded us (and also most reporters); it's perfectly OK, but – save for some unusual 'specials' – wholly unremarkable. / 11.30 pm.

Artigiano NW3   £ 37   ④④④

12a Belsize Ter   (020) 7794 4288   8–2A
We must admit we enjoyed our visit to this "trendy" new Belsize Park Italian; locals, though, proclaim a "shaky start" for a place whose dishes are "more 'designer' than delicious". / 10.30 pm; closed Mon L; set weekday L £24(FP).

L'Artiste Musclé W1   £ 23   ④③②

1 Shepherd Mkt   (020) 7493 6150   3–4B
"A wonderful little corner" – this "cramped", "totally French" Shepherd Market bistro delights regulars despite its "standard (low-end) fare". / 10.30 pm; winter closed Sun L.

Asia de Cuba WC2   £ 55   ③④①

45 St Martin's Ln   (020) 7300 5588   4–4C
The off-the-wall décor of Ian Schrager's (he of NY's Studio 54, Royalton, etc) Manhattanite new Covent Garden hotel is certainly impressive (as is the number of style police in attendance); on a day two visit, the pricey fusion fare in the restaurant did little to distract from the scene, and the beautiful people were already out in force. / Midnight, 1am Sat; closed Sat L.

Ask! Pizza   £ 22   ④③②

160-162 Victoria St, SW1   (020) 7630 8228   2–4B
121-125 Park St, W1   (020) 7495 7760   2–2A
48 Grafton Way, W1   (020) 7388 8108   2–1B
345 Fulham Palace Rd, SW6   (020) 7371 0392   10–1B
1 Gloucester Arcade, SW7   (020) 7835 0840   5–2B
145 Notting Hl Gt, W11   (020) 7792 9942   6–2B
Whiteleys, 151 Queensway, W2   (020) 7792 1977   6–1C
219-221 Chiswick High Rd, W4   (020) 8742 1323   7–2A
222 Kensington High St, W8   (020) 7937 5540   5–1A
Bus' Design Ctr, Upper St, N1   (020) 7226 8728   8–3D
216 Haverstock Hl, NW3   (020) 7433 3896   8–2A
103 St John St, EC1   (020) 7253 0323   9–1A
"A close second to PizzaExpress" – the rise and rise of this "trustworthy" and "cheerful" pizza-and-pasta chain continues. / 11.30 pm.

ASSAGGI W2   £ 40   ❶❶❷

39 Chepstow Pl   (020) 7792 5501   6–1B

A cult following ensures "you can never get a table" at this "terrific" dining room above a Bayswater pub, where "original and different" regional cooking and "very friendly" service make this now the highest-rated Italian in town. / 11.30 pm; closed Sun.

Les Associés N8   £ 32   ❸❷④

172 Park Rd   (020) 8348 8944   1–1C

"Lovely, little local", beloved of Crouch Enders, thanks to charming service and the "great value for money" of its "classic French" menu. / 10 pm; closed Mon & Sat L; no Amex; set Sun L £22(FP).

At Last SW10   £ 25   ❸❸❸

7 Park Wk   (020) 7349 8866   5–3B

Light, bright and very reasonably priced, new bar/brasserie, on the site of the short-lived Simply Nico, Chelsea; it has no great ambitions, but, on an early visit, seemed already to have attracted a (fairly mature) local following. / 11 pm; closed Sun.

Atlantic Bar & Grill W1   £ 45   ⑤⑤❸

20 Glasshouse St   (020) 7734 4888   3–3D

"Dire", "exorbitantly priced" cooking and "awful" service offer little incentive to visit this "large" and "posey" basement bar/restaurant, near Piccadilly Circus; even as a 'scene', it's now "showing its age a bit". / 11.30 pm, bar food until 2.30 am; closed Sat L & Sun L.

The Atlas SW6   £ 23   ❷❷❷

16 Seagrave Rd   (020) 7385 9129   5–3A

"A new start-up worthy of support" – this "Eagle-spawned foodie pub", near Earl's Court 2, offers "generously portioned" Mediterranean grub in a "convivial" setting; "great garden", too. / 10.30 pm; no Amex; no booking.

Atrium SW1   £ 39   ⑤⑤④

4 Millbank   (020) 7233 0032   2–4C

"Because it's the only place near the House of Commons", this "networking" favourite gets away with "bland" food and "poor and stroppy" service; what hope, then, for the quality of public services? / 10 pm; closed Sat & Sun; no smoking area.

AUBERGINE SW10   £ 59   ❶❶❷

11 Park Wk   (020) 7352 3449   5–3B

Gordon Ramsay's move may have robbed this Chelsea address of its headlines, but Willliam Drabble's "tantalising" cooking still makes a visit here a "special treat" – the "unobtrusive" service and "relaxed" setting both outrank the old master's new place. / 10.30 pm; closed Sat L & Sun; set weekday L £34(FP).

Aurora W1 £29 ④④❸
49 Lexington St   (020) 7494 0514   3–2D
The cooking is "slightly amateur" and conditions "crowded",
but the BYO policy at this "candlelit and friendly" Soho café
makes it a "useful" central venue; there is also a "wonderful
courtyard". / 10.30 pm; closed Sun; no Amex.

L'Aventure NW8 £38 ❶❷❶
3 Blenheim Ter   (020) 7624 6232   8–3A
"What a lovely restaurant", typifies reactions to this
"evergreen" St John's Wood "romantic" favourite, where the
Gallic fare is "beautifully presented, and as tasty as it looks".
/ 11 pm; closed Sat L and, in Winter, Sun; no Switch.

The Avenue SW1 £44 ④④❸
7-9 St James's St   (020) 7321 2111   3–4D
"Airy", "bright" and "buzzy" St James's establishment,
whose performance is quite good, judged by the standards
of West End mega-brasseries – that is to say that it's a touch
"overpriced" and service is "erratic". / Midnight, Fri & Sat 12.30am,
Sun 10pm; pre-th. £30(FP).

Axis WC2 £47 ❸❷❸
1 Aldwych   (020) 7300 0300   2–2D
"Smart and sleek" West End basement ("bunker"?) yearling,
whose modern British cooking is often hailed as
"mouthwatering" and "beautifully presented" (though it can
sometimes "fail to ignite"); the slightly "clinical" ambience
especially suits business. / 11.15 pm; closed Sat L & Sun.

Aykoku-Kaku EC4 £45 ❸❸⑤
9 Walbrook   (020) 7248 2548   9–3C
The "great lunchbox" served in the canteen area of this
once-grand, now rather worn, Japanese provides "a very cheap
lunch for the City"; the adjoining restaurant is considerably
more expensive. / 10 pm; closed Sat & Sun; no booking at L.

Ayoush W1 £37 ❸❸❷
58 James St   (020) 7935 9839   3–1A
Omens for this congenial, new, souk-style basement 'club',
north of Oxford Street – already blessed by a visit from
Ms Chelsea Clinton – seem set fair; we found the food
surprisingly good. / 11 pm; closed Sun.

Babe Ruth's £31 ④④❸
O2 Centre, 255 Finchley Rd, NW3   (020) 7433 3388   8–2A
172-176 The Highway, E1   (020) 7481 8181   1–2D
American theme-diners which "could try harder"; especially for
families "with hyperactive kids", however, they do have their
attractions (notably, unusually "good play areas"). / NW3 11 pm -
E1 11.30 pm; 12.30 am, Fri & Sat; no smoking area; E1 no booking -
NW3 parties of 6+ only.

Babur Brasserie SE23 £ 26 ❶❷❸

119 Brockley Rise, Forest HI (020) 8291 2400 1–4D
*"Lovely and delicate" Indian cooking – with excellent regional
specialities – justifies the trip to this Forest Hill subcontinental.*
/ 11.15 pm; closed Fri L; no smoking area; set Sun L £14(FP).

Back to Basics W1 £ 35 ❶❸⑤

21a Foley St (020) 7436 2181 2–1B
*"Great fresh fish" wins universal praise for this "cramped and
basic" Fitzrovian, even though sometimes "sniffy" service
contributes to an atmosphere many find "grim". / 10 pm;
closed Sat & Sun.*

Bah Humbug SW2 £ 27 ④④❶

St Matthew's Church (020) 7738 3184 10–2D
*"Atmospheric, cool and trendy" Brixton veggie, where the
"very good" ambience – if you like Gothic church crypts –
is a greater strength than the "too wholesome to be tasty"
cooking. / 11.30 pm; D only, Sat & Sun open L & D; no Amex.*

Balans £ 29 ④❷❷

60 Old Compton St, W1 (020) 7437 5212 4–3A
239 Brompton Rd, SW3 (020) 7584 0070 5–2C
239 Old Brompton Rd, SW5 (020) 7244 8838 5–3A
*"Cute" staff – who are "friendly whether you're gay or
straight" – account for much of the success of these "sassy"
and "crowded" haunts; Earl's Court is the best-run branch and
Soho the most atmospheric – initial reports from
Knightsbridge are not especially encouraging. / 1 am - W1 Mon-Sat
5 am, Sun 1 am; W1 no booking – SW5 Sat & Sun no booking.*

Bali Sugar W11 £ 43 ❷❷❸

33a All Saints Rd (020) 7221 4477 6–1B
*The Sugar Club's former North Kensington home may be
"quieter now the trendies have gone", but many feel the
"arresting juxtapositions of eclectic ingredients" offered by its
year-old replacement are "better than at the original". / 11 pm;
no smoking area.*

Bam-Bou W1 £ 41 ⑤④❸

1 Percy St (020) 7323 9130 2–1C
*Will Mogens Tholstrup's style (Pasha et al) work outside the
swanky SWs?; it's no surprise that his Fitzrovia newcomer's
allegedly French-Vietnamese food is "appallingly bland" and
"terribly overpriced" (and that's pre-15% service charge), but
the atmosphere lacks the 'wow' which elsewhere saves the
great Dane's bacon. / 11.30 pm; closed Sun.*

Bangkok SW7 £ 28 ❷④④

9 Bute St (020) 7584 8529 5–2B
*For decades now, the "small" menu has been well done at this
"simple" South Kensington Thai; "it's looking a lot less shabby
recently". / 11 pm; closed Sun; no Amex.*

Bangkok Brasserie SW1   £ 26   ❸④❸
48-49 St James's St   (020) 7629 7565   3–3C
"Good value" and St James's don't usually mix, making this
oddly decorated basement something of a puzzle; its set
menus (in particular) offer a *"good choice"* of dishes at
"reasonable prices". / 11pm.

BANK WC2   £ 47   ④④④
1 Kingsway   (020) 7379 9797   2–2D
The *"best of the mega-brasseries"* is *"great for a quick
business dinner"* (and also popular for breakfast); many now
think it *"oversized and overpriced"*, though (and *"don't forget
your earplugs"*). / 11 pm; no Switch; pre-th. £29(FP).

Banners N8   £ 25   ④④❷
21 Park Rd   (020) 8348 2930   1–1C
It's *"worth crossing town"* for the *"legendary"* Sunday brunch
served at this *"nicely casual"* Crouch End bar/diner; service is
"very hit and miss", but, hey, who cares? / 11.30 pm, Fri & Sat
midnight; no Amex & no Switch.

Bar Bourse EC4   £ 39   ❸④❸
67 Queen St   (020) 7248 2200   9–3C
For a *"less formal business lunch"*, this *"lively"* City basement
yearling is a *"good-value"* choice – especially if you go for the
"tasty bar snacks". / L only; closed Sat & Sun.

Bar Gansa NW1   £ 19   ❷④❷
2 Inverness St   (020) 7267 8909   8–3B
"Good quality tapas" and a *"late licence"* make this
happening Camden Town bar a perennial success. / Midnight;
no Amex.

Bar Italia W1   £ 6   ❸❸❶
22 Frith St   (020) 7437 4520   4–2A
"Where else is there at 3 am?" – this *"irresistible"* 24-hour
Soho *"classic"*, famous for the *"best coffee anywhere"* is a
"great place to people-watch" and soak up the *"after-movies
or after-clubbing"* atmosphere. / 4 am, Fri & Sat 24 hours;
no credit cards; no booking.

Bar Japan SW5   £ 24   ❸❸④
251 Old Brompton Rd   (020) 7370 2323   5–3A
"Cheap" and *"reliable"* sushi maintains a steady crowd at this
unpretentious Earl's Court stand-by. / 11 pm.

Barcelona Tapas   £ 20   ❸❸❷
481 Lordship Ln, SE22   (020) 8693 5111   1–4D
1a Bell Ln, E1   (020) 7247 7014   9–2D
1 Beaufort Hs, St Botolph St, EC3   (020) 7377 5222   9–2D
"Good tapas, in a buzzy atmosphere" win a wide following for
the two very different City branches – one in an obscure
basement, the other more prominent at the base of a shiny
skyscraper – of this commendable chain; a *"relaxed"* country
cousin in Dulwich has also been well received. / 10 pm – SE22
11 pm; City branches closed Sat & Sun D.

Barra W1 £ 30 ❸④④

12a Newburgh St (020) 7287 8488 3–2C
*Amiably trendy West Soho newcomer, offering good simple
fish-and-more cookery in cramped surroundings. / 11 pm;
closed Sun.*

Basil St Hotel SW3 £ 33 ❸❷❸

8 Basil St (020) 7581 3311 5–1D
*The "old-fashioned Knightsbridge atmosphere" of this
family-owned hotel makes it a perfect choice for a "bygone-era
breakfast", an "excellent Sunday lunch" or "the best afternoon
tea". / 10 pm; jacket & tie.*

Basilico £ 27 ❷❸④

690 Fulham Rd, SW6 (020) 7384 2633 10–1B
175 Lavender Hl, SW11 (020) 7924 4070 10–2C
*"Great" (but pricey) pizzas are better taken-away from than
eaten-in at the stylish but cramped branches of this promising
new chain. / SW11 10 pm - SW6 10.30 pm; no Amex; no booking.*

Battersea Barge Bistro SW8 £ 18 ⑤❸❷

Nine Elms Ln (020) 7498 0004 10–1D
*It "takes a long time to find" (down a lane opposite New
Covent Garden Market), but the thrill of discovery adds much
to the atmosphere of this funny moored barge – an intriguing
venue for a "cheap and cheerful" gathering. / 11 pm; closed Sun D.*

Battersea Rickshaw SW11 £ 22 ❸❷④

15-16 Battersea Sq (020) 7924 2450 5–4C
*"All the ambience of a three-star hotel in Slough" does little to
dent locals enthusiasm for this Battersea stalwart, with its
"very good and consistent" curries and "smiley" service.
/ 11.30 pm; D only.*

Beach Blanket Babylon W11 £ 36 ⑤④❶

45 Ledbury Rd (020) 7229 2907 6–1B
*"Great ambience but cruddy food" – the famously "jazzy"
décor of this Notting Hill bar/restaurant makes it a "brilliant"
and "fun" venue "for a drink", but "forget eating there".
/ 11 pm.*

Bedlington Café W4 £ 19 ❸④⑤

24 Fauconberg Rd (020) 8994 1965 7–2A
*Fiery cooking won deserved acclaim over the years for this
"unpretentious" and "quirky" Chiswick Thai (by day a 'greasy
spoon'); sadly, though "it's slipped", and is nothing like the
place it was; BYO. / 10 pm; no credit cards; no smoking.*

Beirut Express W2 £ 18 ❷④④

112-114 Edgware Rd (020) 7724 2700 6–1D
*There's "great Lebanese food" to be had at "reasonable
prices" at this otherwise "boring" Bayswater café-takeaway.
/ 1.45 am; no credit cards.*

Beiteddine SW1 £ 32 ❸❸④
8 Harriet St   (020) 7235 3969   2–3A
"Consistent", well-run Lebanese, just off Sloane Street, serving quality cooking in reasonable comfort. / Midnight.

Belair House SE21 £ 40 ❸❸❶
Gallery Rd, Dulwich Village   (020) 8299 9788   1–4C
The "stunning setting" is the undoubted strength of this restaurant housed in a listed Georgian lodge by Dulwich Park; the "good" modern British cooking is increasingly "inconsistent", though, and some find prices "ridiculous". / 10.30 pm.

Belgo £ 30 ⑤④❸
50 Earlham St, WC2   (020) 7813 2233   4–2C
124 Ladbroke Grove, W10   (020) 8982 8400   6–1A
72 Chalk Farm Rd, NW1   (020) 7267 0718   8–2B
Though some still "like the concept" of this Belgian moules/frites (and beer) chain, for many the "gimmick" is now just "old hat"; for 'formula-food' it is amazingly "expensive", especially given the "squashed" conditions and utterly "indifferent" service, charged for at a shocking 15%. / 11.30 pm.

La Belle Epoque SW3 £ 40 ⑤⑤⑤
151 Draycott Ave   (020) 7460 5000   5–2C
Some find themselves "practically alone" in this vast Chelsea "multiplex" – a Gallic brasserie, restaurant and grand oriental totalling 800 covers; it's "not too surprising" – the cooking is "mediocre" and service "appalling". / Midnight.

Bellinis SW13 £ 16 ④❸❸
2-3 Rocks Ln   (020) 8255 9922   10–1A
"Friendly and helpful" service helps make this "reliable" Barnes Italian a local "family pizza" favourite. / 11 pm; no smoking area.

Belvedere W8 £ 44 ❸❸❷
Holland Hs, off Abbotsbury Rd   (020) 7602 1238   7–1D
"At night, overlooking Holland Park, what could be better?" – the "great location" is the special strength of this "tastefully decorated" destination, whose pricey modern British cooking plays second fiddle. / 11 pm; closed Sun D.

Ben's Thai W9 £ 22 ❸❸④
93 Warrington Cres   (020) 7266 3134   8–4A
"Cheap" and "authentic" Thai cooking makes it "hard to get a table" at this sizeable dining room, on the first floor of an impressive Maida Vale boozer (the Warrington Castle). / 10.30 pm; D only; no Amex & no Switch; set weekday L £13(FP).

Bengal Clipper SE1 £ 31 ❷❷❸
Shad Thames   (020) 7357 9001   9–4D
"Different and tasty" cooking "at reasonable prices" (especially given its proximity to the City) makes this smart, if rather suburban, Indian – behind Conran's gastrodrome – worth seeking out. / 11 pm; set Dinner £20(FP).

Benihana   £ 44   ❸❸❸
37 Sackville St, W1   (020) 7494 2525   3–3D
77 King's Rd, SW3   (020) 7376 7799   5–3D
100 Avenue Rd, NW3   (020) 7586 9508   8–2A
"Having food cooked in front of you makes for a fun night out"
– "albeit a pricey one" – at these glossy "teppan-yaki
experiences", which are famed for "ninja waiters" and
"entertaining chefs' tricks"; "kids love it". / 10.30 pm, Fri & Sat
Midnight.

Bentley's W1   £ 53   ❸④❸
11-15 Swallow St   (020) 7734 4756   3–3D
"Superb Stilton and Dover sole" are the sort of thing done
best in the upstairs dining room of this charming, "traditional"
seafood parlour near Piccadilly Circus; it's "rather pricey",
though, and too often spoilt by "patronising" service. / 11.30 pm;
smart casual; pre-th. £35(FP).

Beotys WC2   £ 41   ⑤❸④
79 St Martin's Ln   (020) 7836 8768   4–3B
Something's up at this "comforting" Theatreland "relic" – the
Franco-Greek cooking has been "mediocre" and "overpriced"
for years, but this year the once-faultless service has too often
seemed "pompous" or "overbearing". / 11.30 pm; closed Sun;
no smoking area.

Bersagliera SW3   £ 28   ④❸❸
372 King's Rd   (020) 7352 5993   5–3B
"Loud" and "lively" World's End pizza/pasta joint; it was "once
great" – now it's "fading". / 11.45 pm; closed Sun; no Amex
& no Switch.

Bertorelli's   £ 33   ④❸④
19-23 Charlotte St, W1   (020) 7636 4174   2–1C
44a Floral St, WC2   (020) 7836 3969   4–2D
"Jolly and lively – you can't go wrong", say fans of Groupe
Chez Gérard's "noisy" Italian duo, whose overall performance
is somewhere between "consistent" and "mediocre". / W1 11
pm - WC2 11.30 pm; closed Sun; no smoking area; pre-th. £23(FP).

Beyoglu SW11   £ 19   ❸❷④
50 Battersea Park Rd   (020) 7627 2052   10–1C
"Unsophisticated but tasty" cooking makes this "cramped"
and basic Battersea Turk "good value"; "service can be slow,
but they always welcome you like a long-lost friend". / 11 pm;
no Amex.

Bibendum SW3   £ 59   ❸❸❷
81 Fulham Rd   (020) 7581 5817   5–2C
Hold the front page – Brompton Cross Landmark Stages
Comeback!; it's rather exciting to see this once great modern
French restaurant beginning to regain its old form; it's still
"overpriced" and a bit "snotty", but then it always has been.
/ 10.30 pm.

Bibendum Oyster Bar SW3   £ 34   ❷❷❷
81 Fulham Rd   (020) 7589 1480   5–2C
"Great shellfish, prawns and other tasty cold fruits de mer" win high praise at this *"elegant"* bar in the foyer of the Conran Shop. / 10 pm; no booking.

Bice W1   £ 38   ④❸④
13 Albemarle St   (020) 7409 1011   3–3C
"Food that's just too unimaginative for the prices", served in a *"businesslike"* setting, ensures that such glamour as characterises its NY, Milan, etc siblings is notably absent from this *"uninspiring"* Mayfair basement. / 10.45 pm; closed Sat L & Sun; smart casual.

The Big Chef E14   £ 40   ④④⑤
2nd Fl, Cabot Pl East   (020) 7513 0513   1–3D
The gruesome name change (from 'MPW') is matched by "embarrassing" standards at Canary Wharf's only natural 'business' restaurant, whose "ordinary" cooking, "slow" service and "dead" ambience reflect little credit on the Very Big Name chef who still owns it. / 9 pm; closed Sat & Sun.

Big Easy SW3   £ 33   ④❸❷
334 King's Rd   (020) 7352 4071   5–3C
"Fun fodder" – *"good burgers and cocktails"* – makes this a popular Chelsea destination (especially with kids); beware, though – *"the bill really adds up, and you're not sure how or why"*. / Midnight, Fri & Sat 12.30 am; no smoking area; Fri & Sat, no booking after 7 pm; set weekday L £19(FP).

THE BIRDCAGE W1   £ 56   ❷❸❶
110 Whitfield St   (020) 7323 9655   2–1B
It's "weird and wonderful" to find this "exotic" and "intimate" yearling in such an "awful" location (near Warren Street tube); the "innovative" and "spicy" fusion menu is exciting too, but soaring prices mean some now find it just "too expensive". / 11.15 pm; closed Sat L & Sun; no smoking area.

Bistrot 190 SW7   £ 37   ④④④
189-190 Queen's Gate   (020) 7581 5666   5–1B
The "long downhill drift" continues at this once-brilliant brasserie in the "barren" area near the Albert Hall; cooking is "unreliable" and service "pretty poor". / Midnight.

The Black Truffle NW1   £ 29   – – –
40 Chalcot Rd   (020) 7483 0077   8–3B
The latest Red Pepper group opening is scheduled to open shortly after we go to press; if it matches its stablemates' form, this Primrose Hill Italian will be well worth winkling out. / 10.45 pm; closed Sat L.

Blah! Blah! Blah! W12   £ 23   ❷❸❷

78 Goldhawk Rd   (020) 8746 1337   7–1C
*"Incredibly flavoursome" veggie food, "that never fails to
impress carnivores", wins high praise for this "dark" and
"friendly" Shepherd's Bush fixture; BYO. / 11 pm; closed Sun;
no credit cards.*

Blakes NW1   £ 32   ❷❺❸

31 Jamestown Rd   (020) 7482 2959   8–3B
*Trendy Camden Town boozer, where the "Moroccan-tinged"
grub in the rather "romantic" first floor dining room is
surprisingly good; shame about the "slow, slow, slow" service.
/ 10.30 pm.*

Blakes Hotel SW7   £ 88   ④④❶

33 Roland Gdns   (020) 7370 6701   5–2B
*"She (or he) had better be worth it", if you're contemplating a
visit to this opulent, "dark" and rather "naughty" South
Kensington townhouse hotel basement, famed for its
aphrodisiac qualities; the cooking may be "wonderfully
creative" but it's also "far too expensive". / 11.30 pm.*

Bleeding Heart EC1   £ 33   ❷❷❶

Bleeding Heart Yd, Greville St   (020) 7242 8238   9–2A
*"It's a delight to introduce new diners" to this "difficult-to-find",
"cramped" and "cosy" Holborn cellar, which is as popular for
business lunches as for "romantic" evenings; "solid" French
fare and an "excellent wine list" complete the package.
/ 10.30 pm; closed Sat & Sun.*

BLUE ELEPHANT SW6   £ 44   ❷❷❶

4-6 Fulham Broadway   (020) 7385 6595   5–4A
*It's not only the "unique" and spacious setting – "a bit like
Fantasy Island" – that makes this "great fun" and "romantic"
Fulham Thai once again London's most talked-about ethnic;
the food is "consistently good" (if "expensive"), and service
"friendly" and "attentive". / Midnight, Sun 10.30 pm; closed Sat L;
smart casual.*

Blue Jade SW1   £ 24   ❸❸④

44 Hugh St   (020) 7828 0321   2–4B
*This backstreet Thai brings "good food" to a thin part of
Pimlico; it's "a bit lacking in atmosphere", however. / 11 pm;
closed Sat L & Sun.*

Blue Print Café SE1   £ 40   ④④❷

Design Mus, Butler's Whf   (020) 7378 7031   9–4D
*"Fantastic views" (of the Thames and Tower Bridge) and
"interesting" modern British food win support for this Conran
riversider; those who find it "unimpressive" have gained
ground, however, and service can be "slow". / 11 pm; closed Sun D.*

The Blue Pumpkin SW15 £ 26 ②②②

147 Upper Richmond Rd   (020) 8780 3553   10–2B
*On the site of Putney's Van Gogh (RIP), the same owners have
launched a bright and useful modern British brasserie, which is
notably sensibly priced. / 10.30 pm, Fri & Sat 11 pm; no smoking area.*

BLUEBIRD SW3 £ 45 ⑤④③

350 Kings Rd   (020) 7559 1000   5–3C
*"Conran Restaurants should be ashamed" of this "very
overpriced" and "increasingly disappointing" Chelsea hangar –
"for such a lovely-looking restaurant, it's so incredibly average".
/ 11 pm; pre-th. £27(FP).*

Blues W1 £ 33 ②②❶

42 Dean St   (020) 7494 1966   4–2A
*"Get beyond the deafening bar area" of this "friendly" Soho
joint and you find "welcoming" staff and surprisingly
"interesting" modern British cooking – "nothing too flashy",
of course, "but pitched just right". / 11.30 pm, Thu-Sat midnight;
closed Sat L; set Mon,Tue,Sun dinner (parties 4-) £19(FP).*

Blythe Road Restaurant W14 £ 30 ②④③

71 Blythe Rd   (020) 7371 3635   7–1C
*"Deceptively filling" portions of good-quality (if not particularly
imaginative) modern British grub, make this agreeable
Olympia local a "reliable" choice, even if service is "sometimes
too slow". / 10.30 pm; closed Sat L & Sun.*

Boiled Egg & Soldiers SW11 £ 17 ④④③

63 Northcote Rd   (020) 7223 4894   10–2C
*"If you can beat your way through the nannies and their
charges", this cosy Wandsworth caff (deep in "Nappy Valley")
has a cult following for its "super breakfast/brunches";
nevertheless, it's "expensive for what you get". / 6 pm; L &
afternoon tea only; no credit cards; no booking.*

Boisdale SW1 £ 40 ②②②

13-15 Eccleston St   (020) 7730 6922   2–4B
*"Scotland meets SW1" at this smart and clubby (and recently
expanded) Victoria wine bar, whose devotees applaud "great
cooking", "swift service" and the "fabulous wine list"; a few –
"delighted not to fit in" – dismiss an "extortionately priced"
and "very disappointing" experience. / 10.30 pm.*

Bombay Bicycle Club SW12 £ 30 ②②②

95 Nightingale Ln   (020) 8673 6217   10–2C
*"It's certainly not your average curry house" – "subtle"
cooking and an "airy" and "civilised" setting makes this
Wandsworth Indian one of the best places south of the river;
its "excellent and efficient" takeaways in Battersea (tel 7720
0500), Putney (8785 1188) and Wimbledon (8540 9997)
also have many fans. / 11 pm; D only; closed Sun.*

Bombay Brasserie SW7   £ 42   ❷❸❷
Courtfield Clo, Gloucester Rd   (020) 7370 4040   5–2B
For fans, this grand ("pretentious") South Kensington Indian, with its "lovely" conservatory, is "still the best in London", and serves "yummy" food, "efficiently, if officiously"; that it "trades on its reputation" is a recurrent concern. / Midnight; smart casual.

Bombay Palace W2   £ 32   ❷❷❷
50 Connaught St   (020) 7723 8855   6–1D
"Consistently good", if "somewhat impersonal", Indian, just north of Hyde Park, whose "fresh and tasty" cooking merits greater recognition than it achieves. / 11.30 pm; no smoking area.

Bonjour Vietnam SW6   £ 24   ⑤④④
593-599 Fulham Rd   (020) 7385 7603   5–4A
It may have an eat-all-you-can formula, but too many "poor quality" dishes mean this Fulham oriental "doesn't justify the price". / 11 pm.

La Bouchée SW7   £ 29   ④⑤❷
56 Old Brompton Rd   (020) 7589 1929   5–2B
"Fun" and "cosmopolitan" ("loud" and "cramped") Gallic bistro in South Kensington; the cooking's "reasonable" – lunch and early-evening menus offer best value – but service remains "unacceptably poor". / 11 pm; no Amex & no Switch; pre-th. £20(FP).

Le Bouchon Bordelais SW11   £ 34   ⑤⑤④
5-9 Battersea Rs   (020) 7738 0307   10–2C
"Popularity and cooking have declined, but not the prices" at this "genuinely French, but lazy and unreliable" Battersea bistro; the weekend crèche is an undoubted plus. / 11.30 pm.

Boudin Blanc W1   £ 32   – – –
5 Trebeck St   (020) 7499 3292   3–4B
This "splendid", "old-fashioned" French bistro, in Shepherd Market, famous for the value of its lunch and early-evening set meals, closed for a major expansion in mid-1999; let's hope they don't throw the baby out with the bathwater! / 11 pm; set weekday L £18(FP).

La Bouffe SW11   £ 28   ④❸④
13 Battersea Rs   (020) 7228 3384   10–2C
The quality of the food is "astonishingly variable" – "sometimes very good, sometimes appalling" – at this Gallic bar/restaurant in Battersea. / 11 pm.

Boulevard WC2   £ 26   ❸❸❸
40 Wellington St   (020) 7240 2992   4–3D
"Simple, quasi-French country cooking" and "good value for money" make this "solid" and "unpretentious" bistro a "great Covent Garden stand-by". / Midnight.

The Bow Wine Vaults EC4 £ 29 ④④④
10 Bow Church Yd (020) 7248 1121 9–2C
"Reliable but dreary" City lunching spot; with its quaint location by St Mary-le-Bow, it's best enjoyed outside in summer. / L only; closed Sat & Sun.

The Brackenbury W6 £ 30 ❷❸❸
129-131 Brackenbury Rd (020) 8748 0107 7–1C
"Very good modern British food" and a "friendly", "village" atmosphere ensure that this well known Hammersmith fixture is "always popular"; let's hope the new owners (the Avenue/Circus group) keep up standards. / 10.45 pm; closed Sat L & Sun D; set weekday L £20(FP).

Bradley's NW3 £ 42 ❷❷❸
25 Winchester Rd (020) 7722 3457 8–2A
"Don't tell too many people", implore fans of the "cracking" modern British cooking, "attentive" service and "lovely" atmosphere at this "very good local", "quietly tucked away in Swiss Cottage". / 11 pm; closed Sat L; set weekday L £23(FP).

Brady's SW18 £ 20 ❷❷❸
513 Old York Rd (020) 8877 9599 10–2B
"Plump, moist fish and big fat chips" attract "weekend queues" at this "unpretentious" Wandsworth bistro. / 10.30 pm; closed Sun; no credit cards; no booking.

Brahms SW1 £ 15 ❸④④
147 Lupus St (020) 7834 9075 5–3D
"A welcome return" (for a spell, it traded as a Little Bay), this ultra-budget Pimlico bistro offers "three courses for a fiver", and "exceptional value". / 11.45 pm; no Amex.

Brass. du Marché aux Puces W10 £ 29 ❸❷❷
349 Portobello Rd (020) 8968 5828 6–1A
"Relaxed and uncomplicated", this "cute" Gallic spot in North Kensington – with "really friendly staff" and "tasty" cooking – is some people's idea of "the perfect brasserie". / 11 pm; closed Sun D.

La Brasserie SW3 £ 34 ④④❷
272 Brompton Rd (020) 7584 1668 5–2C
"Improved after the revamp" – admittedly from a low base – this atmospheric South Kensington institution still specialises in "standard", Gallic fare, served rather "lazily"; "great" weekend breakfasts are a highlight. / 11.30 pm; no booking Sat L or Sun L.

Brasserie 24 EC2 £ 39 ❸❸❶
International Financial Centre (020) 7877 7703 9–2C
"Sensational views" – which can now also be enjoyed at night – ensure the 24th-floor dining room at the building formerly known as the NatWest Tower is "consistently full"; the food is "not exciting, but well cooked". / 9 pm; closed Sat & Sun.

Brasserie Rocque EC2 £35 ④❸❸
37 Broadgate Circle (020) 7638 7919 9–2D
*"Boringly reliable and unpretentious", this "workmanlike"
brasserie, in the heart of the Broadgate centre, is "good for
City business"; the quiet location, with many outside tables, is
"great if it's sunny".* / *brasserie 8.30 pm; closed Sat & Sun; bookings only
taken for restaurant.*

Brasserie St Quentin SW3 £37 ④❷❷
243 Brompton Rd (020) 7589 8005 5–2C
*It's still "not as good as before Groupe Chez Gérard took it
over", but standards at this "stylish", "continental"
Knightsbridge brasserie (which nose-dived post-acquisition) are
now at least "sound".* / *11 pm; set Dinner £26(FP).*

Brick Lane Beigel Bake E1 £4 ❷❷④
159 Brick Ln (020) 7729 0616 1–2D
*"Perfect" bagels – "worth travelling half-way across London for
(especially in the wee small hours)" – make this all-hours spot
a deserving East End institution.* / *24 hr; no credit cards.*

Brilliant UB2 £24 ❷❷④
72-76 Western Rd (020) 8574 1928 1–3A
*"Better than home-cooking – the genuine article", says an
(Indian) fan of this celebrated Southall subcontinental;
a minority leaves disgruntled.* / *11 pm; closed Mon, Sat L & Sun L;
no smoking area.*

Brinkley's SW10 £29 ④❸❷
47 Hollywood Rd (020) 7351 1683 5–3B
*The "lively bar, awash with Fulham/Chelsea thirtysomethings"
is the real focus at this "noisy" hang-out, where "fairly decent"
food is enhanced by notably "affordable" wines; there is a
"fabulous outdoor setting for summer".* / *11.30 pm; no Amex.*

La Brocca NW6 £29 ❸❸❷
273 West End Ln (020) 7433 1989 1–1B
*"It has more character than a chain", and locals rave about
the "good-value" and "lively" "warmth" of this West
Hampstead pizzeria; the cooking is "not bad, but lacks
finesse".* / *11 pm.*

Brompton Bay SW3 £26 ❸❷❸
96 Draycott Ave (020) 7225 2500 5–2C
*"Good-value" Brompton Cross newcomer, praised for "fresh
modern food", "affably" served in a "light and airy" setting.*
/ *11 pm; closed Sun D.*

Browns £ 32 ④④❸

47 Maddox St, W1   (020) 7491 4565   3–2C
82-84 St Martin's Ln, WC2   (020) 7497 5050   4–4B
114 Draycott Ave, SW3   (020) 7584 5359   5–2C
*"A poor relation to Oxford and Cambridge's 'parental visit'
restaurants" – this Bass-owned English brasserie chain has
"'lost it' with expansion"; "there's a nice buzz – just don't
waste your money on the food!" / 10 pm - WC2 midnight; no smoking
area, WC2 & W1; set Sun L £22(FP).*

Bu San N7 £ 24 ❸❸④

43 Holloway Rd   (020) 7607 8264   8–2D
*"Very good and spicy Korean food" still wins praise for this
rather faded oriental, near Highbury & Islington tube.
/ 11.30 pm; closed Sat L & Sun L; no Amex; set weekday L £14(FP).*

Bubb's EC1 £ 45 ④④④

329 Cent Mkts, Farringdon St   (020) 7236 2435   9–2A
*"Excellent for long City lunches" – traditionalists applaud the
solid bourgeois cuisine and quality wines at this "most French
of restaurants", occupying quaint rooms on the corner of
Smithfield Market. / 10 pm; closed Sat & Sun.*

Buchan's SW11 £ 34 ④❸❸

62-64 Battersea Br Rd   (020) 7228 0888   5–4C
*It has a "nice buzz", but the food at this bright modern
Scottish bar/restaurant by Battersea Bridge is variable and
"can be very disappointing". / 10.45 pm; set weekday L £22(FP).*

Buona Sera £ 26 ❸④❷

43 Drury Ln, W1   (020) 7836 8296   4–2D
289a King's Rd, SW3   (020) 7352 8827   5–3C
22 Northcote Rd, SW11   (020) 7228 9925   10–2C
*"Bustling, noisy and fun, with good prices", the Clapham
original of this "reliable" mini-chain has spawned two offspring
worth remembering; the new Covent Garden branch is a
useful central option, while Chelsea (formerly 'The Jam') has
intriguing double-decker tables. / SW11 midnight -
W1, SW3 11.30 pm; W1 closed Sun, SW3 closed Mon; no Amex.*

Busabong Too SW10 £ 30 ❸④④

1a Langton St   (020) 7352 7414   5–3B
*"It always satisfies", say regulars at this "friendly", if at times
"quiet" World's End Thai. / 11.15 pm; D only.*

Busabong Tree SW10 £ 33 ❷❷❸

112 Cheyne Walk   (020) 7352 7534   5–4B
*"Authentic" cooking and "always friendly" service make it well
worth seeking out this "low-key" and rather obscurely located
Chelsea Thai; there's a "very nice garden". / 11.15 pm;
smart casual.*

The Butlers Wharf Chop-house SE1   £ 44   ④④❸
36e Shad Thames   (020) 7403 3403   9–4D
*It's "not bad, for a Conran restaurant" (especially the
"great-value bar"), but, in spite of its "superb views", this
modern-style Tower Bridge-side chophouse is "in no way
memorable"; surely Blighty's cooking deserves a better
showcase than somewhere this "overpriced" and "average"?
/ 11 pm; closed Sat L & Sun D; set always available £22(FP).*

Byron's NW3   £ 35   ④④❸
3a Downshire HI   (020) 7435 3544   8–2A
*Some feel that this Hampstead townhouse, seemingly
"designed for romance", "is nicer than it seems to get credit
for" – that's because service is too often "poor" and the
modern British grub rarely better than "conventional". / 11 pm;
no smoking area.*

Cactus Blue SW3   £ 33   ④④❷
86 Fulham Rd   (020) 7823 7858   5–2C
*"Nondescript" southern American food is the least attraction
at this impressively decorated Chelsea bar/restaurant – "don't
eat there, drink" (or go for the "excellent jazz brunch").
/ 11.45 pm; D only, Sat & Sun open L & D.*

Café 209 SW6   £ 17   ❸①❸
209 Munster Rd   (020) 7385 3625   10–1B
*"Relaxed, no-fuss, BYO" Thai, which younger Fulhamites
pronounce "always a hoot" – indeed, all the hooting makes it
"noisy"; the "bantering" owner is Joy – "by name and nature".
/ 10.45 pm; D only; closed Sun; no credit cards.*

Café Bohème W1   £ 29   ④④❶
17 Old Compton St   (020) 7734 0623   4–2A
*"It's really the ambience you go for (especially in the wee small
hours)" to this "always buzzing" and "loud" – but also "cosy"
and "unpretentious" – Soho hang-out; it's a "better bar than it
is a restaurant". / 2.45 am, Thu-Sat open 24 hours, Sun 11.30 pm.*

Café Coq WC2   £ 24   ④④④
154-156 Shaftesbury Ave   (020) 7836 8635   4–2B
*"Simple" chicken 'n' chips chain-prototype, near Cambridge
Circus; some think it "a good idea", but, given the ratings, it's
hard to get too excited about its impending 'roll out'. / 11 pm;
closed Sun L.*

Café de la Place SW11   £ 22   ④❸❸
11-12 Battersea Sq   (020) 7978 5374   5–4C
*Useful all-day Battersea bistro, applauded for its breakfasts
and its "large menu choice". / 11 pm; no Amex.*

Café de Maya NW3   £ 19   ❸❷④
38 Primrose HI Rd   (020) 7209 0672   8–3B
*Pleasant and spacious, and perhaps somewhat
under-appreciated Primrose Hill Thai, a little way off the main
restaurant drag. / 11 pm; D only; no Amex; no smoking area.*

Café de Paris W1 £ 50 ⑤⑤④

3 Coventry St   (020) 7734 7700   4–4A
*"You go to dance, not eat" – if you have any sense, that is –
at this Art Deco nightclub, just off Leicester Square; its
mezzanine restaurant is a "poseurs" paradise, serving
"disappointing and unoriginal food". / 10.45 pm (bar 3 am); D only;
closed Sun & Mon.*

Café Delancey NW1 £ 25 ④④④

3 Delancey St   (020) 7387 1985   8–3B
*It's "buzzing on Sunday mornings", when the "good brunch"
comes into its own at this large and "easy-going" Camden
Town brasserie; at other times, it's supremely mediocre.
/ 11.30 pm, Sun 10 pm; no Amex.*

Café des Amis du Vin WC2 £ 37 ④❸❸

11-14 Hanover Pl   (020) 7379 3444   4–2D
*The cooking is still only "average" at this "nicely refurbished"
bistro, down an alley by the Royal Opera House; the
(unchanged) basement bar, with its "fine cheese board" and
"good wines", remains a "very good" rendezvous. / 11.30 pm;
closed Sun; pre-th. £24(FP).*

Café du Jardin WC2 £ 36 ❸④❸

28 Wellington St   (020) 7836 8769   4–3D
*A "safe haven" in Covent Garden, offering "good" modern
British cooking in an "attractive" environment; those in the
know say "sit downstairs", and advocate the "good-value" set
meals (lunch and pre-theatre) over dining à la carte. / Midnight;
set weekday L £21(FP).*

Café du Marché EC1 £ 36 ❷❷❶

22 Charterhouse Sq   (020) 7608 1609   9–1B
*"Relax – forget the City for a couple of hours", at this "very
attractive", "rustic" favourite on the fringe of Smithfield, which
offers "reliable" French cooking and "friendly" service; it's
"very different in the evenings", when romantics replace suits,
and there's jazz. / 10 pm; closed Sat L & Sun; no Amex.*

Café Emm W1 £ 23 ❸④❸

17 Frith St   (020) 7437 0723   4–2A
*"Food that's affordably priced for Soho", if "basic", ensures
that this "young" and "loud" bargain eatery is "always
crowded". / 10.30 pm, Fri & Sat 12.30 am; closed Sat L & Sun L; no Amex;
book L only.*

Café Fish W1 £ 32 ❸❸④

36-40 Rupert St   (020) 7287 8989   4–3A
*"Reliable", "good-quality", "fresh" fish makes this "noisy"
central stand-by (from Groupe Chez Gérard) a "better than
expected" venue for a light meal, and a 'natural' pre- or
post-theatre. / 10.30 pm; no smoking area.*

Café Flo £ 28 ⑤⑤④

11 Haymarket, SW1 (020) 7976 1313 4–4A
103 Wardour St, W1 (020) 7734 0581 3–2D
13 Thayer St, W1 (020) 7935 5023 2–1A
51 St Martin's Ln, WC2 (020) 7836 8289 4–4C
89 Sloane Ave, SW3 (020) 7225 1048 5–2C
676 Fulham Rd, SW6 (020) 7371 9673 10–1B
25-35 Gloucester Rd, SW7 (020) 7589 1383 5–1B
127 Kensington Ch St, W8 (020) 7727 8142 6–2B
334 Upper St, N1 (020) 7226 7916 8–3D
205 Haverstock HI, NW3 (020) 7435 6744 8–2A
38-40 Ludgate HI, EC4 (020) 7329 3900 9–2A
The branches may look "breezy, bright and pleasant", but this Gallic-owned chain's Gallic cooking is "generic" and "pricey for what it is"; "it's better than Café Rouge, but so is Burger King". / 11.30 pm, Sun 11 pm; set always available £19(FP).

Café Grove W11 £ 22 ④④❷

253a Portobello Rd (020) 7243 1094 6–1A
"You must sit on the balcony" – with its "brilliant view of the market" – to appreciate why people seek out this otherwise ordinary Notting Hill café. / winter 5 pm, summer 10.30 pm; winter, L only; summer, closed Sat D & Sun D; no credit cards.

Café Indiya E1 £ 23 ❷❷❸

30 Alie St (020) 7481 8288 9–3D
The "thoughtful and interesting" cooking at this "cheerful" east-City Indian bears comparison with that of its well-known neighbour, Café Spice Namaste, which used to occupy this site. / 11 pm; closed Sat & Sun.

Café Japan NW11 £ 24 ❷❷④

626 Finchley Rd (020) 8455 6854 1–1B
You're "enthusiastically greeted" at this Golders Green oriental, which is "always busy", thanks to a "wide range of dishes at reasonable prices", not least "top-quality sushi". / 10.30 pm; closed Mon L & Tue L; no Amex; no smoking area.

Café Laville W2 £ 29 ⑤④❷

453 Edgware Rd (020) 7706 2620 8–4A
Little Venice café whose "quiet and idyllic setting", over the canal, is perfect for breakfast; the food "could be improved", though, and service can be "slow". / 10 pm; no Amex; no smoking area.

Café Lazeez £ 34 ❸❸❷

21 Dean St, W1 (020) 7434 9393 4–2A
93-95 Old Brompton Rd, SW7 (020) 7581 9993 5–2C
88 St John St, EC1 (020) 7253 2224 9–1B
"A refreshing change from the usual Indian" – this "funky and stylish" group offers "unusual adaptations of traditional dishes", with an emphasis on lighter food; the "attractive, bare-bricked" Smithfield newcomer outscores its longer-in-the-tooth South Kensington parent; the new Soho branch opens in November '99. / EC1 9 pm - SW7 12.30 am; Sun 10.30 pm; EC1 closed Sun; SW7, no smoking area; set Sun L £23(FP).

Café Med £ 29 ④④❸

22-25 Dean St, W1 (020) 7287 9007 4–2A
2 Hollywood Rd, SW10 (020) 7823 3355 5–3B
184a Kensington Pk Rd, W11 (020) 7221 1150 6–1B
320 Goldhawk Rd, W6 (020) 8741 1994 7–1B
21 Loudon Rd, NW8 (020) 7625 1222 8–3A
2 Wandsworth Common N'side, SW18 (020) 7228 0914 10–2C
370 St John's St, EC1 (020) 7278 1199 8–3D
*"Adequate" brasserie staples (including "great grills") and
"good ambience" are the strengths of this growing chain.*
/ 11.30 pm.

Café Milan SW3 £ 35 ④④❸

312-314 King's Rd (020) 7351 0101 5–3C
*"They may have spent millions on the décor", but this
"fashionable" new Chelsea antipasti bar/restaurant misses its
mark – yes, it attracts a "cosmopolitan" crowd, but the food is
only "passable", and service can be "slow" and "rude".*
/ 11.30 pm.

Café Mozart N6 £ 19 ❸④❸

17 Swains Ln (020) 8348 1384 8–1B
*"Dozy" service takes the edge off this useful 'mitteleuropean'
pâtisserie/bistro, near Hampstead Heath, which has some
especially nice outside tables; it's most popular for breakfast.*
/ 10 pm; no Amex; no smoking; no booking at L.

Café Pacifico WC2 £ 27 ④④❸

5 Langley St (020) 7379 7728 4–2C
*Covent Garden cantina – once the best Mexican in town –
which "continues to decline", now serving "standard" fare in a
rather "tatty" environment. / 11.45 pm; bookings taken Sun-Tue only.*

Café Pasta £ 22 ④❸④

15 Greek St, W1 (020) 7434 2545 4–2A
184 Shaftesbury Ave, WC2 (020) 7379 0198 4–2B
2-4 Garrick St, WC2 (020) 7497 2779 4–3C
270 Chiswick High Rd, W4 (020) 8995 2903 7–2A
229-231 Kensington High St, W8 (020) 7937 6314 5–1A
373 Kensington High St, W8 (020) 7610 5552 7–1D
8 Theberton St, N1 (020) 7704 9089 8–3D
200 Haverstock Hl, NW3 (020) 7431 8531 8–2A
94 Upper Richmond Rd, SW15 (020) 8780 2224 10–2B
*New owners PizzaExpress have done little to improve the
"passable" (at best) cooking of this high street chain;
(branches of PE's home-grown failure, Pasta di Milano, now
also trade under this name). / 11 pm-midnight; some branches have
no smoking areas; not all branches take bookings.*

Café Portugal SW8 £ 28 ❷❷④

5a & 6a Victoria Hs, S Lambeth Rd (020) 7587 1962 10–1D
*"Lovely" service adds much to the enjoyment of a Portuguese
dinner at this "unusual" family-run Vauxhall café. / 10.30 pm;
no Amex.*

Café Rouge   **£ 26**   ⑤⑤⑤

15 Frith St, W1   (020) 7437 4307   4–2A
46-48 James St, W1   (020) 7487 4847   3–1A
34 Wellington St, WC2   (020) 7836 0998   4–3D
27-31 Basil St, SW3   (020) 7584 2345   5–1D
390 King's Rd, SW3   (020) 7352 2226   5–3B
855 Fulham Rd, SW6   (020) 7371 7600   10–1B
102 Old Brompton Rd, SW7   (020) 7373 2403   5–2B
31 Kensington Pk Rd, W11   (020) 7221 4449   6–1A
Whiteleys, W2   (020) 7221 1509   6–1C
227-229 Chiswick High Rd, W4   (020) 8742 7447   7–2A
158 Fulham Palace Rd, W6   (020) 8741 5037   7–2C
98-100 Shepherd's Bush Rd, W6   (020) 7602 7732   7–1C
2 Lancer Sq, Kensington Ch St, W8   (020) 7938 4200   5–1A
30 Clifton Rd, W9   (020) 7286 2266   8–4A
6 South Grove, N6   (020) 8342 9797   8–1B
18 Chalk Farm Rd, NW1   (020) 7428 0998   8–2B
38-39 High St, NW3   (020) 7435 4240   8–1A
120 St John's Wood High St, NW8   (020) 7722 8366   8–3A
Hay's Galleria, Tooley St, SE1   (020) 7378 0097   9–4D
39-49 Parkgate Rd, SW11   (020) 7924 3565   5–4C
248 Upper R'mond Rd, SW14   (020) 8878 8897   10–2A
200 Putney Br Rd, SW15   (020) 8788 4257   10–2B
40 Abbeville Rd, SW4   (020) 8673 3399   10–2D
20 Cabot Sq, E14   (020) 7537 9696   1–3D
140 Fetter Ln, EC4   (020) 7242 3469   9–2A
Hillgate Hs, Limeburner Ln, EC4   (020) 7329 1234   9–2A
"Horrendous food and service" continue to win a torrent of brickbats for this under-powered faux-Gallic bistro chain.
/ 11 pm - City, E14 & W2 earlier; City, E14 & W2 closed some or all Sat & Sun.

Café Spice Namaste   **£ 31**   ❷❸❸

247 Lavender Hl, SW11   (020) 7738 1717   10–2C
16 Prescot St, E1   (020) 7488 9242   1–2D
Cyrus Todiwala's "very interesting" (and often "exceptional") Indian cooking justifies the trip to the large, "bright" and "modern" original, near Tower Bridge; the inferior Battersea offshoot is a bit of a red herring. / 10.30 pm, Sat 10 pm; E1 closed Sat L & Sun - SW11 D only except Sun when L & D.

Caffè Nero   **£ 10**   ❷❸❸

225 Regent St, W1   (020) 7491 0763
43 Frith St, W1   (020) 7434 3887
62 Brewer St, W1   (020) 7437 1497
79 Tottenham Court Rd, W1   (020) 7580 3885
2 Lancaster Pl, WC2   (020) 7836 6346
29 Southampton St, WC2   (020) 7240 3433
32 Cranbourn St, WC2   (020) 7836 6772
65-72 Strand, WC2   (020) 7930 8483
66 Old Brompton Rd, SW7   (020) 7589 1760
53 Notting Hl Gt, W11   (020) 7727 6505
1-5 King St, W6   (020) 8741 9939
7 Jamestown Rd, NW1   (020) 7482 6969

Caffè Nero (continued)
1 Hampstead High St, NW3   (020) 7431 5958
22-24 Wormwood St, EC2   (020) 7588 4848
Winchester House, London Wall, EC2   (020) 7588 6001
"One of the better chains", say reporters of these upmarket
outlets, which provide "a good choice of pastries" and
"excellent" coffee, as well as pizza and pasta. / 8 pm-11 pm - City
branches earlier - Frith St 2 am; 4 am Thu-Sun; City branches closed Sat
& Sun; no credit cards; no booking.

Caffè Uno   £ 24   ⑤④④
100 Baker St, W1   (020) 7486 8606   2–1A
28 Binney St, W1   (020) 7499 9312   3–2A
5 Argyll St, W1   (020) 7437 2503   3–1C
64 Tottenham Court Rd, W1   (020) 7636 3587   2–1C
24 Charing Cross Rd, WC2   (020) 7240 2524   4–3B
37 St Martin's Ln, WC2   (020) 7836 5837   4–4C
805 Fulham Rd, SW6   (020) 7731 0990   10–1B
106 Queensway, W2   (020) 7229 8470   6–1C
11 Edgware Rd, W2   (020) 7723 4898   6–1D
163-165 Chiswick High Rd, W4   (020) 8742 1942   7–2A
9 Kensington High St, W8   (020) 7937 8961   5–1A
62 Upper St, N1   (020) 7226 7988   8–3D
4 South Grove, N6   (020) 8342 8662   8–1B
40-42 Parkway, NW1   (020) 7428 9124   8–3B
122 St John's Wood High St, NW8   (020) 7722 0400   8–3A
375 Lonsdale Rd, SW13   (020) 8876 3414   10–1A
The "Italianate atmosphere" is "not bad for a chain", but
otherwise these pasta-and-pizza stops are let down by
slapdash standards. / 10 pm-Midnight; some branches have no smoking
areas.

La Cage Imaginaire NW3   £ 29   ④❸❸
16 Flask Walk   (020) 7794 6674   8–1A
"OK, but rather overpriced" Gallic spot, whose small premises
have a dead cute location in Hampstead's lanes. / 11 pm, Sat
11.30 pm; closed Mon.

Calabash WC2   £ 24   ❸④⑤
38 King St   (020) 7836 1976   4–3C
London's only pan-African menu is the special attraction of this
dated basement, underneath a Covent Garden cultural centre;
it makes a "cheep and cheerful" experience that's a little
"different". / 10.30 pm; closed Sat L & Sun; no Switch.

Caldesi W1   £ 34   ❸❷④
15-17 Marylebone Ln   (020) 7935 9226   3–1A
"Trusty local Italian", near the Wigmore Hall; it's "a bit dressy
and old-fashioned" for some tastes. / 11 pm; closed Sat L & Sun;
no smoking area.

FSA

Calzone £22 ④④④

335 Fulham Rd, SW10 (020) 7352 9797 5–3B
352a King's Rd, SW3 (020) 7352 9790 5–3C
2a Kensington Pk Rd, W11 (020) 7243 2003 6–2B
35 Upper St, N1 (020) 7359 9191 8–3D
66 Heath St, NW3 (020) 7794 6775 8–1A
For a "good, cheap meal", these quite stylish, "easy/friendly" pizzerias have their proponents; they were once exceptional, but now they're "nothing special". / Midnight - SW3 11.45 pm - SW10 Fri & Sat 12.45 am.

Cambio de Tercio SW5 £33 ❸❷❷

163 Old Brompton Rd (020) 7244 8970 5–2B
"Really good fun" – this stylish South Kensington spot serves some "good Spanish food", and has a "friendly" attitude. / 11 pm.

Camden Brasserie NW1 £29 ❸❷❷

216 Camden High St (020) 7482 2114 8–2B
"Popular, busy, and good value", this "very unpretentious and relaxing" fixture provides "quality food for all ages". / 11.30 pm; no Amex.

La Candela W8 £37 ④❷④

135 Kensington Ch St (020) 7727 5452 5–1A
Spring '99 Kensington trattoria opening which could as well have debuted in '89 (or '79, for that matter); it offers a solid, fairly traditional package, rather expensively. / 11 pm; closed Sat L & Sun.

Cantaloupe EC2 £28 ❷❸❶

35-42 Charlotte Rd (020) 7613 4411 9–1D
"Hip-crowd" Clerkenwell spot, liked not just for the "loud" and "funky" vibe of the bar (which itself does good snacks), but also for the "unusual and interesting" modern British dishes in the restaurant (at the rear). / Midnight; bar menu only Sat L & Sun; no Amex.

The Canteen SW10 £39 ❷❷❷

Chelsea Harbour (020) 7351 7330 5–4B
"Only the location in dismal Chelsea Harbour is a let-down", at this "brilliant", if nowadays slightly unsung, modern British "all-rounder"; it reliably delivers "top food and top service" in a "unique" setting. / 11 pm, Fri & Sat midnight; closed Sat L & Sun.

Cantina del Ponte SE1 £40 ④⑤④

36c Shad Thames (020) 7403 5403 9–4D
"On a warm evening", "unsurpassable views" can make Conran's Thames-side Italian "perfect for relaxation"; ratings for the "bland" Italian grub (mostly pizzas) have at last scraped off rock bottom, but service remains "truly appalling". / 10.45 pm.

Cantina Italia N1 £26 ❷❷❸

19 Canonbury Ln (020) 7226 9791 8–2D
"Basic and cheap" Islington Italian yearling, which is "good all round", especially if you sit upstairs. / 11 pm; closed Mon L; no Amex.

52

Cantina Vinopolis SE1 £ 26 ②③②
1 Bank End   (020) 7940 8333   9–3C
*Cathedral-like railway arches lend drama to the brasserie at
the South Bank's new wine theme-park; an early visit found
simple, reasonably priced cooking, good enough to make the
place a destination in itself (and – as you might hope – an
interesting and extensive wine list).* / 10.45 pm; no Amex.

Cantinetta Venegazzú SW11 £ 29 ③④③
31–32 Battersea Sq   (020) 7978 5395   5–4C
*This year-old Battersea Italian (with "lovely outside seating,
if you can ignore the traffic") is hailed by some as a foodie
mecca; many, though, just find it rather "boring".* / 10.30 pm; set
weekday L £17(FP).

Canyon TW10 £ 37 ④④③
Riverside   (020) 8948 2944   1–4A
*With a "heavenly riverside setting", "attractive" design, and –
not least – little in the way of local competition, it's no wonder
this Richmond newcomer (part of the Montana group) is
already "massively popular"; its southwest USA menu is
"frustrating", though – it "sounds good, but it's disappointing".*
/ 11 pm; no smoking area.

La Capannina W1 £ 34 ④②④
24 Romilly St   (020) 7437 2473   4–3A
*It "looks very old-fashioned" nowadays, but they "always make
you welcome" at this old-school, "dull" but "reliable" Soho
trattoria.* / 11.30 pm; closed Sat L & Sun; no Switch.

Capital Hotel SW3 £ 75 ③②③
22-24 Basil St   (020) 7589 5171   5–1D
*"Formal" and pricey Knightsbridge hotel dining room, whose
quiet competence has long offered a "consistent" culinary
benchmark; initial reports give cause to question whether new
chef Eric Chavot is keeping up standards.* / 11 pm; dinner, jacket &
tie; set weekday L £36(FP).

LE CAPRICE SW1 £ 47 ②①①
Arlington Hs, Arlington St   (020) 7629 2239   3–4C
*The engine purrs so smoothly at this ultra-"chic" modern
British "perennial" near the Ritz that there are always
doubters who "can't understand the fuss"; to its legions of
devotees, though, it's just "overall wonderful" – "surviving its
new ownership with flying colours" – and "always booked".*
/ Midnight.

Caraffini SW1 £ 34 ②①②
61-63 Lower Sloane St   (020) 7259 0235   5–2D
*"Good value for money" and "fun waiters who are
professionals" make this "bustling" and "friendly" Italian near
Sloane Square a great local favourite – "in spite of the noise".*
/ 11.30 pm; closed Sun.

Caravaggio EC3   **£ 43**   ④④④
107-112 Leadenhall St   (020) 7626 6206   9–2D
*In the heart of the Square Mile (by Lloyds) – but "not too
City" in feeling – this large and "buzzy" Italian is a popular
business destination, in spite of "ordinary" cooking and tables
which are "too close". / 10 pm; closed Sat & Sun.*

Caravan Serai W1   **£ 25**   ④❸⑤
50 Paddington St   (020) 7935 1208   2–1A
*The fact that it's "different" is now the chief selling point of
this rather "rusty", rug-filled Marylebone Afghani. / 11 pm, Fri
& Sat 11.30 pm; no smoking area.*

Carnevale EC1   **£ 28**   ❷❸④
135 Whitecross St   (020) 7250 3452   9–1B
*"Great little vegetarian" near the Barbican; the place may be
"way too cramped", but the cooking is "inventive" and
"cheap". / 10.30 pm; closed Sat L & Sun; no Visa, Mastercard or Amex; set
weekday L £17(FP).*

Casale Franco N1   **£ 32**   ❸⑤❸
rear of 134-137 Upper St   (020) 7226 8994   8–3D
*"Pizzas to die for" and other "good" Italian cooking have long
made this large but "intimate" Islington trattoria (hidden down
an alleyway) a notable local fixture; service is needlessly
"stroppy". / 11.30 pm, Sun 9 pm; closed Mon ; no Amex; no smoking area;
book L only.*

The Castle SW8   **£ 20**   ④④❸
115 Battersea High St   (020) 7228 8181   10–1C
*This "difficult-to-find" Battersea backstreet boozer shines on a
sunny day on account of its nice, "quiet" garden; the grub's
OK, and reasonably priced. / 9.45 pm; no Amex.*

Cave W1   **£ 49**   ❷❸❸
161 Piccadilly   (020) 7409 0445   3–3C
*"The lobster and caviar are excellent" – and prices "not
unreasonable" – at the grand but quite wackily decorated
adjunct to Piccadilly's Caviar House; its "light" atmosphere
best "suits lunch", as evenings can be quiet. / 9 pm, Thu–Sat
10.30 pm; closed Sun.*

Cecconi's W1   **£ 63**   ⑤⑤⑤
5a Burlington Gdns   (020) 7434 1509   3–3C
*"The well-heeled seem to love it", and there are reporters who
would eat "daily" at this self-important Mayfair Italian "if it
weren't so expensive"; the overwhelming view, however, is that
it's the "biggest rip-off ever". / 11.15 pm; closed Sun; jacket & tie.*

Centuria N1   **£ 25**   ❸④④
100 St Paul's Rd   (020) 7704 2435   1–1C
*"Mammoth portions" of Italian cooking "better than you'd
expect in a pub" are offered at this "otherwise slightly dull"
north Islington local; the bar area is nicer than the dining
room. / 11 pm; closed weekday L; no Amex.*

Chada SW11 £28 ②❸④
208-210 Battersea Park Rd   (020) 7622 2209   10–1C
"Excellent food in smart Thai surroundings" has made this
"small" Battersea oriental "good for over a decade" now; it
"lacks atmosphere". / 11 pm, Fri & Sat 11.30 pm; closed Sat L;
smart casual.

The Chapel NW1 £26 ②④❸
48 Chapel St   (020) 7402 9220   6–1D
"Great grub is served with good grace" (if no great alacrity) at
this popular gastropub, near Edgware Road tube; it's "difficult
getting a table" at peak times. / 9.50 pm.

Chapter Two SE3 £34 ❸❸④
43-45 Montpelier Vale   (020) 8333 2666   1–4D
Though undeniably a "great local asset", this modern British
establishment looking onto Blackheath has "no originality",
and "raises expectations above its performance". / 10.30 pm, Fri
& Sat 11.30 pm.

Charco's SW3 £34 ④❸④
1 Bray Pl   (020) 7584 0765   5–2D
"An oasis off the King's Road", say regulars at this "friendly",
"relatively undiscovered" modern British restaurant (under a
wine bar), which is "seldom busy". / 10.30 pm; closed Sun; pre-th.
£24(FP).

Che SW1 £50 ④④④
23 St James's St   (020) 7747 9380   3–4D
"A waste of a potentially stunning location", this elevated St
James's newcomer "lacks atmosphere", and many find its
modern British fare "way overpriced"; it can be "nice for
business", though, with its "interesting cigar room" and
"commendable wine list". / 11.30 pm; closed Sat L & Sun; set
weekday L £29(FP).

Chelsea Bun Diner SW10 £18 ❸④❸
9a Lamont Rd   (020) 7352 3635   5–3B
"Titanic fry-ups" at "good-value" prices make this "fun and
lively" diner Chelsea's number one "hangover breakfast" point
– at other times, the BYO policy is the principal attraction;
they "need a no-smoking area". / 11 pm; no Amex.

Chelsea Kitchen SW3 £11 ④❸④
98 King's Rd   (020) 7589 1330   5–2D
"Basic", "fast", "reliable" and "cheap" – and only 200 yards
from Sloane Square! / 11.45 pm; no credit cards; no smoking area; need
4+ to book.

The Chelsea Ram SW10 £26 ②④②
32 Burnaby St   (020) 7351 4008   5–4B
"Delicious pub grub at reasonable prices" and an "attractive
interior" guarantee that this obscurely located Chelsea
"hang-out" is often "too busy"; the food has "slipped" slightly,
though. / 10 pm; no Amex; no booking.

Cheng Du NW1   £31   ③③③

9 Parkway   (020) 7485 8058   8–3B
"Always dependable" Camden Town Chinese with "polite"
service and civilised décor. / 11.30 pm; no Amex & no Switch.

CHEZ BRUCE SW17   £38   ❶❶②

2 Bellevue Rd   (020) 8672 0114   10–2C
This "great neighbourhood restaurant" overlooking
Wandsworth Common elicits a hymn of praise – from
reporters right across London – for its "top quality",
"inventive" and "good value" modern British cooking and its
"lovely, friendly" service. / 10.30 pm; closed Sun D; booking: max 6.

Chez Gérard   £30   ④③③

31 Dover St, W1   (020) 7499 8171   3–3C
8 Charlotte St, W1   (020) 7636 4975   2–1C
119 Chancery Ln, WC2   (020) 7405 0290   2–2D
45 East Ter, Covent Gdn, WC2   (020) 7379 0666   4–3D
3 Yeoman's Row, SW3   (020) 7581 8377   5–2C
84-86 Rosebery Ave, EC1   (020) 7833 1515   8–4D
64 Bishopsgate, EC2   (020) 7588 1200   9–2D
14 Trinity Sq, EC3   (020) 7480 5500   9–3D
"Reliable steak and chips" has been at the heart of the
success of this consistent chain, whose attractive branches win
most praise as "good-value business lunch places"; some
wonder if the formula isn't becoming rather "tired". / 10 pm-
11.15 pm; Charlotte St closed Sat L - Dover St closed Sun L - EC1 closed Sat L
& Sun D - Chancery Ln & EC2 closed Sat & Sun - EC3 closed Sun;
no smoking areas.

Chez Liline N4   £30   ❶③⑤

101 Stroud Green Rd   (020) 7263 6550   8–1D
Arguably "the best exotic fish restaurant in town" may have a
"lousy" Finsbury Park location, "uninspiring" décor and
sometimes "slow" service, but it offers "excellent value" and is
"worth a detour". / 10.30 pm; closed Sun.

Chez Moi W11   £40   ③❶②

1 Addison Ave   (020) 7603 8267   6–2A
"A touch camp, but good for wooing", this "old-fashioned"
Gallic fixture in Holland Park is still a "favourite", even if the
cuisine – like the "red and velvety" décor – is "too rich" for
some tastes. / 11 pm; closed Sat L & Sun; set weekday L £25(FP).

Chez Nico at Ninety
Grosvenor House Hotel W1   £89   ②③④

90 Park Ln   (020) 7409 1290   3–3A
Even those lauding "exceptional" food at Nico Ladenis's
Mayfair temple of gastronomy admit that it's a "very dull"
place, and increasingly the view is that the whole performance
is "very ordinary, for the price". / 11 pm; closed Sat L & Sun;
no Switch; jacket & tie.

Chezmax SW10 £41 ❶❶❷

168 Ifield Rd (020) 7835 0874 5–3A
"Superb" and *"inspired"* Gallic cooking and *"amazing"* service
– the maître d' is *"awesome"* – are carving out a notable
reputation for this obscurely sited Chelsea-fringe basement;
"it's equally good for romance or a good night out". / 11 pm;
closed Mon & Sun.

Chiang Mai W1 £32 ❶④⑤

48 Frith St (020) 7437 7444 4–2A
This Soho stalwart's *"authentic"*, *"imaginative"* and *"subtle"*
Thai cuisine is the best of its type in the West End; the catch?
– the atmosphere can be *"deathly"*. / 11 pm; closed Sun L; no Amex.

Chicago Rib Shack SW7 £27 ④④④

1 Raphael St (020) 7581 5595 5–1C
"Kids love the great rack of ribs" at this *"noisy and fun"*
Knightsbridge institution – *"it's all pretty unhealthy, but
sometimes that's what you want"*. / 11.45 pm; no smoking area;
no booking Sat.

China Blues NW1 £35 ④④❸

29-31 Parkway (020) 7482 3940 8–3B
"Great music at weekends" is the biggest strength of this quite
stylish Camden Town oriental, whose cooking is *"average"* and
"overpriced". / 11 pm; smart casual; no smoking area.

China City WC2 £25 ❸④④

25a Lisle St (020) 7734 3388 4–3A
"Delicious dim sum" is the highlight at this huge Chinese, set
back in its own courtyard – *"one of the more tolerable
restaurants in the vicinity of Chinatown"*. / 11.45 pm;
no smoking area; Sun, no lunch bookings.

China House W1 £35 – – –

160 Piccadilly (020) 7499 6996 3–3C
Huge, ambitious newcomer, near the Ritz, which will hopefully
bring some much-needed sparkle to the Chinese restaurant
scene; downstairs will be informal – upstairs, the 'Clipper'
dining room draws its style from inter-war seaplanes. / 11.30 pm.

China Jazz W1 £52 ⑤⑤⑤

12 Berkeley Sq (020) 7499 9933 3–3B
Mega-*"swanky"* new Mayfair oriental whose *"delusions of
grandeur"* have already led it into receivership; as we go to
press, a relaunch is planned. / Midnight, Sun 10 pm; closed Sat L
& Sun D; jacket & tie.

Chinon W14 £35 ❷④④

23 Richmond Way (020) 7602 4082 7–1C
Does this *"absolute one-off"* near Shepherd's Bush risk
becoming 'normal'?; though praise remains very generous for
the *"sublime"* Gallic fare, its rating slipped a fraction this year,
while the infamously *"strange"* atmosphere scored higher.
/ 10.45 pm; D only; closed Sun.

Chiswick Restaurant W4   £ 35   ❷❸④

131-133 Chiswick High Rd   (020) 8994 6887   7–2B
"Interesting" modern British cooking is the cornerstone of this popular neighbourhood restaurant's success; its setting is attractive, but "noisy" and "tight for space". / 11 pm; closed Sat L & Sun D; set weekday L £20(FP).

Chor Bizarre W1   £ 39   ❸❷❷

16 Albemarle St   (020) 7629 9802   3–3C
Fans praise the "fabulous" food at this "exotic" Mayfair Indian, but it's still "not on a par with the interesting décor". / 11.30 pm; no smoking area.

Christian's W4   £ 30   ❸❸❸

1 Station Pde   (020) 8995 0382   1–3A
The open kitchen at this slightly offbeat Chiswick "local" delivers quite ambitious (but "variable") Anglo-French cooking; service "can be on the slow side". / 10.30 pm; closed Mon & Sun.

Christopher's WC2   £ 44   ④❸❸

18 Wellington St   (020) 7240 4222   4–3D
"Perfect for posh steak and chips" (or seafood), this "chic" American benefits from a "stunning" ("grandiose") Covent Garden setting whose "well spaced tables" are ideal for business; ratings fell this year, and prices are "high" – "but who cares, on expenses?" / 11.45 pm; closed Sun D; smart casual; pre-th. £27(FP).

Chuen Cheng Ku W1   £ 27   ❸④④

17 Wardour St   (020) 7437 1398   4–3A
"Still the best dim sum" (if you like ordering from trollies) is the highlight of this huge, Chinatown landmark, which otherwise subscribes to the iffy standards of the area. / 11.45 pm; no smoking area.

Chunk WC2   £ 9   ❸❸④

9 Adelaide St   (020) 7836 9550   4–4C
Just by Trafalgar Square, this bright and agreeable, if fairly pricey, soup and sandwich stop is doubtless the prototype of (yet another) chain. / L only; closed Sat & Sun; no credit cards; no smoking.

Churchill Arms W8   £ 15   ❷④❸

119 Kensington Ch St   (020) 7792 1246   6–2B
"The best Thai food ever, and as cheap as anything" ensures it's "impossible to get a table" at this very well known Kensington pub-annexe; beware – "if you haven't booked, the waitresses can be scary". / 9.30 pm; closed Sun D; no Amex; no lunch bookings.

Chutney Mary SW10   £ 42   ❷❸❸

535 King's Rd   (020) 7351 3113   5–4B
"Consistently good" cooking, which "may not all be authentic, but is exciting and delicious", has made this "spacious and airy" Indian "with a twist" the best known subcontinental in town, in spite of its distant-Chelsea location. / 11.30 pm; no smoking area; set weekday L £27(FP).

Chutneys NW1 £16 ❸④④
124 Drummond St (020) 7388 0604 8–4C
"Good-value buffets" (at lunch and all day Sunday) of "tasty
and varied" grub makes it worth remembering this Indian
veggie, near Euston. / 11 pm; no Amex & no Switch;
Sun, need 10+ to book.

Cibo W14 £40 ❷❸❸
3 Russell Gdns (020) 7371 6271 7–1D
"Intimate" (if vaguely "weird") Olympia Italian whose
"delicious" (if pricey) cooking and "unusual" wines make it
quite a "favourite"; "make sure you get a good table – some
are cramped". / 11 pm; closed Sat L & Sun D; smart casual.

Cicada EC1 £31 ④④❸
132-136 St John St (020) 7608 1550 9–1B
"Self-consciously trendy" Smithfield bar/restaurant, serving
"hit-and-miss" fusion fare. / 10.45 pm; closed Sat L & Sun;
no smoking area.

Circus W1 £42 ④④④
1 Upper James St (020) 7534 4000 3–2D
The "funky" basement bar is the undoubted star at this
"stark" Soho minimalist; some think the restaurant "stylish",
but many feel it's "unexciting" in every respect – "the same as
hundreds of other restaurants round town". / Midnight, Fri
& Sat 12.30 am; closed Sun D; pre-th. £29(FP).

City Brasserie EC3 £51 ④❸④
56 Mark Ln (020) 7480 6789 9–3D
"Lacking the buzz of its previous location", but still serving
"overpriced City fare", this vaguely Deco-ish basement
presents a "hard-to-remember" experience. / 9 pm; closed Sat
& Sun.

City Miyama EC4 £51 ❷❷④
17 Godliman St (020) 7489 1937 9–3B
This "stark" City Japanese is "expensive but worth it"; the
teppan-yaki and sushi bars find most favour – "the restaurant
itself is fine, but atmosphere-free". / 9.30 pm; closed Sat D & Sun.

CITY RHODES EC4 £55 ❷❷❸
New Street Sq (020) 7583 1313 9–2A
"Exquisite" modern British cooking and "extremely helpful"
and "efficient" staff create "a very good atmosphere for
business" at Gary R's dining room, just off Fleet Street –
reporters' top choice for an "expensive" City lunch. / 9 pm;
closed Sat & Sun.

Claridges Restaurant W1 £70 ④❸❷
Brook St (020) 7629 8860 3–2B
"Impressive and elegant" it may be, but the charming Art
Deco dining room of Society's favourite hotel only really sets
pulses racing at breakfast, which is "exceptional in every way".
/ 10.45 pm; jacket & tie.

CLARKE'S W8   £ 46   ❶❶❷

124 Kensington Ch St   (020) 7221 9225   6–2B

Sally Clarke's "always spot-on" cooking offers "simplicity at its best" from "focussed" modern British menus (which, at dinner, offer no choice); many find her "very pleasant" restaurant, near Notting Hill Gate, "romantic" – especially upstairs.
/ 10 pm; closed Sun; no smoking area.

CLUB GASCON EC1   £ 33   ❶❷❷

57 West Smithfield   (020) 7796 0600   9–2B

"Foie gras in every conceivable permutation" is part of the "exceptional and different" repertoire which has made this unusual newcomer – specialising in Gascony's "gutsy" cuisine – the foodie hit of the year; an "excellent and unusual wine list" is a bonus. / 11 pm; closed Sat L & Sun; no Amex.

Coast W1   £ 48   ④④④

26b Albemarle St   (020) 7495 5999   3–3C

"Echoey" and "sterile", and with "no buzz, despite its size", this ultra-minimalist Mayfair venture earns little affection, despite its wacky design; the "inventive" modern British may be "pretentious", but it's still better than at many similarly trendy places. / 11.45 pm.

Coffee Republic   £ 6   ❸❷❷

2 South Molton St, W1   (020) 7629 4567
37 Gt Marlborough St, W1   (020) 7734 5529
38 Berwick St, W1   (020) 7437 2328
88 Wardour St, W1   (020) 7287 8948
18 Garrick St, WC2   (020) 7240 1323
234 Strand Law Courts, WC2   (020) 7583 2456
80 Strand, WC2   (020) 7836 6660
178 Fulham Rd, SW10   (020) 7373 0919
157 King's Rd, SW3   (020) 7351 3178
72 Old Brompton Rd, SW7   (020) 7823 8120
8 Pembridge Rd, W11   (020) 7229 6698
58 Queensway, W2   (020) 7792 3600
280 Chiswick High Rd, W4   (020) 8995 7772
87 Charterhouse St, EC1   (020) 7253 8161
25 Exchange Sq, EC2   (020) 7588 5130
47 London Wall, EC2   (020) 7588 2220
59-60 Cornhill, EC3   (020) 7623 2926
74 Leadenhall Mkt, EC3   (020) 7626 1993
147 Fleet St, EC4   (020) 7353 0900
30-32 Ludgate Hl, EC4   (020) 7329 2522

"Coffee to die for" (not least the "fantastic choice of flavoured lattes") made this bright and stylish chain one of reporters' "best in town" for a caffeine fix. / 6 pm-10 pm - City branches earlier - W2 & Wardour St 11 pm; City & Law Courts branches closed Sat & Sun; no credit cards; no bookings.

Coins W11   £ 25   ❸④❷

105-107 Talbot Rd   (020) 7221 8099   6–1B

"Cool" diner "hang-out", that's "great for watching all the wannabe beautiful people" of Notting Hill; the "fantastic Sunday brunch" is a major attraction. / L only; no Amex.

The Collection SW3   £ 43   ④⑤❸
264 Brompton Rd   (020) 7225 1212   5–2C
The "meat market" bar at this glitzy Brompton Cross hang-out
"tends to predominate" – some do "love the galleried dining
area above", but service is "unsmiling", and the "expensive"
modern British food comes in "small portions". / 11.30 pm;
closed Sun.

Le Colombier SW3   £ 35   ❸❸❷
145 Dovehouse St   (020) 7351 1155   5–2C
This popular Gallic brasserie in a Chelsea back street has a
"relaxed", very "grown-up" atmosphere and, for the summer,
a "lovely" terrace; the grub is dependable but "not cheap".
/ 11 pm.

Como Lario SW1   £ 37   ④❸❸
22 Holbein Pl   (020) 7730 2954   5–2D
"Reliable but boring" trattoria, long popular as a "friendly"
haven near Sloane Square; it's "lost its touch", though, with
food declined "from OK to bland", and ambience to
"average". / 11.30 pm; closed Sun; smart casual.

CONNAUGHT W1   £ 70   ❸❶❷
Carlos Pl   (020) 7499 7070   3–3B
"Splendid", panelled Mayfair dining room whose dependable
Anglo-French cooking remains resolutely "unfashionable and
calorific"; service is legendarily "perfect". / 10.45 pm;
Grill closed Sat L; jacket & tie for dinner, jacket for lunch; appreciated if guests
try to refrain from smoking.

Conrad Hotel SW10   £ 44   ❷❷❸
Chelsea Harbour   (020) 7823 3000   5–4B
A "mind-boggling array of scrumptious food" makes it worth
seeking out the "amazing" Sunday brunch – to which our
ratings relate – at this otherwise unremarkable Chelsea
marina-side hotel. / 10.30 pm; no smoking area.

Il Convivio SW1   £ 40   – – –
143 Ebury St   (020) 7730 4099   2–4A
Long the home of Mijanou (RIP), this rather obscure Belgravia
townhouse site is, as we go to press, being relaunched as an
Italian by the Taberna Etrusca group; (the price given is our
guesstimate). / 10.30 pm; closed Sat L & Sun.

The Cook House SW15   £ 34   ❷❷④
56 Lower Richmond Rd   (020) 8785 2300   10–1A
"Robust" modern British cooking from a "short" menu is
applauded at this "cramped" and "chaotic" Putney spot; the
BYO policy helps make for a "guaranteed good evening".
/ 11 pm; D only; closed Sun & Mon; no Amex.

Coopers Arms SW3 £ 24 ③④②
87 Flood St   (020) 7376 3120   5–3C
*"Brilliant modern pub with an old edge", in deepest Chelsea;
most praise its "good-value" and "unpretentious" cooking,
though it's been a "bit unreliable recently". / 10 pm;
Sun, no booking.*

Coq d'Argent EC3 £ 49 ④④③
1 Poultry   (020) 7395 5000   9–2C
*"Typically Conran" City yearling – albeit one with a "fantastic"
6th-floor location – offering cooking which is "nothing special"
at "bank robbery" prices; "crazy" table-turning demands are a
recurrent complaint. / 10 pm; closed Sat L & Sun D; set Sun L £32(FP).*

Cork & Bottle WC2 £ 27 ④④②
44-46 Cranbourn St   (020) 7734 7807   4–3B
*"Hidden" and "clubby" Leicester Square "stalwart" which
remains a popular and "convenient" central watering-hole; the
"simple" food is no more than OK, however, and many think
the good wine list "the main reason to visit". / 11.30 pm,
Sun 10 pm; no smoking at lunch; no booking after 6.30 pm.*

Corney & Barrow WC2 £ 30 ③②③
116 St Martin's Ln   (020) 7655 9800   4–4B
*"A great arrival for the area" (just north of Trafalgar Square),
this stylish offshoot of the eminent City wine bar chain is a
useful rendezvous and "fills a niche" for "good pre-theatre"
dining. / 11.15 pm; closed Sun D; no booking.*

Costa's Fish Restaurant W8 £ 15 ②①④
18 Hillgate St   (020) 7727 4310   6–2B
*"Much better, cheaper fish than nearby Geale's" (its famous
neighbour) is found at this "consistent" chippy, just off Notting
Hill Gate. / 10.30 pm; closed Mon & Sun; no credit cards.*

Costa's Grill W8 £ 13 ④③③
12-14 Hillgate St   (020) 7229 3794   6–2B
*"Going for 40 years", this "homely" Greek off Notting Hill
Gate can still make a "relaxed" stand-by; the complaint that
"it used to be decent – not any more", is too often heard,
however. / 10.30 pm; closed Sun; no credit cards; no smoking area.*

Cottons NW1 £ 28 ④③②
55 Chalk Farm Rd   (020) 7482 1096   8–2B
*"Unforgettable rum cocktails" and a "great happy hour" are
the highpoint at this Camden Caribbean; the cooking's "not
worth it". / 11 pm, Thu-Sat 11.45 pm; no smoking area.*

The County Hall Restaurant SE1 £ 42 ⑤④④
Queens Walk   (020) 7902 8000   2–3D
*"The view is great" but "there's no getting away from the hotel
feel" at this year-old dining room (overlooking Westminster
from the South Bank); "blandly executed" cooking is served
"unemotionally" and "at a price". / 11 pm; no smoking at breakfast;
pre-th. £28(FP).*

The Cow W11 £ 32 ❸❸❸

89 Westbourne Park Rd   (020) 7221 0021   6–1B
*"Very trendy" Notting Hill boozer, whose cosy upstairs dining
room offers a modern British menu that's "unusual but a bit
overpriced"; the "fun", "noisy" and "smoky" downstairs bar
serves "great seafood".* / 11 pm; D only; no Amex.

Coyote Café W4 £ 27 ❸❸❸

2 Fauconberg Rd   (020) 8742 8545   7–2A
*"Great margaritas", hearty portions of Tex-Mex nosh and a
few nice outside tables are the attractions of this
neighbourhood bar/café, in deepest Chiswick.* / 10 pm;
closed Mon L; no large bookings on Fri & Sat.

Cranks £ 14 ④④④

23 Barrett St, W1   (020) 7495 1340   3–1B
8 Marshall St, W1   (020) 7437 9431   3–2D
9-11 Tottenham St, W1   (020) 7631 3912   2–1B
17-19 Great Newport St, WC2   (020) 7836 5226   4–3B
Unit 11, 8 Adelaide St, WC2   (020) 7836 0660   4–4C
Concourse Level, 15 Cabot Pl, E14   (020) 7513 0678   1–3D
*Gripes about "bland, overpriced food" linger, but this
long-established veggie chain is beginning to haul itself off the
ropes, and now wins more praise for its "quick, reliable and
healthy" fare.* / 7 pm-11 pm; some branches closed part of weekend; some
branches no credit cards; no smoking; no booking.

The Crescent SW3 £ 24 ④❷❷

99 Fulham Rd   (020) 7225 2244   5–2C
*"Very interesting" wines (from an "exhaustive", 200-strong list)
are twinned with "rather boring" food at this "sophisticated
but unpretentious" Brompton Cross wine bar-cum-diner.*
/ 11.30 pm; no booking.

The Criterion W1 £ 43 ❸⑤❶

Piccadilly Circus   (020) 7930 0488   3–3D
*It's a pity that "disobliging" and "elusive" service mars so
many visits to this "exquisite" neo-Byzantine chamber – its
school-of-MPW cooking may not be remarkable, but it is
competent by the standards of the larger West End places.*
/ Midnight, Sun 10.30 pm.

Cross Keys SW3 £ 33 ④❸❷

1 Lawrence St   (020) 7349 9111   5–3C
*"Not very pub-like", former Chelsea boozer, whose rear
conservatory houses "such a lovely restaurant", serving fairly
good modern British fare in a "fun" and "buzzy" atmosphere.*
/ 11 pm; set weekday L £20(FP).

The Crown SW3 £ 25 ❷❸④

153 Dovehouse St   (020) 7352 9505   5–2C
*New Chelsea back street gastroboozer, with "friendly" staff
and a "great mixture of good traditional pub grub and modern
British cooking"; it can get "smoky".* / 10 pm; no Amex.

Cuba Libre N1   £ 26   ⑤④❸
72 Upper St   (020) 7354 9998   8–3D
*It's "fun" and has a "nice" setting, but this impressively
themed Islington hang-out's cooking is "ordinary" at best.
/ 11 pm, Fri & Sat midnight; no Amex; set weekday L £16(FP).*

Cucina NW3   £ 29   ❸❸④
45a South End Rd   (020) 7435 7814   8–2A
*"Good" Italian cooking and "charming" service help make this
"busy" (although rather "overlit" and "echoey") neighbourhood
spot a local hit in the void that is Hampstead. / 10.30 pm, Fri
& Sat 11 pm; closed Sun D; smart casual.*

Da Mario SW7   £ 29   ④❸④
15 Gloucester Rd   (020) 7584 9078   5–1B
*There's "always a crowd" at this well-established, "efficient and
friendly" Italian (a PizzaExpress in disguise), near the Albert
Hall; the disco cellar suits budget dine-and-bops. / 11.30 pm;
no Switch; book for disco.*

Dakota W11   £ 37   ④④❷
127 Ledbury Rd   (020) 7792 9191   6–1B
*"Trendy" and "packed", it may be, but this Notting Hill
yearling's once "imaginative" American cooking is "going
downhill" – it's "not so much Deep South as deeply
disappointing" – and service is often "terrible"; good outside
terrace. / 10.45 pm.*

Dan's SW3   £ 36   ④❸❷
119 Sydney St   (020) 7352 2718   5–3C
*With its "lovely conservatory" and "great garden", this
"pretty", long-established Chelsea townhouse restaurant
makes a "good summer venue"; it's "let down by average
food". / 10.30 pm; closed Sun D.*

Daphne NW1   £ 24   ❸❷❸
83 Bayham St   (020) 7267 7322   8–3C
*"Very Greek, very friendly, very good" – this long-established
Camden Town spot, with its "fabulous roof terrace", attracts a
more-than-local following; "the fish specials are hugely
recommended". / 11.30 pm; closed Sun; no Amex; set weekday L £16(FP).*

Daphne's SW3   £ 41   ④④❷
110-112 Draycott Ave   (020) 7589 4257   5–2C
*"Still a little pretentious, but very enjoyable"; now the smart
crowd is moving on from this Brompton Cross Italian, it is
reverting to a happier obscurity – a "discreet and romantic
place" with OK cooking and somewhat "inattentive" service.
/ 11.30 pm.*

Daquise SW7   £ 22   ④④❸
20 Thurloe St   (020) 7589 6117   5–2C
*"The dated ambience, not the food, is the point" of this "old
favourite" South Kensington café (stuck in Warsaw, circa
1955), where "fellow diners are full of character". / 10.45 pm;
no Amex; no smoking area.*

De Cecco SW6 £30 ❸❷❷

189 New King's Rd   (020) 7736 1145   10–1B
"When it's on form", this large, "upbeat" Parson's Green
trattoria is a "great local spot", with "fair prices" and a
"buzzing" atmosphere. / 10.45 pm; closed Sun.

Deals £28 ⑤⑤⑤

14-16 Foubert's Pl, W1   (020) 7287 1001   3–2C
Chelsea Harbour, SW10   (020) 7795 1001   5–4B
Broadway Centre, W6   (020) 8563 1001   7–2C
"Disappointing all-round" diners, whose only saving grace is
that "kids love them". / 11 pm, Sat & Sun 11.30 pm - W1 1.30 am Fri
& Sat; W1 closed Sun D.

Deco SW10 £24 ❸❸❸

294 Fulham Rd   (020) 7351 0044   5–3B
The modern British cooking may have no great ambitions,
but it's "actually quite good" at this distant-Chelsea newcomer;
a good atmosphere" and the décor's "touch of deco"
commend it to locals. / 11 pm; closed Sun D; no Amex.

Defune W1 £43 ❷❸⑤

61 Blandford St   (020) 7935 8311   2–1A
"Truly Japanese" fixture, near Baker Street, whose devotees
proclaim it "the best in town" (especially for sushi); there's
zilch in the way of décor, though. / 10.30 pm; closed Sun; set
weekday L £26(FP).

Del Buongustaio SW15 £33 ❶❷❷

283 Putney Br Rd   (020) 8780 9361   10–2B
"Original" and "consistently excellent" cooking (and "exciting
wines", too) makes this externally unpromising but "intimate"
Putney Italian a very popular southwest London destination.
/ 10.30 pm; closed Sat L; set weekday L £22(FP).

Delfina Studio Café SE1 £33 ❸❸❷

50 Bermondsey St   (020) 7357 0244   9–4D
"A gem in Bermondsey" – "light" and "fresh" dishes,
"charming" staff and a "lovely" setting make this airy gallery a
useful and quite fashionable lunchtime rendezvous. / L only;
closed Sat & Sun.

La Delizia £24 ❸④④

63-65 Chelsea Manor St, SW3   (020) 7376 4111   5–3C
246 Old Brompton Rd, SW5   (020) 7373 6085   5–2A
The shine is going off these "neighbourhood jewel" Chelsea
pizzerias; they were once a trio, but the wonderfully
Eurotrashy branch at the Farmer's Market is sadly no more.
/ Midnight; no credit cards; no booking in summer.

Denim WC2 £35 ⑤④④

4a Upper St Martin's Ln   (020) 7497 0376   4–3B
Groovily glazed and video-banked West End newcomer
bar/restaurant; "love it as a bar – eat elsewhere". / Midnight,
Sun 10 pm.

The Depot SW14   **£ 27**   ❸④❷
Mortlake High St   (020) 8878 9462   10–1A
*"Beautiful views of the river" are the highlight at this
"child-friendly" Barnes spot, which is "excellent for Sunday
lunch"; the grub has "improved" of late.* / 11 pm; no smoking area.

Dibbens EC1   **£ 31**   ❸❷❸
2 Cowcross St   (020) 7250 0035   9–1A
*Smart and simple Smithfield newcomer (on the site of Mange
2, RIP), with its eye on the business lunching market; service is
efficient, but we found the modern British fare a touch
ordinary for the price – others are more generous.* / 11 pm;
closed Sat & Sun.

Diverso W1   **£ 42**   ❷❸④
85 Piccadilly   (020) 7491 2222   3–4C
*The grandly rustic décor may be "dull", but this Mayfair
Italian's "good" and (appropriately) "diverse" cooking arguably
deserves a wider following than it has; it can be "excellent for
business".* / 11.30 pm; closed Sun L.

Diwana Bhel-Poori House NW1   **£ 16**   ❷❸④
121 Drummond St   (020) 7387 5556   8–4C
*"Authentic Indian vegetarian food at incredibly low prices"
continues to draw a wide following to this basic, very '60s spot,
in the 'Little India' by Euston Station; the "stunning lunch
value" is well known; BYO.* / 11.30 pm; no smoking area; Fri–Sun no
booking; set weekday L £9(FP).

Dixie's Bar & Grill SW11   **£ 21**   ④⑤❷
25 Battersea Rs   (020) 7228 7984   10–2C
*It's the "lively" and "noisy" atmosphere that keeps this
Battersea "local" Tex/Mex "busy" – not the "basic brunch and
burgers".* / 11.30 pm.

Dôme   **£ 24**   ⑤⑤❸
57-59 Old Compton St, W1   (020) 7287 0770   4–3A
32 Long Acre, WC2   (020) 7379 8650   4–2C
8 Charing Cross Rd, WC2   (020) 7240 5556   4–4B
354 King's Rd, SW3   (020) 7352 2828   5–3B
194-196 Earl's Court Rd, SW5   (020) 7835 2200   5–2A
Kensington Ct, W8   (020) 7937 6655   5–1A
341 Upper St, N1   (020) 7226 3414   8–3D
58-62 Heath St, NW3   (020) 7431 0399   8–1A
57-59 Charterhouse St, EC1   (020) 7336 6484   9–1A
4 St Paul's Churchyard, EC4   (020) 7489 0767   9–2B
*"Bad" faux-Gallic cooking and "terrible" service ensure that
this Whitbread chain – an attractive pastiche of inter-war Left
Bank style – is best enjoyed as a breakfast stop or "when on
your own for a coffee, roll, etc".* / 10.30 pm-11 pm; EC1 closed Sat &
Sun; some branches have no smoking areas.

don Fernando's TW9 £ 22 ❸❸❷

27f The Quadrant   (020) 8948 6447   1–4A

"Great tapas" make it worth knowing about this lively, large
Spaniard, next to Richmond BR station; *"service is abrupt, but
that's in keeping with the character of the place"*. / 11 pm;
no Amex.

Don Pepe NW8 £ 25 ❸❸❸

99 Frampton St   (020) 7262 3834   8–4A

The oldest tapas bar in town, just around the corner from
Lords, still wins local praise for its *"excellent service and
home-made dishes"*. / Midnight; closed Sun.

DORCHESTER GRILL
DORCHESTER HOTEL W1 £ 59 ❷❶❶

53 Park Ln   (020) 7629 8888   3–3A

With its *"sumptuous, old-fashioned"* Spanish Baronial
décor, *"impressive"* (but *"not condescending"*) service and
"dependable" cooking, this *"grand"* Mayfair grill is a
worthy representative of *"English tradition at its best"*.
/ 11 pm; smart casual; pre-th. £40(FP).

Dorchester, Oriental
Dorchester Hotel W1 £ 70 ❸❷④

53 Park Ln   (020) 7629 8888   3–3A

The cooking – *"on a par with Hong Kong"* – is *"almost worth
the prices"* at this swanky Mayfair Chinese; some think the
décor *"chic"* – we're with those who find it *"silkily off-putting"*.
/ 11 pm; closed Sat L & Sun; smart casual; set weekday L £25(FP).

La Dordogne W4 £ 32 ❸❷❷

5 Devonshire Rd   (020) 8747 1836   7–2A

"You feel you are in France" at this *"cosy"* and *"reliable"*
Chiswick *"classic"*; it offers *"good, unfancy cooking"* and
"service to match". / 11 pm; closed Sat L & Sun; set weekday L £18(FP).

Dover Street W1 £ 43 ⑤⑤④

8-9 Dover St   (020) 7629 9813   3–3C

"Lots of fun in the evening", say fans of the *"good atmosphere
for eating and dancing"* at this *"lively"* Mayfair cellar; the food
is *"average"*, at best, though, and some are *"disgusted"* by the
level of service. / 3 am; closed Sat L & Sun; no jeans.

Down Mexico Way W1 £ 29 ⑤④❶

25 Swallow St   (020) 7437 9895   3–3D

"Only go for the bar and dancing", at this atmospheric and
"noisy" Mayfair Mexican; the *"ghastly"* grub is good for
"parties only". / 11.45 pm, Sun 10.30 pm.

Drones SW1 £ 38 ④❸④

1 Pont St   (020) 7259 6166   2–4A

Pretty but *"characterless"* modern British Belgravian; in distant
times, this was a notable address – now it's barely a blip on
the radar. / 11 pm.

The Duke of Cambridge N1   £ 24   ❸❸❷

30 St Peters St   (020) 7359 3066   1–2C

All-organic Islington pub newcomer whose cooking is "tasty and interesting" (but also "pricey"); locals say it's a "relaxing" place, but we found it gloomy. / 10.30 pm; closed Mon L; no Amex; no smoking area.

The Eagle EC1   £ 22   ❷④❷

159 Farringdon Rd   (020) 7837 1353   9–1A

"Fight to get a table" if you want to enjoy the "gutsy" Mediterranean cooking which has won fame for this "cramped and smoky" gastropub (it was London's first), on the fringe of Smithfield. / 10.30 pm; closed Sun D; no credit cards; no booking.

East One EC1   £ 25   ④④❸

175-179 St John St   (020) 7566 0088   9–1A

Some still praise the "great concept" of this once-"trendy", "create-your-own-dish" place, north of Smithfield; the novelty's wearing thin, though – increasingly it's just seen as "an unexciting, upmarket Mongolian Barbecue". / 11.30 pm; closed Sat L & Sun D; set weekday L £13(FP).

Eat   £ 8   ❷❸❸

3 Duke Of York St, SW1   (020) 7930 0960
37 Tothill St, SW1   (020) 7222 5855
16a Soho Sq, W1   (020) 7287 7702
39 Villiers St, WC2   (020) 7839 2282
62 London Wall, EC2   (020) 7374 9555
Exchequer Ct, 33 St Mary Axe, EC3   (020) 7623 4413
170 Fleet St, EC4   (020) 7583 2585

"Yummy soups" and a "wonderful selection" of "different" sandwiches leave reporters drooling over this expanding take-away chain; we're in the mean minority who think it's rather "expensive". / L only; City branches closed Sat & Sun - W1, SW1 & WC2 closed Sun; no credit cards; no smoking; no booking.

Ebury Street Wine Bar SW1   £ 34   ④❸❸

139 Ebury St   (020) 7730 5447   2–4A

The "cosy" atmosphere is a greater draw than the "OK", but "expensive" cooking at this "bustly" and "smoke-filled" Belgravia stalwart. / 10.30 pm; closed Sun L.

Eco   £ 25   ❷④❸

162 Clapham High St, SW4   (020) 7978 1108   10–2D
4 Market Row, Brixton Market, SW9   (020) 7738 3021   10–2D

"Electric atmosphere and top pizzas" have made the oddly decorated, 'original' Clapham branch a "very trendy" (if "noisy", "smoky" and "uncomfortable") south London phenomenon; the Brixton Market branch – where you can BYO – actually came first (as Pizzeria Franco), and was re-badged this year. / SW4 11 pm, Sat 11.30 pm - SW9 L only; SW9 closed Wed & Sun; SW4 Mon-Fri no smoking area; SW9 no booking.

Ed's Easy Diner £21 ❸❸❷

12 Moor St, W1 (020) 7439 1955 4–2A
Trocadero, W1 (020) 7287 1951 3–3D
362 King's Rd, SW3 (020) 7352 1956 5–3B
O2 Centre, 255 Finchley Rd, NW3 (020) 7431 1958 8–2A
*"You can't go far wrong" perching on a stool at these "retro"
American diners – they offer "perfect burgers" and
"milkshakes to die for".* / Midnight - SW3 & NW3 11 pm - all branches
1 am, Fri & Sat; no booking.

Efes Kebab House £24 ④❷❷

1) 80 Great Titchfield St, W1 (020) 7636 1953 2–1B
2) 175-177 Gt Portland St, W1 (020) 7436 0600 2–1B
*"Bustling" and "courteous" Marylebone "old favourites",
whose "relatively cheap" and "solid" Turkish cooking is
recovering from a patch of "inconsistency"; the belly-dancing
at Efes 2 offers "great entertainment".* / 11.30 pm, Fri & Sat 3 am;
1 closed Sun.

1837 at Brown's Hotel W1 £71 ④④❸

Albemarle St (020) 7408 1837 3–3C
*An "incredible wine list" ("especially for wine by the glass") is
the sole notable feature of this old-fashioned Mayfair hotel
dining room, relaunched a year ago; the modern French fare is
"laughably overpriced", and service "friendly but so slow".*
/ 10.30 pm; closed Sat L & Sun; no smoking area; set weekday L £36(FP).

Elena's L'Etoile W1 £39 ❸❶❷

30 Charlotte St (020) 7636 7189 2–1C
*"You're in safe hands" (Elena Salvoni is the doyenne of
London's maîtresses d') at this "slick" and "professional"
old-style bourgeois Fitzrovian; the "classic" Gallic fare is
"competently produced".* / 11 pm; closed Sat L & Sun; smart casual.

Elistano SW3 £26 ❷❷❷

25-27 Elystan St (020) 7584 5248 5–2C
*It's the "perfect local Italian", say devotees of this "crowded",
"noisy" and "fun" Chelsea backstreet trattoria.* / 11 pm;
closed Sun.

Emile's £24 ❸❷❸

144 Wandsworth Br Rd, SW6 (020) 7736 2418 10–1B
96-98 Felsham Rd, SW15 (020) 8789 3323 10–2B
*"Cheerful", "local", "living room-style" French restaurants,
in Fulham and Putney; they are praised for their "good-value
set-price menus", but the ratings are grist to the mill of those
who say the food is "going downhill".* / 11 pm; D only; closed Sun;
no Amex.

The Engineer NW1 £35 ❸④❷

65 Gloucester Ave (020) 7722 0950 8–3B
*"Overcrowded", Primrose Hill gastropub hailed for its "great,
relaxed atmosphere", "beautiful garden" and "beautiful
punters"; "everything is fresh, and portions are generous", with
the "great Sunday brunch" perhaps the leading attraction.*
/ 10.30 pm; no Amex.

English Garden SW3 £ 46 ❸❶❷

10 Lincoln St (020) 7584 7272 5–2D
The "delightful" and "romantic" atmosphere (especially
"in the conservatory"), "pleasant" modern British cooking
and "impeccable" service have long maintained the popularity
of this Chelsea fixture. / 10 pm; set Sun L £27(FP).

English House SW3 £ 43 ⑤❸❸

3 Milner St (020) 7584 3002 5–2D
"Twee but very romantic" Chelsea townhouse with
"accommodating" staff; "the tables are too close together",
though, and the English cooking "flat" at best. / 11 pm; set
weekday L £20(FP).

Enoteca Turi SW15 £ 33 ❷❶❸

28 Putney High St (020) 8785 4449 10–2B
"Super", "innovative" cooking and "genuine, attentive" service
(as well as a wine list of real interest) make it worth seeking
out this undramatic-looking Italian, near Putney Bridge. / 11 pm;
closed Sat L & Sun; smart casual.

The Enterprise SW3 £ 32 ④❸❷

Walton St (020) 7584 3148 5–2C
"Always lively, always fun" – this "easy-going" converted pub is
usually "packed to the gills" with quite a "wacky" crowd (well,
by Knightsbridge standards); the food is not really the point.
/ 11 pm; smart casual; book Mon-Fri L only.

Esarn Kheaw W12 £ 23 ❷⑤④

314 Uxbridge Rd (020) 8743 8930 7–1B
Shepherd's Bush "gem", offering "great, spicy and authentic"
north Thai cooking "at a bargain price"; as a place, it's "not
fun", though, and service is very "indifferent". / 11 pm;
closed Sat L & Sun L.

Escaped Cafe SE10 £ 17 ❸❸④

141 Greenwich South St (020) 8692 5826 1–3D
Boho, BYO Greenwich café, best for breakfast; it can be pretty
dull at night. / 10.30 pm; no credit cards.

L'Escargot W1 £ 40 ❷❷❷

48 Greek St (020) 7437 2679 4–2A
"Excellent cooking", "friendly and attentive" service and a
"charming" atmosphere have finally come together again at
this reviving Gallic classic in the heart of Soho – now a top
all-round West End choice; upstairs, the suitably adorned
Picasso Room offers pricier fine dining. / 11.30 pm; closed Sat L
& Sun.

L'Estaminet WC2 £ 37 ④④④

14 Garrick St (020) 7379 1432 4–3C
"Twee", "traditionally French" Theatrelander; some used to
tip it as a "reliable" central stand-by, but gripes of "weary"
standards all round put even that in jeopardy. / 11 pm; closed Sun;
pre-th. £20(FP).

Euphorium N1   £ 38   ❷④❸
203 Upper St   (020) 7704 6909   8–2D
*Maybe it's just too "painfully trendy" – even for Islington's
"groovy thirtysomethings" – as the "surprisingly good" cooking
here can't be the reason this place is "often quiet"; (it has a
useful neighbouring bakery and café). / 10.30 pm; closed Sun D;
no smoking area.*

Fairuz W1   £ 30   ❷❸④
3 Blandford St   (020) 7486 8108   2–1A
*"Marvellous, fresh food" (if you choose well) makes this
"pleasant" little Lebanese restaurant a useful, new addition to
Marylebone. / 11 pm.*

Fakhreldine W1   £ 39   ❸❸④
85 Piccadilly   (020) 7493 3424   3–4C
*"Airport lounge-like" Mayfair Lebanese whose "very
authentic", if "expensive", cooking has made it an enduring
success; it's really a late-night place – by day, "book a table
overlooking Green Park". / Midnight; smart casual.*

Il Falconiere SW7   £ 26   ❸❷④
84 Old Brompton Rd   (020) 7589 2401   5–2B
*"Old-style Italian food and waiters who spoil the kids rotten" is
the sort of formula which makes this "well priced" South
Kensington trattoria a "dependable" stand-by. / 11.45 pm;
closed Sun.*

La Famiglia SW10   £ 44   ❸④❸
7 Langton St   (020) 7351 0761   5–3B
*The garden is "a joy", and the cooking at this "pricey",
"Chelsea crowd" trattoria in World's End is "still pretty good";
regulars just love the place, but others find that "awful",
"un-jolly Italian" service "outweighs other merits". / 11.45 pm.*

Fat Boy's W4   £ 26   ❸❷④
10a Edensor Rd   (020) 8994 8089   10–1A
*"A cut above the average", this Chiswick Thai offers "good
value" (with the ability to BYO "a bonus"); "it's worth a trip to
eat outside in summer". / 11 pm; closed Sat L; no Amex.*

Faulkner's E8   £ 19   ❶❸⑤
424-426 Kingsland Rd   (020) 7254 6152   1–2D
*"Except for the impossible location", this eminent East Ender
wins consistent acclaim thanks to "the best fish and chips
around"; BYO. / 10 pm; no Amex; no smoking area.*

Feng Shang NW1   £ 30   ❷❸❸
Opp 15 Prince Albert Rd   (020) 7485 8137   8–3B
*A "totally different Chinese experience" – "outstandingly
presented" food, "polite" service and a "wonderful setting" –
makes for a fun night out at this festive barge, at the top of
Regent's Park. / 11 pm; no Switch.*

Ffiona's W8 £ 26 ❸❷❷

51 Kensington Ch St (020) 7937 4152 5–1A
A "real patronne", "good home cooking", a "friendly
atmosphere and "reasonable prices" make a "rare"
combination at this "intimate" Kensington bistro. / 11.30 pm;
D only, Sun open L & D.

**Fifth Floor at
Harvey Nichols SW1** £ 51 ④❸❸

Knightsbridge (020) 7235 5250 2–3A
As "a pleasant lunch location", many laud this "swish"
("pretentious") dining room atop the glam Knightsbridge
department store; as usual it wins less support at dinner time
(when the neighbouring bar is an infamous "pick-up joint").
/ 11.30 pm; closed Sun D.

**Fifth Floor at
Harvey Nichols (Café) SW1** £ 36 ❸❸❷

Knightsbridge (020) 7823 1839 2–3A
"Unfussy and cool" – Harvey Nics's top-floor café "is as nice
as the restaurant is underwhelming"; "good salads", the "best
coffee" and jazz evenings number among its attractions.
/ 10.30 pm; closed Sun D; book eve only.

Fileric £ 9 ❸❸④

57 Old Brompton Rd, SW7 (020) 7584 2967 5–2C
12 Queenstown Rd, SW8 (020) 7720 4844 10–1C
"It feels like France" at these simple cafés, which offer
"excellent strong coffee" and "great pastries". / 8 pm; no booking.

Fina Estampa SE1 £ 27 ❸❷④

150 Tooley St (020) 7403 1342 9–4D
A "Peruvian novelty", not far from Tower Bridge; the
"interesting and tasty" fare ("fantastic" fish soup, in particular)
is well liked, but doesn't get the raves it once did. / 10.30 pm;
closed Sun.

La Finca £ 19 ④④❷

96-98 Pentonville Rd, N1 (020) 7837 5387 8–3D
185 Kennington Ln, SE11 (020) 7735 1061 10–1D
"Don't go for the food" (or service, for that matter), but these
"loud 'n' lively" tapas bars offer "fun" options in thin areas.
/ 11.15 pm Fri & Sat N1 1.30 am, SE11 11.30 pm.

FireBird W1 £ 45 – – –

23 Conduit St (020) 7493 7000 3–2C
Eye-catching migrant from NYC's Theater District, scheduled
to touch down in Mayfair in November; Tsarist Russia is the
theme, with cooking – and prices – to match.

First Floor W11 £ 36 ⑤⑤④

186 Portobello Rd (020) 7243 0072 6–1B
Presumably, it's the "interesting" décor which sustains this
Notting Hill spot in the face of numerous reports of "terrible"
cooking and "truly appalling" service; "stay away". / 11.30 pm.

fish! SE1 £30 ②②④

Cathedral St (020) 7836 3236 9–4C
*The "greenhouse-like" Borough Market prototype of this
ambitious new chain, has made a good start with its "fresh
and simple" fish and "efficient" service; coming soon –
openings in Battersea, Canary Wharf, Marylebone and
Smithfield.* / 11 pm; closed Sun; no smoking area.

Floriana SW3 £53 ②④③

15 Beauchamp Pl (020) 7838 1500 5–1C
*It's a shame that the "divine" Italian cooking at this
"sophisticated" Knightsbridge newcomer is "aimed at the
cost-insensitive" and comes in such "small portions";
"the chief obstacle to enjoyment", however, is the
"exceptionally slooooow service".* / 11 pm; closed Sun;
set weekday L £35(FP).

Florians N8 £29 ③③②

4 Topsfield Parade (020) 8348 8348 1–1C
*"Friendly and continental-feeling" Hornsey linchpin; the "very
good-value bar menu" is preferred to the "slightly
disappointing modern Italian cooking" in the rear restaurant.*
/ 10.45 pm; no Amex.

La Fontana SW1 £37 ③②③

101 Pimlico Rd (020) 7730 6630 5–2D
*"Very warm and welcoming", small Pimlico Italian, known for
its truffles (in season); its dated style now seems positively
'period'.* / 11 pm; no Switch.

Food for Thought WC2 £16 ②④③

31 Neal St (020) 7836 0239 4–2C
*"Some of the best, wholesome veggie food in London"
maintain the continuing crush at this "tiny" Covent Garden
basement café; "scrummy puddings somehow undo all the
good work of the other dishes".* / 8.15 pm; closed Sun D;
no credit cards; no smoking; no booking.

Footstool SW1 £33 ⑤④③

St John's, Smith Sq (020) 7222 2779 2–4C
*"Lovely arched vaults" add atmosphere at this Westminster
crypt, but "absence of local competition" allows it to be
"hopelessly awful and incompetent".* / L only but buffet concert eves;
closed Sat & Sun except when eve concerts; no smoking area; pre-th. £22(FP).

Formula Veneta SW10 £34 ③②②

14 Hollywood Rd (020) 7352 7612 5–3B
*Stylish, "fun" and "friendly" distant-Chelsea Italian; as ever,
some say the cooking's "slipping".* / 11.15 pm; closed Sun.

Four Regions SE1 £36 ②①③

County Hall (020) 7928 0988 2–3D
*South Bank Chinese offering "interesting" fare and "great
views of the Houses of Parliament"; it's housed in the
ponderous former GLC banqueting suite, so outside tables are
to be preferred.* / 11.30 pm.

Fox & Anchor EC1 £ 22 ❷④❷
115 Charterhouse St (020) 7253 4838 9–1B
"Guinness and a full English breakfast, perfect", say fans of the "astounding" fry-ups – "you can feel your arteries clogging up" – at this Smithfield institution. / 10 pm, weekends 10.30 pm; closed Sun.

The Fox Reformed N16 £ 24 ④❸❷
176 Stoke Newington Ch St (020) 7254 5975 1–1C
"Informal" Stoke Newington wine bar – a "backgammon player's paradise" – that's useful "for a coffee and snack, or a full meal"; you can sit in the "nice garden, if you get there early". / 10.30 pm.

Foxtrot Oscar SW3 £ 28 ④④④
79 Royal Hospital Rd (020) 7352 7179 5–3D
"Unchanging" local for Chelsea toffs, where "good burgers" are the highlight of the "snack-type fodder". / 11 pm.

Francofill SW7 £ 26 ④❸④
1 Old Brompton Rd (020) 7584 0087 5–2C
"Simple" snacks at "not unreasonable" prices make this Gallic bar/bistro a "good stand-by" in the environs of South Kensington tube. / 11 pm; no smoking area.

Frederick's N1 £ 38 ❷❷❷
106 Camden Pas (020) 7359 2888 8–3D
"A sense of occasion" attaches to this old Islington warhorse, with its lofty conservatory; the "good-value" modern British cooking has improved of late, and "slick" service contributes to a "smooth" overall experience. / 11.30 pm; closed Sun; smart casual; no smoking area; set Sat Lunch £24(FP).

French House W1 £ 32 ❷❷❷
49 Dean St (020) 7437 2477 4–3A
The "food is back on form" – with a vengeance – at this "cosy", "intriguing" and "romantic" dining room, above the famous Soho pub; as at its sibling, St John, the modern British menu is "uncompromising". / 11.15 pm; closed Sun.

Friends SW10 £ 28 ❸④❷
6 Hollywood Rd (020) 7376 3890 5–3B
"Trendy" and "fun" new Chelsea pizzeria (complete with a wood-burning oven and a "fabulous buffet table"); the setting is "rather cramped", though, and service "questionable". / 11.30 pm; closed L Mon-Fri; no Amex.

Frith Street Restaurant W1 £ 35 ❸❷❸
63-64 Frith St (020) 7734 4545 4–2A
Chef Stephen Terry's early departure from this "sparely" decorated Soho venture rendered a brilliant newcomer relatively ordinary; a visit under the new-régime found competent and generously priced modern British cooking, but little culinary sparkle. / 10.45 pm; closed Sat L & Sun.

Frocks E9 £ 28 ❸②②

95 Lauriston Rd (020) 8986 3161 1–2D
"Wonderful local bistro", near Victoria Park, which is best
known for its all-day weekend breakfasts; service – long a
weakness – *"has improved"*. / 11 pm; closed Mon & Sun D;
no Sunday bookings.

Front Page SW3 £ 25 ❸④❸

35 Old Church St (020) 7352 2908 5–3C
"Tasty pub grub" (that's *"cheap"*, for Chelsea) makes this
stylish boozer a useful stand-by. / 10 pm.

Fryer's Delight WC1 £ 8 ❸❸④

19 Theobald's Rd (020) 7405 4114 2–1D
Quintessential Formica chippy, near Gray's Inn, offering
good-value stodge in no-nonsense surroundings; you can BYO.
/ 10 pm; closed Sun; no credit cards.

Fuego EC3 £ 26 ④④⑤

1a Pudding Ln (020) 7929 3366 9–3C
*"Very tacky in the evening, but competent tapas for a quick
business lunch"* – this *"dive of a bar"*, near the Monument,
makes a slightly *"different"* City stand-by. / 9.30 pm; closed Sat
& Sun; smart casual.

Fung Shing WC2 £ 32 ❶④⑤

15 Lisle St (020) 7437 1539 4–3A
"The best Chinese food in Chinatown" (*"excellent seafood"*,
in particular) is consistently found at this *"exceptional
oriental"*; there's *"no real atmosphere"*, though. / 11.30 pm.

Futures EC2 £ 25 ❸❸❸

2 Exchange Sq (020) 7638 6341 9–1D
"Yummy veggie treats" in a *"good setting"* – a modern café
amidst the Broadgate complex – makes this a useful City
option. / L only; closed Sat & Sun; no smoking at L.

Futures EC3 £ 9 ❷❸-

8 Botolph Alley (020) 7623 4529 9–3C
"When you can't face another sandwich", canny City types
head for this ace veggie take-away, near Monument; *"its worth
the 1pm queue"*. / L only; closed Sat & Sun; no credit cards; no smoking;
no booking.

Galicia W10 £ 23 ❸④❸

323 Portobello Rd (020) 8969 3539 6–1A
"Moody" waiters add authenticity to this long-established
North Kensington tapas bar. / 11.30 pm; closed Mon; set weekday L
£12(FP).

Gallipoli £ 22 ❷①❷

102 Upper St, N1   (020) 7359 0630   8–2D
120 Upper St, N1   (020) 7226 8099   8–3D
An "amazing-value" combination of "fresh" Turkish food
(served in "huge portions"), supremely "friendly" staff and a
"lively" atmosphere makes these "wonderfully cheap and
cheerful" Islington cafés "deservedly popular" – "it's best to
book". / 11 pm; Fri & Sat 11.30 pm; no Amex.

Garlic & Shots W1 £ 27 ④④❸

14 Frith St   (020) 7734 9505   4–2A
Despite "garlic in everything, including the beer and ice
cream", some (perhaps anaesthetised by one slammer too
many) report "amazingly good food" at this "frantic" Soho
bar/restaurant. / 11.15 pm, Fri & Sat 12.15 am; D only; no Amex;
no booking.

Gastro SW4 £ 27 ④④❷

67 Venn St   (020) 7627 0222   10–2D
"Very French" café, opposite the Clapham Picture House;
it's "great for brunch", but otherwise some find its culinary
attractions "dubious". / Midnight; no credit cards; no smoking area;
need 15+ to book.

The Gasworks SW6 £ 29 ⑤④❶

87 Waterford Rd   (020) 7736 3830   5–4A
London's "weirdest place ever" is a "gem" (if you like this sort
of thing); the food is "disgusting" and the service "hysterical",
but it's the amazing, decadent, antique-filled setting which can
make it a "great night out". / 11 pm; D only, open Wed-Sat only;
no credit cards.

The Gate W6 £ 27 ❶❷❷

51 Queen Caroline St   (020) 8748 6932   7–2C
"Revolutionary" cooking makes this "hard-to-find"
Hammersmith spot – with its "great staff" and "laid back"
atmosphere – "the best veggie in London". / 10.45 pm; closed Sat L
& Sun.

El Gaucho SW3 £ 26 ❸④❸

Chelsea Farmers' Mkt, 125 Sydney St   (020) 7376 8514   5–3C
"Wow the steaks are good!"; the only real gripe about this
"very good" Argentinean meat-shack in Chelsea Farmer's
Market is that it's "incredibly crammed"; an on-licence has
been applied for, but you can still BYO. / 11 pm; Fri & Sat,
11.30 pm; no credit cards; no booking in summer.

Gaucho Grill £ 36 ❷④❸

19-25 Swallow St, W1   (020) 7734 4040   3–3D
64 Heath St, NW3   (020) 7431 8222   8–1A
12 Gracechurch St, EC3   (020) 7626 5180   9–3C
"Paradise for meat-lovers"; few chains equal the standards of
this Dutch-owned group, which offers "perfect hunks of steak"
(and "great chips") in innovatively themed settings; a useful
new City branch has opened, just off Gracechurch Street.
/ 11.45 pm - EC3 11 pm; EC3 closed Sat & Sun (except breakfast).

Gaudi EC1 £ 42 ❸④❸

63 Clerkenwell Rd   (020) 7608 3220   9–1A

Is the Spanish cooking at this Clerkenwell two-year-old "sublime", or is it "difficult to find such bad food nowadays"?; is the ambience "wonderful" or "terrible"?; does "everything work" or is the service "dodgy"? – rarely does a place inspire such a cornucopia of contradictory comments. / 10.30 pm; closed Sat L & Sun; set weekday L £26(FP).

LE GAVROCHE W1 £ 97 ❷❶❸

43 Upper Brook St   (020) 7408 0881   3–2A

For traditionalists, "the best French food in town" (not to mention "the best wine list") makes this "slightly stuffy" Mayfair stalwart "a true corner of paradise"; "outrageous" prices irritate some, making "the best quality set lunch in London" all the more attractive. / 11 pm; closed Sat & Sun; jacket & tie.

Gay Hussar W1 £ 34 ④❶❷

2 Greek St   (020) 7437 0973   4–2A

This "trip down memory lane" offers "dependable" and "traditional" Hungarian nosh in a "convivial" 'old Soho' setting; for those with long memories, though, "mediocrity has replaced eminence". / 10.45 pm; closed Sun; smart casual.

Geale's W8 £ 23 ❸❸④

2 Farmer St   (020) 7727 7969   6–2B

Many think "new owners are improving standards" at this veteran chippy, off Notting Hill gate (owned by the Geale family, 1945-1999); a "lick of paint" and better service have been welcomed – the jury is out on the cooking, but most still find it "good value". / 10.30 pm; closed Sun.

Geeta NW6 £ 16 ❷❷④

59 Willesden Ln   (020) 7624 1713   1–1B

"An outstanding record of excellence" justifies a trip to this grotty-looking but "good-value" Kilburn Indian. / 10.30 pm, Fri & Sat 11.30 pm; no Switch.

George & Vulture EC3 £ 30 ④❷❷

3 Castle Ct   (020) 7626 9710   9–3C

"Food better than the menu would suggest" is just one of the attractions at this wonderful City "museum", where little seems to have changed since Dickens's day. / L only; closed Sat & Sun; jacket & tie.

Ghillies £ 30 ❸❸❸

271 New King's Rd, SW6   (020) 7371 0434   10–1B
20 Bellevue Rd, SW17   (020) 8767 1858   10–2C

"Cosy" Parson's Green and Wandsworth bistros whose "good selection" of dishes (including "very good fish and chips") helps make them ideal locals. / 10.45 pm.

Gili Gulu WC2 £18 ⑤⑤④
50-52 Monmouth St (020) 7379 6888 4–2B
*"The all-you-can-eat-buffet is the only thing worth mentioning",
say critics of this conveyor belt café, near Covent Garden;
other offerings are too often "terrible". / 11 pm; no smoking;
no booking.*

Giraffe £22 ❷❷❶
6-8 Blandford St, W1 (020) 7935 2333 2–1A
46 Rosslyn Hl, NW3 (020) 7435 0343 8–2A
*Can these "cool", "sparkily decorated", "'70s ambience"
newcomers revolutionise our perception of chain restaurants?;
with their "enthusiastic young staff" and "enormous portions"
of "surprisingly good" food, they could... if they can keep it
up. / NW3 11.30 pm - W1 11.15 pm; no smoking; no booking.*

Gladwins EC3 £50 ❷❷❸
Minster Ct, Mark Ln (020) 7444 0004 9–3D
*"Imaginative food and cheerful service" make this not
especially characterful spot a "very good City restaurant";
"tables at a respectable distance" help justify high prices.
/ L only; closed Sat & Sun.*

Glaisters £28 ④④❸
4 Hollywood Rd, SW10 (020) 7352 0352 5–3B
8-10 Northcote Rd, SW11 (020) 7924 6699 10–2C
36-38 White Hart Ln, SW13 (020) 8878 2020 10–1A
*They have a "fun" atmosphere and attractive décor (and, in
SW10, a nice garden), but in most respects these
younger-scene bistros are "simply mediocre". / 11.30 pm.*

The Glasshouse TW1 £37 ❶❸❸
14 Station Parade, Kew (020) 8940 6777 1–3A
*"Following in the footsteps of Chez Bruce" (same owner), this
"superb" newcomer is already "well worth the drive to Kew"
on account of its "brilliant" menu of "imaginative" modern
British cooking; "service doesn't match up", though. / 10.30 pm;
closed Sun D.*

Globe Restaurant NW3 £30 ❸❷❸
100 Avenue Rd (020) 7722 7200 8–2A
*There's no real consensus on this "poorly located" Swiss
Cottage spot; for some, its conservatory-like setting helps make
it like a "West End restaurant", with "interesting" modern
British menus and "humorous" staff – others decry
"oversized" bills for "boring" food. / 11 pm; closed Sat L; set
weekday L £15(FP).*

Golden Dragon W1 £22 ❷④❸
28-29 Gerrard St (020) 7734 2763 4–3A
*"Great dim sum" is the highlight of this "plain" Chinatown
behemoth, but get ready for service "at 100 mph", and which
can be "offensive". / 11.30 pm, Fri & Sat midnight.*

The Good Cook W11   £21   ④⑤⑤

The Tabernacle, Powis Sq   (020) 7565 7808   6–1B
"Echoey" café at a Notting Hill community centre, whose favourable press crits left us bemused; we found erratic modern British fare and "overstretched" service. / L only; no Amex; set weekday L £12(FP).

Good Earth SW3   £32   ❸❷④

233 Brompton Rd   (020) 7584 3658   5–2C
Long-established Knightsbridge Chinese, which may be "pricey", but serves some "excellent dishes". / 10.45 pm.

Goolies W8   £36   ❸❷❸

21 Abingdon Rd   (020) 7938 1122   5–1A
"Fun all round" and "fairly priced", say fans of this small modern British bar/restaurant, just off Kensington High Street, for a "local" place it attracts a surprisingly wide-ranging following. / 10.30 pm; set weekday L £22(FP).

Gopal's of Soho W1   £26   ❷④④

12 Bateman St   (020) 7434 1621   4–2A
It looks bog-standard, but this "cramped" Soho curry house remains "a cut above average" (if not quite up to its recent stellar standards). / 11.15 pm; smart casual.

GORDON RAMSAY SW3   £68   ❶❷❸

68-69 Royal Hospital Rd   (020) 7352 4441   5–3D
The TV "hysterics" may be difficult to stomach, but not so Ramsay's "perfect and masterful" cooking which has clearly established his Chelsea yearling as the capital's culinary number one; service is so good it's "nearly intrusive", though, and the special charm of the 'old' Aubergine has not been transplanted to here. / 11 pm; closed Sat & Sun; set weekday L £43(FP).

Gordon's Wine Bar WC2   £19   ④❷❶

47 Villiers St   (020) 7930 1408   4–4D
"Great as ever", London's oldest wine bar offers a good, inexpensive wine selection to accompany its "super cheeses" and "reasonable" and "freshly cooked" plats du jour; its dark corners are ideal "for illicit encounters", and there's a wonderful terrace. / 9 pm; closed Sun; no Amex; no booking.

Goring Hotel SW1   £48   ④❶❷

15 Beeston Pl   (020) 7396 9000   2–4B
"Mr Goring knows how to train his staff", and "good old-fashioned service" is the key strength of this family-owned Victoria hotel; "ordinary" cooking means it best suits breakfast or business. / 10 pm; closed Sat L.

Le Gothique SW18   £32   ④❸❷

The Royal Victoria Patriotic Bldg, Fitzhugh Gr, Trinity Rd
(020) 8870 6567   10–2C
"Wonderful setting but poor food" is still the story at this Wandsworth venture, located in an extraordinary Victorian Gothic folly; there's a "lovely garden" in the cloisters. / 10.30 pm; closed Sat L & Sun.

Gourmet Pizza Company £ 25 ❸④④

7-9 Swallow St, W1 (020) 7734 5182 3–3D
Gabriels Whf, 56 Upper Ground, SE1 (020) 7928 3188 9–3A
18 Mackenzie Walk, E14 (020) 7345 9192 1–3D
"Inventive, tasty pizzas" in a "fun" setting make this one of the better chains in town; the Gabriel's Wharf branch, with its outside seating and "lovely river views", is "always full".
/ 10.45 pm; W1 & E14, no smoking area; need 8+ to book.

Gow's EC2 £ 40 ④❸④

81-82 Old Broad St (020) 7920 9645 9–2C
"It is so convenient for much of the City" (near Liverpool Street) that it's perhaps no surprise that this "dark and dingy" fish parlour "needs a rocket putting under it". / L only; closed Sat & Sun; smart casual.

Goya SW1 £ 31 ④④❷

34 Lupus St (020) 7976 5309 2–4C
"Cosy tapas bar in Pimlico", which is "always buzzing", even though the food's "not great"; downstairs, there's a "simple" restaurant. / 11.30 pm, midnight for tapas; no smoking area.

Granita N1 £ 33 ❷❷④

127 Upper St (020) 7226 3222 8–2D
"Well-balanced and intelligently cooked" modern British food maintains a large north London fan club for this well-known Islington eatery; as ever, its stark setting is too "cool" and "noisy" for some people. / 10.30 pm; closed Mon & Tue L; no Amex & no Switch.

Grano W4 £ 42 ❷❷❸

162 Thames Rd (020) 8995 0120 1–3A
The team from Tentazioni have hit the ground running at this "excellent" newcomer, near Kew Bridge, delivering some "imaginative" (and "deceptively filling") modern Italian cooking; it's "expensive for the location", though, and some complain of a "lack of atmosphere". / 10.30 pm; closed Mon L, Sat L & Sun D.

The Grapes E14 £ 37 ❸❸❸

76 Narrow St (020) 7987 4396 1–2D
"The great river view from the upper room" and some "wonderfully fresh fish, simply done and simply served" make this "tiny", characterful Limehouse pub one of the best options in Docklands. / 9.15 pm; closed Sun.

Great Eastern Dining Room EC2 £ 30 ❷❷❷

54 Great Eastern St (020) 7613 4545 9–1D
"Cool" new Italian bar/restaurant which is already "too popular" with Shoreditch hipsters; the surprise is that the "simple" cooking is "well prepared", and that service is "friendly". / 10.30 pm; closed Sat L & Sun.

Great Nepalese NW1   £19   ③②④
48 Eversholt St   (020) 7388 6737   8–3C
"Vegetable dishes and Nepalese specialities can be superb" at
this *"friendly"* but *"drab"* subcontinental, by Euston Station.
/ 11.30 pm; no Switch.

The Green Olive W9   £34   ②①②
5 Warwick Pl   (020) 7289 2469   8–4A
"A real surprise in Maida Vale", this *"terrific neighbourhood
Italian"*, by Clifton Nurseries, impresses with its *"good food"*,
"nice wines", *"caring service"* and *"value for money"*; it can be
"romantic" too, but *"you must sit upstairs"*. */ 10.45 pm; D only
Mon-Fri; Sat & Sun open L & D.*

Green's SW1   £52   ④③③
36 Duke St   (020) 7930 4566   3–3D
A *"thoroughly English classic in the heart of St James's"*, much
beloved of the Establishment; it's *"expensive"*, and rather
"hit-and-miss", but at best serves *"deliciously fresh fish and
the best seafood"*. */ 11 pm; closed Sun in summer.*

Greenhouse W1   £44   ③②②
27a Hays Mews   (020) 7499 3331   3–3B
"Americans love" this *"consistently good"* updated-traditional
British restaurant, hidden away in Mayfair; its setting is
"pleasant", and some find it *"romantic"*, but lunches in
particular can suffer from a *"dull business clientele"*. */ 11 pm;
closed Sat L; smart casual.*

Grenadier SW1   £37   ③④②
18 Wilton Rw   (020) 7235 3074   2–3A
It's *"touristy"* and *"too busy"*, but this *"tucked-away"* Belgravia
mews pub is rightly famed for its *"fantastic sausages"* (and its
Bloody Marys, too); the rear restaurant (to which the price
relates) is less of an attraction. */ 9.30 pm.*

Gresslin's NW3   £35   ④④⑤
13 Heath St   (020) 7794 8386   8–2A
Has Hampstead's notorious indifference finally got to the
"imaginative and professional" patron of the area's former
leading light?; the room has always been *"horrid"*, but the
service is now *"haphazard"* and the modern British cooking
"rather unmemorable". */ 10.30 pm; closed Mon L & Sun D; no Amex;
no smoking area.*

Grissini SW1   £42   ②②③
Hyatt Carlton Tower, 2 Cadogan Pl   (020) 7858 7171   2–4A
"Stylish" Belgravia hotel restaurant whose *"fantastic"* Italian
cooking and *"obliging"* service don't get the following which
fans think it merits; the culprits seem to be the expense and,
to some, *"a lack of ambience"*. */ 10.45 pm; no smoking area.*

Grumbles SW1 £ 27 ⑤④④
35 Churton St (020) 7834 0149 2–4B
*It's amazing the way this "very '60s" Pimlico bistro still garners
support in some quarters as a "great local" as it's "not what it
was" – the food is "dull" and "expensive", and service is
"slow". / 11.45 pm.*

The Guinea W1 £ 49 ②④❸
30 Bruton Pl (020) 7499 1210 3–2B
*"The steak and kidney pie is a must" at this "cosy, dark and
charming" Mayfair pub dining room (which also does a decent
steak); it's "just what Americans think England should be like".
/ 11 pm; closed Sat L & Sun.*

Gung-Ho NW6 £ 27 ❷❸❸
330-332 West End Ln (020) 7794 1444 1–1B
*The "best Chinese around" – down West Hampstead way,
anyhow – is very popular, and offers "consistently healthy"
food in a "nice" environment. / 11.30 pm; no Amex.*

Ha Ha £ 25 ❸❸④
43-51 Gt Titchfield St, W1 (020) 7580 7252 2–1B
273 Camden High St, NW1 (020) 7482 0767 8–2B
*Some report "unexpectedly good food in an informal setting"
at this new chain of "alternatives to All Bar One". / W1 11 pm -
NW1 10 pm; W1 closed Sat & Sun.*

Halcyon Hotel W11 £ 61 ❷❸❸
129 Holland Pk Ave (020) 7221 5411 6–2B
*There's no 'right answer' about the dining room of this discreet
Holland Park villa hotel, beloved of celebs; for fans, it's a
"romantic" place ("especially al fresco"), with "terrific"
modern British food and "charming" service – for detractors,
it's "expensive", "hotely" and "dull". / 10.30 pm, Fri & Sat 11 pm;
closed Sat L; smart casual; set weekday L £39(FP).*

Halepi £ 30 ❸❸❷
18 Leinster Ter, W2 (020) 7262 1070 6–2C
48-50 Belsize Ln, NW3 (020) 7431 5855 8–2A
*An odd duo comprising a "dark and intimate" Bayswater
Greek taverna and its new, shinier Hampstead offshoot; fans
applaud the "lively" spirit at both sites – sceptics just can't see
it. / W2 12.30 am - NW3 10 am.*

The Halkin SW1 £ 66 ❸④④
5 Halkin St (020) 7333 1234 2–3A
*Is this grandly minimalist Belgravian a "civilised spot with
discreet service and fabulous modern Italian food" or
"ludicrously overpriced, and undeniably a hotel restaurant for
rich business execs"? – the latter camp is slightly the more
convincing of the two. / 10.45 pm; closed Sat L & Sun L; smart casual;
set weekday L £35(FP).*

Hanover Square W1   £ 29   ④④④
25 Hanover Sq   (020) 7408 0935   3–2C
"Very good wines" are the key strength of this Mayfair cellar
wine bar, which is an obscure sibling of the famous Cork &
Bottle – there's *"a similar unevenness in the cooking"*.
/ 10.30 pm; closed Sun; smart casual; no smoking area.

Harbour City W1   £ 26   ❷⑤⑤
46 Gerrard St   (020) 7439 7859   4–3B
"Superb dim sum" make this large venue one of Chinatown's
most notable; *"in the evenings, it's not good value"*, though,
and service is *"barking"*. / 11.15 pm, Fri & Sat 11.45 pm; set weekday L
£17(FP).

Hard Rock Café W1   £ 27   ④❸❷
150 Old Park Ln   (020) 7629 0382   3–4B
"The queue says it all", proclaim fans of this Mayfair *"legend"*
– the original of the worldwide chain – which is *"still rocking"*
(*"too loud"*); standards, though, are being *"diluted"*. / 12.30 am,
Fri & Sat 1 am; no Switch; no smoking area; no booking.

Hardy's W1   £ 33   ❷❷❸
53 Dorset St   (020) 7935 5929   2–1A
"Marylebone's friendliest wine bar" offers *"happily eclectic"*
cooking, *"great-value"* wines, and an atmospheric setting.
/ 10.30 pm; closed Sat & Sun.

Havana   £ 26   ⑤④❸
17 Hanover Sq, W1   (020) 7629 2552   3–1C
490 Fulham Broadway, SW6   (020) 7381 5005   5–4A
*"The music and dancing are the reasons to go – don't expect
much of the food"* at these *"loud but fun"* Latin Americans, in
Mayfair and Fulham. / W1 11.45 pm - SW6 midnight (tapas until 2 am);
Sun 10.30 pm; SW6 D only.

The Havelock Tavern W14   £ 27   ❶④❷
57 Masbro Rd   (020) 7603 5374   7–1C
"Arrive early to nab your table" to enjoy the *"imaginative"* and
"consistent" cooking at this *"relaxed"* and *"buzzy"* Olympia
gastropub – it can be *"impossibly crowded and smoky"* and
service is *"shambolic"*. / 10 pm; no credit cards; no booking.

Haweli SW13   £ 22   ❷❷❸
7 White Hart Ln   (020) 8876 4441   10–1A
For *"a good west London curry"* – *"herby/spicy but not very
hot"* – this Barnes fixture has its moments. / Midnight.

Heather's SE8   £ 20   ❸❸❸
74 McMillan St   (020) 8691 6665   1–3D
"Well worth a trip to Deptford", say fans of this *"marvellous"*,
"eat-all-you-can" veggie, in a large converted pub; service can
be slack. / 11 pm, 9 pm Sun; closed Mon; no credit cards; no smoking.

Helter Skelter SW9 £ 33 ➋➋④
50 Atlantic Rd (020) 7274 8600 10–2D
"An increasingly discovered hidden gem"; this "fun" and
"funky" Brixton café may be "cramped", "smoky" and
"too busy", but fans brave such hardships for the "tasty
and interesting" cooking and "charming" service. / 11 pm,
Fri & Sat 11.30 pm; D only, except Sun L.

Hilaire SW7 £ 51 ➋➋➋
68 Old Brompton Rd (020) 7584 8993 5–2B
"Friendly" and "reliable" bourgeois South Kensington spot,
where a loyal fan club hails "consistently excellent" French
cooking; it's "comfortable" but "a little cramped", which some
find "romantic". / 11 pm; closed Sat L & Sun.

Hodgson's WC2 £ 32 ④➌➌
115 Chancery Ln (020) 7242 2836 2–2D
"Handsome", "airy" early-Victorian room (with an interesting
glazed ceiling) that provides a "spacious" business-lunching
environment in "a fairly barren area", the modern British
cooking is "not bad". / 10 pm; closed Sat & Sun.

Home EC1 £ 26 ➌➋➊
100-106 Leonard St (020) 7684 8618 9–1D
Deeply "chilled" bar, near Old Street, where "cool" staff
deliver some "surprisingly good" cooking in the "relatively
calm, curtained-off dining room". / 10 pm; closed Sat L & Sun;
no Amex.

home (Between Six & Eight) W1 £ 45 – – –
1 Leicester Sq (020) 7909 1177 4–4A
As we go to press, a much-hyped clubby 'scene' opens, which
claims its scale and style will transcend its terrifyingly un-hip
Leicester Square location; the restaurant promises Asian
cuisine from an ex-Vong chef and panoramic city views –
price is our guesstimate. / Midnight.

The Honest Cabbage SE1 £ 28 ➌➋④
99 Bermondsey St (020) 7234 0080 9–4D
"Chunky, wholesome, heaving plates of fresh and nourishing
food", not to mention "charming" staff, win plaudits for this
"straightforward" Bermondsey gastropub. / 10 pm; closed Sun D;
no Amex.

Hope & Sir Loin EC1 £ 35 ➋➌④
94 Cowcross St (020) 7253 8525 9–1B
"Lunch isn't possible" after a "huge and splendid" breakfast at
this well known Smithfield pub. / L only; closed Sat & Sun.

Hornimans SW4 £ 22 ④④④
69 Clapham Common S'side (020) 8673 9162 10–2D
"The best bit is the outside seating area" at this bistro beside
Clapham Common; many locals judge the food "excellent
value" – some non-residents "wouldn't feed it to the cat".
/ 11 pm; D only; no Amex; pre-th. £15(FP).

Hot John's N1 £ 25 ④④④
105 Upper St (020) 7704 9902 8–3D
Islington newcomer whose too often "disappointing" southern American cooking and "terrible" service do not augur well for the chain-ambitions it seems to harbour. / 11 pm; no Amex.

House on Rosslyn Hill NW3 £ 33 ④④❷
34 Rosslyn Hl (020) 7435 8037 8–2A
"Buzzing" hang-out of Hampstead's gilded youth; it's "good for brunch", but food and service generally are well "below average". / Midnight; no Amex; no lunch bookings.

Hudson's NW1 £ 34 ④❸❷
239 Baker St (020) 7935 3130 8–4B
It's a "great place to relax", aver enthusiasts for this popular Putney fixture, liked for its "pleasant" service and inexpensive "burgers-to-Thai" menu. / 10.30 pm.

Hujo's W1 £ 27 ④❶④
11 Berwick St (020) 7734 5144 3–2D
"Plain" and "variable" cooking has knocked ratings at this "basic" but very "friendly" modern British bistro (previously seen as a "good and inexpensive" central stand-by); it's in a "not particularly nice part of Soho". / Midnight; closed Sun; pre-th. £18(FP).

Hunan SW1 £ 29 ❶❷④
51 Pimlico Rd (020) 7730 5712 5–2D
"There is much happy slurping" at this idiosyncratic and intimate Chinese near Pimlico Green – the cooking is "excellent", especially if you "leave the choice to them"; "slapdash" service is not unknown. / 11.15 pm; closed Sun.

I Thai, The Hempel W2 £ 80 ④⑤❸
31-35 Craven Hl Gdns (020) 7298 9001 6–2C
You either love ("touches all the senses") or hate ("pretentious in every way") the dining room of Lady Weinberg's "out-of-this-world", minimalist Bayswater townhouse hotel; the prices are "outrageous", of course, but the "beautifully presented" East-West dishes are "almost worth it". / 11 pm.

Ibla W1 £ 35 ❸④④
89 Marylebone High St (020) 7224 3799 2–1A
Many still applaud this innovative Marylebone Italian for its "different" and "delicious" cooking and its "intimate" style; it's "inconsistent", though, and some feel it "under-delivers". / 10.30 pm; closed Sun; no Amex.

Icon SW3 £ 44 ❸❸❸
19 Elystan St (020) 7589 3718 5–2C
"Good, modern French cooking" and a "pleasant" overall experience are making a success of this small and "attractively decorated" Chelsea yearling; service can be "erratic". / 11.30 pm; closed Sun; set weekday L £24(FP).

Idaho N6 £ 39 ④④❸

13 North HI (020) 8341 6633 1–1C
"New but extremely noisy" Highgate southwest American
(a Montana group production) offering at best "innovative
but not outlandish" cooking (and at worst "a strange menu
that needs to settle down"); we preferred the brasserie to the
restaurant above – there's also a garden. / 11.30 pm.

Ikeda W1 £ 53 ❷❷④

30 Brook St (020) 7629 2730 3–2B
"Superb sushi" is the mainstay of Mr Ikeda's long-established
Mayfair Japanese. / 10.30 pm, Sat 10 pm; closed Sat L & Sun; no Switch;
smart casual; set weekday L £34(FP).

Ikkyu £ 24 ❷❸❸

67 Tottenham Ct Rd, W1 (020) 7636 9280 2–1C
7 Newport Pl, WC2 (020) 7439 3554 4–3B
"Authentic Japanese neighbourhood restaurants", well known,
in particular, for their "good and cheap sushi"; the original
(W1) branch is "much the better of the two". / 10.30 pm - WC2
Fri & Sat 11.30 pm; W1, closed Sat & Sun L; W1 no Switch; WC2
no smoking area.

Imperial City EC3 £ 33 ❸❷❸

Cornhill (020) 7626 3437 9–2C
"Good food, and a change for the City"; the "reliable" Chinese
restaurant in the "glamorous" and "cavernous" cellars of the
Royal Exchange is always "good for business". / 9 pm; closed Sat
& Sun.

Inaho W2 £ 29 ❶❸④

4 Hereford Rd (020) 7221 8495 6–1B
"The long waits are for a good reason" at this "tiny" and
"cramped" Japanese café in Bayswater – the chef is preparing
"impeccable", very "affordable" sushi and other "exceptional"
dishes; "you get warm service… when it finally comes". / 11 pm;
closed Sat L & Sun; no Amex & no Switch; set weekday L £15(FP).

L'Incontro SW1 £ 55 ④❸④

87 Pimlico Rd (020) 7730 6327 5–2D
"Very expensive and nothing special" – given the odious
impression of "complacency" emanating from this
quintessentially '80s, Pimlico Italian, the news (as we go to
press) of an imminent refurb is all the more welcome.
/ 11.30 pm; closed Sat L & Sun L; smart casual; set weekday L £32(FP).

India Club WC2 £ 19 ❸❷④

143 Strand (020) 7836 0650 2–2D
"Odd but good-value", "Formica-chic" stalwart (on the second
floor of a small Aldwych hotel), whose "basic but brilliantly
authentic" curries have a devoted following; BYO, or grab a
pint from the hotel bar. / 11 pm; closed Sun; no credit cards; need 6+ to
book.

Indian Ocean SW17   £21   ❷❸❸
216 Trinity Rd   (020) 8672 7740   10–2C
"Above-average" Wandsworth Indian, with *"friendly"* service.
/ 11.30 pm.

Indigo WC2   £40   ❸❷❸
1 Aldwych   (020) 7300 0400   2–2D
"An elegant and simple atmosphere and superior food" make
the mezzanine dining room of this chic new Covent
Garden-fringe hotel a useful business venue; we're with the
minority who find the cooking *"bland"* and *"expensive"*.
/ 11.15 pm.

Indigo W1   £28   ❸④❸
75 Beak St   (020) 7287 1840   3–2D
Trendy but intimate West Soho newcomer, where we found
quite good cooking – only time will tell if that's enough to
exorcise the jinx which seems to haunt this small site.
/ 10.30 pm; set always available £19(FP).

Ishbilia SW1   £29   ❸❷④
9 William St   (020) 7235 7788   2–3A
"Crowds of street-wise Middle-Easterners" and *"excellent"*
meze *"lend much authenticity"* to this otherwise anonymous
Knightsbridge spot; service is *"very helpful"*. / Midnight; no Switch.

Isola SW1   £60   – – –
145 Knightsbridge   (020) 7838 1044   5–1D
First announced over a year ago, Oliver Peyton's Knightsbridge
newcomer has been a long time in coming, so lets hope this
large Italian (overseen by Frenchman Bruno Loubet) is worth
the wait; the basement is to house the slightly less ambitious
Osteria d'Isola (£45).

Istanbul Iskembecisi N16   £18   ❷❸❸
9 Stoke Newington Rd   (020) 7254 7291   1–1C
"Pleasant" Dalston Turk that offers *"good food, very cheap"*;
offal is the spécialité de la maison. / 5 am.

Italian Kitchen WC1   £28   ❸❸❸
43 New Oxford St   (020) 7836 1011   2–1C
"Good-value, tasty Italian food" makes this *"pleasingly
unpretentious"* north Covent Garden spot a worthwhile
Theatreland destination; fingers crossed, it won't be
transformed into a 'Maggiore's', like its erstwhile sibling.
/ 11 pm; restricted booking Fri & Sat.

It's £17 ❸❷❸

15a Air St, W1 (020) 7734 4267 3–3D
60 Wigmore St, W1 (020) 7224 3484 3–1B
74 Southampton Row, WC1 (020) 7405 2876 2–1D
128 Holland Pk Ave, W11 (020) 7243 1106 6–2A
17-20 Kendal St, W2 (020) 7724 4637 6–1D
404 Chiswick High Rd, W4 (020) 8995 3636 7–2A
197 Baker St, NW1 (020) 7486 6027 2–1A

The volume of feedback isn't huge, but reporters rate this emerging "cheap and cheerful" pizza-and-more chain higher than many of its better known competitors; it's certainly not exciting, but it is "good value". / 10.30 pm; .

Itsu SW3 £25 ❸❸❸

118 Draycott Ave (020) 7584 5522 5–2C

Glossily gimmicky, conveyor-belt bar/restaurant, near Brompton Cross (formerly called t'su); its "interesting sushi" concept is "quite expensive", but the "new menu is a great improvement". / 11 pm; smoking only in bar; no booking.

THE IVY WC2 £47 ❷❶❶

1 West St (020) 7836 4751 4–3B

"Without peer"; this "consistently satisfying" Theatrelander is still (new owners notwithstanding) reporters' No 1 Favourite, thanks to its "simple" and "reliable" modern British cooking and "superb" service (and "you can watch the stars", too); "it would be even better if you could get in". / Midnight; set Saturday lunch £28(FP).

Iznik N5 £21 ❷❸❶

19 Highbury Pk (020) 7354 5697 8–2D

"Much loved" Islington Turk; it has "good-value" cooking and "welcoming" service, but it's the "superb", "romantic" atmosphere which earns its cult following. / 11 pm; no Amex.

Japanese Canteen £22 ⑤⑤⑤

5 Thayer St, W1 (020) 7487 5505 3–1A
305 Portobello Rd, W10 (020) 8968 9988 6–1A
19-21 Exmouth Mkt, EC1 (020) 7833 3521 9–1A
394 St John St, EC1 (020) 7833 3222 8–3D

It's not only purists who are outraged by the "shoddy representation" of Japanese food (and its "hit-and-miss" realisation) at these "very sparse", "cold" and "uninviting" establishments. / City & W10 11 pm - W1 9 pm, Sat 6 pm; City branches closed Sun L - W1 closed Sun; W1 no credit cards; no smoking area - W1 no smoking; W1 no booking.

Jason's W9 £38 ❷❷❶

Opposite 60 Blomfield Rd (020) 7286 6752 8–4A

"Sitting with a view of the canal" (near Little Venice) is the best place to enjoy "fabulous fish" (with "imaginative" Mauritian twists), according to the many devotees of this "small" and "friendly" fixture. / 10.30 pm; closed Sun D.

Jenny Lo's Tea House SW1   £19   ❸②④
14 Eccleston St   (020) 7259 0399   2–4B
Belgravia "canteen", popular for its "filling and healthy"
oriental fare – in particular "good noodles" – and "the best
herbal teas". / 10 pm; closed Sun; no credit cards; no booking.

Jim Thompson's SW6   £28   ④④❷
617 King's Rd   (020) 7731 0999   5–4A
The "fun" atmosphere at this stylishly decorated oriental suits
parties for the young-at-heart; there is the odd complaint of
"terrible slop", but the cooking is mostly "decent". / 11 pm.

Jimmy's W1   £15   ④❷❸
23 Frith St   (020) 7437 9521   4–2A
"Cheap" Greek veteran, in a Soho basement; it's "still a
favourite", especially for the impecunious. / 11 pm, Thu, Fri & Sat
11.30 pm; closed Sun; no Amex.

Jin Kichi NW3   £24   ❷❸❸
73 Heath St   (020) 7794 6158   8–1A
"Great sushi" is amongst the attractions of this "functional but
delicious" Hampstead Japanese; "it's just like being in Tokyo –
the only complaint is that there are too many smokers".
/ 11 pm; D only, Sat & Sun open L & D.

Jindivick N1   £33   ④❸④
201 Liverpool Rd   (020) 7607 7710   8–3D
Inconsistent standards hold back enthusiasm for what some
say is an "underrated" Islington venue; the "superb brunch"
is widely praised, particularly by parents – the number of
"New Labour babies" can make it "like a playground".
/ 10.45 pm; closed Mon L & Sun D; no Amex; no smoking area; set D £20(FP).

Joe Allen WC2   £31   ④❸❷
13 Exeter St   (020) 7836 0651   4–3D
This "lively", "late-night" Theatreland basement is "just as
good as the one in NYC", and "great for star-spotting and
impromptu piano-playing"; top choice is the "great burgers"
(not listed on the menu). / 12.45 am; no smoking area.

Joe's Brasserie SW6   £31   ④④❸
130 Wandsworth Br Rd   (020) 7731 7835   10–1B
Fulham "local", which maintains its twentysomething following
in spite of cooking that "lacks oomph", to say the least. / 11 pm.

Joe's Café SW3   £40   ❸❸❷
126 Draycott Ave   (020) 7225 2217   5–2C
"For the shoppers of Brompton Cross", this "fashionable"
brasserie offers a "simple light menu" of "relatively stylish"
food, and "great people-watching"; the return of evening
opening is on the cards as we go to press. / L only.

Joy King Lau W1   **£ 21**   **❷❸**④
3 Leicester St   (020) 7437 1132   4–3A
"Excellent", reasonably priced cooking and "wonderful service
for a Chinese" make this one of the best bets in Chinatown.
/ 11.30 pm; no Switch.

Julie's W11   **£ 44**   ④④**❶**
135 Portland Rd   (020) 7229 8331   6–2A
"Sexy, crazy, great" – the "lovely nooks and corners" of this
"intimate", Gothic/Baroque Holland Park labyrinth make
"a wonderful place to hide away with your loved one"; even
the starry-eyed, though, can see the cooking's "past it".
/ 11.15 pm; closed Sat L.

Julie's Bar W11   **£ 32**   ④**❷❶**
137 Portland Rd   (020) 7727 7985   6–2A
"Low lighting and interesting décor" lends Julie's neighbouring
bar much of the magic of its parent; "the food seems to have
improved" – not, in truth, difficult. / 10.30 pm.

Kalamaras W2   **£ 22**   **❸❷❸**
66 Inverness Mews   (020) 7727 5082   6–2C
"Still cheerful", this "fun" taverna – obscurely located in a
Bayswater mews – offers reasonable cooking (and the BYO
policy is a boon); its former renown, however, is but a memory.
/ 11 pm; D only; no Switch.

Kaspia W1   **£ 41**   **❸❷❸**
18-18a Bruton Pl   (020) 7493 2612   3–2B
"If caviar is your thing", this discreet Mayfair mews dining
room is for you; it is, of course, "outrageously expensive".
/ 11.30 pm; closed Sun; no Switch; smart casual.

Kastoori SW17   **£ 19**   **❶❷**④
188 Upper Tooting Rd   (020) 8767 7027   10–2C
"An absolute delight – who needs meat?"; the "refreshingly
different" vegetarian fare at this "well-run" Tooting South
Indian/East African is as "fabulous" as the atmosphere is
"dull". / 10.30 pm; closed Mon L & Tue L; no Amex & no Switch.

Kavanagh's N1   **£ 30**   **❷❷❸**
26 Penton St   (020) 7833 1380   8–3D
"An undiscovered gem in otherwise over-discovered Islington";
this "great local" can be "variable", but usually provides "good
value" cooking and "friendly" service. / 10.30 pm; closed Mon
& Sun D; no Amex; set weekday L £19(FP).

Kaya Korean W1   **£ 42**   ④**❸**⑤
42 Albemarle St   (020) 7499 0622   3–3C
London's grandest Korean, near the Ritz, may serve
"good-quality" food but it's "very expensive for what you get",
and this is possibly "the dullest restaurant in the world".
/ 10.45 pm; closed Sun L.

Ken Lo's Memories SW1   £ 40   ❷❷④

67-69 Ebury St   (020) 7730 7734   2–4B
*Fans forgive the "decidedly dated décor" of this eminent and
long-established Belgravian, thanks to the notably "high
standard" of its Chinese cuisine. / 10.45 pm; closed Sun L;
smart casual.*

Ken Lo's Memories of China W8   £ 37   ❷❷④

353 Kensington High St   (020) 7603 6951   7–1D
*"Good but pricey" Kensington oriental, which does not yet
quite match the lofty culinary standards of the Belgravia
original. / 11.15 pm; closed Sun L.*

Kensington Place W8   £ 39   ❸❸❷

201-205 Kensington Ch St   (020) 7727 3184   6–2B
*Loyal fans say we're "harsh" about this seminal, if
"uncomfortable" and "noisy", modern British 'goldfish bowl',
just off Notting Hill, but the fact is that its ratings have been
inexorably heading south; can recent purchasers the
Avenue/Circus group turn it round? – time will tell. / 11.45 pm,
Sun 10.15 pm; set weekday L £22(FP).*

Kettners W1   £ 23   ⑤④❷

29 Romilly St   (020) 7734 6112   4–2A
*Will no one rescue "poor old Kettners"?; this "palatial",
once-elegant Soho landmark is "showing its age", serving
"expensive pizza and burgers" in a "tired" setting; still "you
can always get a table" nowadays. / Midnight; smart casual;
no booking.*

Khan's W2   £ 16   ❸⑤❸

13-15 Westbourne Grove   (020) 7727 5420   6–1C
*"Fast and fun"; this notorious Bayswater "institution" – whose
service is "brisk"-going-on-"rude" – may be as relaxing as an
Indian railway station, but it doles out "cheap" grub to a
surprisingly grateful public. / 11.45 pm.*

Khan's of Kensington SW7   £ 21   ❷❷❸

3 Harrington Rd   (020) 7581 2900   5–2B
*"Good-value" South Kensington Indian with "above-average"
cooking and staff who give "personal attention". / 11.15 pm, Fri
& Sat 11.45 pm; no smoking area; set weekday L £13(FP).*

Khyber Pass SW7   £ 20   ❷❸⑤

21 Bute St   (020) 7589 7311   5–2B
*The "worst décor ever" is amply compensated for by "cheap"
and "consistently good" cooking at this tiny Indian, near South
Kensington tube. / 11.30 pm; no Switch; set weekday L £12(FP).*

King's Road Café SW3   £ 20   ④④❸

208 King's Rd   (020) 7351 6645   5–3C
*For an in-store snackbar, Habitat's café is a cut above the
norm; the food is "fresh", and "as the place is run by Italians,
they really understand kids". / open shop hours only, until 5.30 pm;
L only; no Amex; no smoking area; no booking at weekends.*

Krungtap SW10 £ 20 ④❷④
227 Old Brompton Rd   (020) 7259 2314   5–2A
"Cheap and cheerful Thai café" in Earl's Court; it's *"lost its charm"* since the fire, though, *"lovely"* service notwithstanding. / 10.30 pm; no Amex.

Kulu Kulu W1 £ 18 ❷❸④
76 Brewer St   (020) 7734 7316   3–2D
"Top quality" conveyor-belt sushi *"at good prices"* make this tiny Soho café a great place to *"eat and run"*. / 10 pm; closed Sun; no Amex; no smoking; no booking.

Kundan SW1 £ 32 ❷❷⑤
3 Horseferry Rd   (020) 7834 3211   2–4C
"Very dated", cavernous Westminster basement Pakistani, whose *"beautiful"* cooking is hailed as *"the best"* by its (rather small) fan club. / Midnight; closed Sun.

Kwan Thai SE1 £ 29 ❸❷④
The Riverfront, Hay's Galleria   (020) 7403 7373   9–4D
"Efficient", *"attentive"* staff and *"consistent"*, *"tasty"* cooking make this (to some, rather *"sterile"*) riverside Thai, a useful stand-by, a few minutes' walk from London Bridge. / 10 pm; closed Sun; no smoking area.

The Ladbroke Arms W11 £ 24 ❸❸❷
54 Ladbroke Rd   (020) 7727 6648   6–2B
"A real pub, with good food and beer, and without pretensions" – which is all the more remarkable, as it's on the fringe of Notting Hill; when it's sunny, arrive early to *"grab a table"* outside. / 9.45 pm; no Amex.

Lahore Kebab House E1 £ 18 ❶④⑤
2 Umberston St   (020) 7488 2551   1–2D
"If you can ignore the squalor", it's *"seriously worth journeying across town"* for the *"incredible food at rock bottom prices"* – *"the best kebabs in the world!"* – at this infamous East Ender; BYO. / 11.45 pm; no credit cards.

The Landmark Hotel NW1 £ 58 ④❸❷
222 Marylebone Rd   (020) 7631 8000   8–4A
"The Winter Garden is a great setting for brunch" (or afternoon tea) at this attractive Marylebone hotel, complete with soaring atrium – the cooking is otherwise rather *"slack"*. / 10.45 pm; closed Sat L & Sun D; smart casual; no smoking area; set weekday L £39(FP).

Lanes, Four Seasons Hotel W1 £ 46 ⑤④⑤
Park Ln   (020) 7499 0888   3–4A
Like us, reporters *"cannot believe"* that this new *"Post House-style"* restaurant got past the doorman of any Mayfair hotel – let alone one with the proud heritage of the once-*"acclaimed"* Inn on the Park. / 11 pm; no Switch; no smoking area.

The Lanesborough W1 £ 52 ④❷❶
Hyde Pk Corner   (020) 7259 5599   2–3A
*"They don't seem to pull it off, foodwise", but the large
conservatory-restaurant of this mega-swanky hotel, with
"enough plants to rival Kew", offers consolation in the form of
"good-value set menus", "terrific English breakfasts" and "very
good afternoon teas".* / Midnight.

Langan's Bistro W1 £ 30 ④❸❸
26 Devonshire St   (020) 7935 4531   2–1A
*"Inconsistent" Marylebone bistro, whose intimate scale and
tranquillity present a stark contrast with its Mayfair
stable-mate.* / 11 pm; closed Sat L & Sun.

Langan's Brasserie W1 £ 40 ④❸❷
Stratton St   (020) 7493 6437   3–3C
*This famously "fun" Mayfair brasserie – long a top
out-of-towner's choice for a Big Night Out – is still "wonderfully
glamorous", for many people; it's "living on its reputation",
though, and even fans admit the food "isn't great".* / 11.45 pm;
closed Sat L & Sun.

Langan's Coq d'Or SW5 £ 41 ④❸❸
254-260 Old Brompton Rd   (020) 7259 2599   5–3A
*A "good all-round performance, marred by high prices" is the
general view on this "pleasant enough", genuinely
Gallic-looking Earl's Court brasserie; we're with those who say
it's plain "overpriced" – £12.50 for bangers and mash?* / 11 pm;
closed Mon.

Lansdowne NW1 £ 27 ❸④❷
90 Gloucester Ave   (020) 7483 0409   8–3B
*"Down-to-earth" Primrose Hill gastropub, whose "great
Sunday lunch" is something of an institution; "very inconsistent
service" is a perennial bugbear.* / 10 pm; closed Mon L; no Amex; book
Sun L only.

La Lanterna SE1 £ 25 ❸❷❷
6–8 Mill St   (020) 7252 2420   1–3D
*"Bustling", "squashed" family-run Italian, five minutes from
Tower Bridge, liked for its "good-value" approach and
"courteous" and "welcoming" service.* / 11 pm; closed Sat L.

Latitude SW3 £ 32 ⑤④❸
165 Draycott Ave   (020) 7589 8464   5–2C
*Pricey, oriental newcomer near Brompton Cross, whose
approach suggests that the 'L' in the name is redundant; with
its "mean" portions and "noisy" setting, the place is
presumably meant more as a bar than a restaurant?* / 11.45 pm;
closed Sun; no booking.

Latymers W6 £ 20 ❷❷④
157 Hammersmith Rd   (020) 8741 2507   7–2C
*"Great Thai food for a fiver" and "very good" service make it
worth braving the "smoky" back room of this "grim-looking"
Hammersmith gin palace.* / 10 pm; closed Sun; no booking at lunch.

Laughing Gravy SE1 £32 ❸❷❸

154 Blackfriars Rd (020) 7721 7055 9–4A

An uninspiring location, near the east end of The Cut, means few have stumbled across this bistro newcomer; some of those who have come across it pronounce it "a real find", and we thought it a pleasant all-rounder. / 11 pm; closed Sat L & Sun.

Launceston Place W8 £41 ❷❶❶

1a Launceston Pl (020) 7937 6912 5–1B

This "delightful" gem – "tucked away" in a Kensington townhouse – was bought by the Avenue/Circus group in mid '99; with its "grown-up", "drawing room" ambience, it's long been one of the capital's most enjoyable modern British restaurants – let's hope they don't wreck it! / 11.30 pm; closed Sat L & Sun D; pre-th. £27(FP).

Laurent NW2 £23 ❷❷⑤

428 Finchley Rd (020) 7794 3603 1–1B

"The best couscous anywhere" has long inspired pilgrimage to this "consistent", if "no-frills", Cricklewood "gem". / 11 pm; closed Sun; no Switch.

Lavender £26 ❷❷❸

112 Vauxhall Walk, Embankment, SE11 (020) 7735 4440 10–1D
61 The Cut, SE1 (020) 7928 8645 9–4A
171 Lavender Hl, SW11 (020) 7978 5242 10–2C
24 Clapham Rd, SW9 (020) 7793 0770 10–1D

"Reliable comfort food" in a "rather basic" setting is proving a winning formula for this "lively", "young" chain, which is "taking over south London". / 11 pm.

Lawn SE3 £36 ❸④❸

1 Lawn Terrace (020) 8355 1110 1–4D

You "don't have to go 'up West' nowadays" if you want a proper modern British dinner in the wastes of Blackheath; since its acquisition by the Bank group, however, the place hasn't inspired quite the same degree of confidence. / 11 pm; closed Mon L & Sun D.

Leith's W11 £48 ❷❶❷

92 Kensington Pk Rd (020) 7229 4481 6–2B

Notting Hill gastronomic stalwart, which won much more support this year for its "excellent" modern British cooking, "superb" wine list, "solid" service and "romantic" setting; for a vocal minority, though, the whole approach remains "a bit '80s". / 11.30 pm; closed Mon L, Sat L & Sun.

Leith's Soho W1 £44 ❸❸④

41 Beak St (020) 7287 2057 3–2D

"Rather clinical" Soho yearling, whose modern British cooking divides opinion; those who find it "consistently of a high standard" somewhat outnumber those who say it's "at best ordinary". / 11.15 pm; closed Sat L & Sun.

Lemonia NW1   £ 25   ④❶❷
89 Regent's Pk Rd   (020) 7586 7454   8–3B
*"As welcoming as ever" – the long-serving and "very friendly"
staff are what really make this "popular" and "noisy" Primrose
Hill fixture; the Greek fare is "reasonable", if not up to its past
best.* / 11.30 pm; closed Sat L & Sun D; no Amex; set weekday L £15(FP).

Leonardo's SW10   £ 32   ❸②❸
397 King's Rd   (020) 7352 4146   5–3B
*"The new owners are 'having a go'" at this "timeless" World's
End trattoria which has been a "welcoming family restaurant
over the last 25 years".* / 11.45 pm; closed Sun D; set weekday L
£20(FP).

The Lexington W1   £ 30   ④❸❸
Lexington St   (020) 7434 3401   3–2D
*"Intimate", oddball Soho fixture, with proportions "a bit like a
railway carriage"; as ever it's "the good-value early-evening
deal" which wins most unequivocal praise – other results are
"not very memorable".* / 11 pm; closed Sat L & Sun; booking:
deposit taken.

Lindsay House W1   £ 48   ❶❶❷
21 Romilly St   (020) 7439 0450   4–3A
*Richard Corrigan has really hit his stride at this "beautiful"
Soho townhouse, whose "unusual" (ring-to-enter) set-up is
part of its "intimate" and "discreet" appeal; on a good day, his
"gorgeous, superbly executed" modern British grub is among
the best in town.* / 11 pm; closed Sat L & Sun.

Lisboa Patisserie W10   £ 6   ❶❷④
57 Golborne Rd   (020) 8968 5242   6–1A
*"Custard tarts to die for" have brought fame to this "grotty"
but trendy Portuguese pâtisserie in North Kensington.* / 8 pm;
no credit cards; no booking.

The Little Bay NW6   £ 16   ④❸❷
228 Belsize Rd   (020) 7372 4699   1–2B
*"Simple, cheap, fun" – this ultra-budget Kilburn bistro may be
"basic", but it's "always a bargain".* / Midnight; no credit cards.

Little Havana WC2   £ 33   ⑤⑤❸
Queens House, 1 Leicester Pl   (020) 7287 0101   4–3B
*The food "isn't up to much", and service can be "confused",
but those who have stumbled into this large Cuban-themed
joint, above Leicester Square, applaud the "genuine
entertainment" value which makes it "good for large parties".*
/ 12.30 pm; closed Sat L.

Little Italy W1   £ 36   ④❷❷
21 Frith St   (020) 7734 4737   4–2A
*"Hectic, but fantastic if you're in the right mood", this Soho
Italian really comes into its own in the early hours; it's "not
cheap", though, and you have to manoeuvre "large plates at
small tables".* / 4 am, Sun midnight.

The Little Square W1   £ 28   ④❸④
3 Shepherd Mkt   (020) 7355 2101   3–4B
*Tiny and "cramped" modern British bistro yearling in
Shepherd Market whose "friendliness and convenience"
make it a decent stand-by.* / 10.45 pm.

LIVEBAIT   £ 42   ❸④⑤
21 Wellington St, WC2   (020) 7836 7161   4–3D
43 The Cut, SE1   (020) 7928 7211   9–4A
*"This fish has gone off"; Groupe Chez Gérard continues its
"disastrous" devaluation of this once "fresh and lively"
concept, which is now really "beginning to feel like a chain" –
"expensive", "noisy", "too casual" and with "indifferent"
cooking; Waterloo is still much better than Covent Garden.*
/ 11.30 pm; closed Sun; no smoking areas; set weekday L £28(FP).

Lobster Pot SE11   £ 41   ❶❷❸
3 Kennington Ln   (020) 7582 5556   1–3C
*We think the "very surreal" discovery of a "wonderfully
kitsch", "authentically French" fish restaurant hard by the
Elephant & Castle leads reporters to over-egg their
appreciation of its cooking; we're with the minority who find it
"rather expensive" for what it is, if of a "high standard".*
/ 11 pm; closed Mon & Sun; smart casual.

Lola's N1   £ 35   ❸❷❷
359 Upper St   (020) 7359 1932   8–3D
*Though its "ambitious" modern British cooking can be
"variable", this "pretty", "light" and "airy" establishment, over
Islington's Antiques Market is establishing itself as a top north
London address.* / 11 pm.

Lomo SW10   £ 21   ❸❷❷
222-224 Fulham Rd   (020) 7349 8848   5–3B
*"Chic" but "laid-back", this "excellent modern tapas café" –
newly washed up on the Chelsea 'Beach' – is "really friendly"
and "trying hard".* / 11.30 pm; no booking.

The Lord Palmerston N19   £ 22   ④④❸
33 Dartmouth Park Hl   (020) 7485 1578   8–1B
*Archway gastropub, where – thanks to the "interesting", if not
consistent, cooking – it's "hard to get a seat".* / 10 pm; closed
Mon L; no Amex; no booking.

Lou Pescadou SW5   £ 39   ❸❸❸
241 Old Brompton Rd   (020) 7370 1057   5–3A
*"Brightly lit", "authentically French" (and sometimes
"arrogant") Earl's Court fish restaurant of long standing; its
ever-fluctuating standards are currently on an up.* / Midnight; set
weekday L £21(FP).

Luc's Brasserie EC3   £ 34   ②②②
17-22 Leadenhall Mkt   (020) 7621 0666   9–2D
"Full of life" and with *"City food about as good as it gets"*, this *"excellent"*, *"unpretentious"* Gallic bistro makes a top choice around Lloyds; it's *"not the place for a serious business lunch"*. / L only; closed Sat & Sun; no Switch.

Luigi Malones   £ 24   ⑤④④
3 Charing Cross Rd, WC2   (020) 7925 0457   4–4B
73 Old Brompton Rd, SW7   (020) 7584 4323   5–2B
Some do praise *"enormous pizzas"* and *"meaty burgers"* at this diner duo; too many, though, report that *"even with low expectations, I was disappointed"*. / 11pm.

Luigi's WC2   £ 46   ④④④
15 Tavistock St   (020) 7240 1789   4–3D
"It may be a bit passé, but they still do the basics pretty well", say devotees of this attractively housed, old-school Covent Garden Italian; we're with those who see it as *"average"* and *"overpriced"*. / 11.30 pm; closed Sun; smart casual; pre-th. £26(FP).

Luigi's Delicatessen SW10   £ 26   ②⑤④
359 Fulham Rd   (020) 7351 7825   5–3B
"Fantastic pizzas" (and other good, simple dishes) *"in chaotic Italian style"* make this *"cramped"* Chelsea 'Beach' deli/diner a huge hit with *"a Eurotrash crowd that's happy to rough it"*. / 10.30 pm; closed Sun; no Amex; no booking.

Luna Nuova WC2   £ 31   ④❸❸
22 Short's Gdns   (020) 7836 4110   4–2C
"Reliable" pizza and pasta makes this north-Covent Garden basement a *"convenient"* (if slightly *"characterless"*) central option — *"great for kids and gossipy lunches"*. / 11.30 pm; no smoking area; pre-th. £21(FP).

Lunch   £ 16   ②②④
Lincoln's Inn Fields, WC2   (020) 7404 3110   2–1D
60 Exmouth Mkt, EC1   (020) 7278 2420   8–4D
"Fresh" and *"functional"* post-modernist cafés, offering a *"tempting and healthy array of bakes, salads, snacks and soups"*; *"get there early before the best dishes run out"*. / L only; closed Sat & Sun; no credit cards; EC1 no smoking at L; no booking.

Lundum's SW7   £ 32   ❸①❸
119 Old Brompton Rd   (020) 7373 7774   5–2B
The *"personal"*, *"family"* touch is what really distinguishes this otherwise *"bland"* South Kensington newcomer (on the site of Shaws, RIP); *"if you've been desperate for Danish cooking"*, it *"fills a niche"*, but beware the *"overpriced"* wines. / 11 pm; closed Sun D.

Ma Goa SW15   £ 28   ②②❸
244 Upper Richmond Rd   (020) 8780 1767   10–2B
"Carefully executed Goan home-cooking" and *"keen"* and *"friendly"* service make this family-run Putney bistro an *"interesting"* destination. / L only; Sun, open L & D; closed Mon.

Mackintosh's Brasserie W4   £ 29   ④④❸
142 Chiswick High Rd   (020) 8994 2628   7–2B
*"Relaxed" and "friendly" all-day Chiswick stand-by, popular
locally for its "varied menu" (even if the cooking's "not great");
it's best enjoyed for a "lazy weekend brunch".* / Midnight;
no smoking area; no booking.

Made in Italy SW3   £ 26   ❷④❸
249 King's Rd   (020) 7352 1880   5–3C
*"Very fresh pastas and pizza" win strong praise for this
"basic", "fun" and "friendly" Chelsea spot, though service can
be "moody".* / 11.30 pm; D only; no Amex; to book need 6+.

Madhu's Brilliant UB1   £ 22   ❷❷④
39 South Rd   (020) 8574 1897   1–3A
*"Always as brilliant as its name", say fans of this "very
reasonably priced" Southall curry house a couple of minutes
from the BR station; it's a step-sibling to the original Brilliant,
and some say it's similarly "overrated".* / 11.30 pm; closed Tue, Sat L
& Sun L.

Maggie Jones's W8   £ 33   ④❸❶
6 Old Court Pl   (020) 7937 6462   5–1A
*"For those winter days", the "dark", "cosy" and "rustic" charm
of this "eccentric" Kensington fixture is just the job; it comes in
"generous" portions, but the dated Anglo/French cooking is a
"bit overpriced" and "complacent".* / 11 pm.

Maggiore's Italian Kitchen WC2   £ 30   ④④④
17-21 Tavistock St   (020) 7379 9696   4–3D
*A parable of what can go wrong with '90s London restaurants
– this formerly cheap, basic and tasty Covent Garden spot has
been given a fancy face-lift and now charges "inflated" prices
for its "production line" creations.* / 11.45 pm.

Magno's Brasserie WC2   £ 36   ⑤④④
65a Long Acre   (020) 7836 6077   4–2D
*What a shame this pre-theatre stand-by didn't close for a
revamp while the builders were in at the neighbouring Opera
House; it's "gone downhill" in a big way.* / 11.30 pm; closed Sat L
& Sun L.

Maison Bertaux W1   £ 5   ❷❸❸
28 Greek St   (020) 7437 6007   4–2A
*"The coffee is only okay" at this "Soho institution" (London's
oldest pâtisserie, est. 1871), "but they have some of the best
pastries in London".* / 8.30 pm; no credit cards; no smoking area.

Maison Novelli EC1   £ 52   ❸④④
29 Clerkenwell Gn   (020) 7251 6606   9–1A
*Fans extol J-C Novelli's "beautifully presented" Gallic fare at his
City-fringe flagship; others who encounter "food promising
more than it delivers", poor service and a need to "make your
own" atmosphere conclude that it is "not very special".* / 11 pm;
closed Sat L & Sun.

Malabar W8   £ 24   ②②②
27 Uxbridge St   (020) 7727 8800   6–2B
The feel is "upmarket", but prices offer "good value" at this wonderfully "consistent" and justifiably well-known Indian, just off Notting Hill Gate. / 11.15 pm; no Amex; set Sun L £13(FP).

Malabar Junction WC1   £ 29   ②③②
107 Gt Russell St   (020) 7580 5230   2–1C
"Subtle" and "fresh" south Indian food is slowly drawing the following this "pleasant" but "underrated" Bloomsbury conservatory/restaurant deserves. / 11.30 pm; no Switch; no smoking area.

La Mancha SW15   £ 28   ③③②
32 Putney High St   (020) 8780 1022   10–2B
Prominently-located Putney bar which is "great for a pre-cinema bite", and liked by younger locals for its "fever pitch" atmosphere; "always great tapas" are preferred to the restaurant fare. / Mon-Thu 11 pm, Fri-Sun 11.30 pm.

Mandalay W2   £ 17   ②①④
444 Edgware Rd   (020) 7258 3696   8–4A
"Charming", "cheerful" owners and Burmese cooking (Indian with an oriental twist) "which is definitely out of the ordinary" set apart this "cheap, cheap, cheap" café, round the corner from Lords. / 10.30 pm; closed Sun; no smoking; set weekday L £11(FP).

Mandarin Kitchen W2   £ 27   ①④⑤
14-16 Queensway   (020) 7727 9012   6–2C
"Heavenly" seafood (including "the best lobster in London") makes it worth braving the "bizarre" '70s décor of this eminent Bayswater Chinese; service is "friendly", too, "considering the turnover". / 11.30 pm.

Mandeer WC1   £ 23   ③④④
8 Bloomsbury Way   (020) 7242 6202   2–1D
"Cheap", "canteen-style" Bloomsbury Indian, offering "simple" and "well prepared" vegetarian cooking; the new premises aren't a patch on the old, though. / 10 pm; closed Sun; no smoking.

Mandola W11   £ 24   ③④②
139 Westbourne Grove   (020) 7229 4734   6–1B
"The ambience is still there, but what's happened to the food?", is the gist of too many reports on this "fun" and "different" ("scatty") Bayswater-fringe Sudanese (where the cooking used to be notably "delicious"); perhaps it's just become "too popular"; BYO. / 10.30 pm; no credit cards.

Mango Room NW1   £ 27   ②③①
10 Kentish Town Rd   (020) 7482 5065   8–3B
"Vibrant" décor, a "chilled" atmosphere, and "really friendly" staff – not to mention "original" modern British cooking (with a Caribbean twist) – win high praise for this "cool" Camden Town spot. / 11 pm; no Amex.

Manna NW3 £26 ③④④

4 Erskine Rd (020) 7722 8028 8–3B
"A real veggie" on Primrose Hill; *"when it's good, it's really
good, but…"*. / 11 pm; closed Mon; no Amex; no smoking.

Manorom WC2 £23 ③③④

16 Maiden Ln (020) 7240 4139 4–3D
"Pleasantly small" Covent Garden Thai, where sometimes
"rude" service can let down the generally *"friendly"*
atmosphere. / 11 pm; closed Sat L & Sun.

Manzi's WC2 £39 ②③③

1 Leicester St (020) 7734 0224 4–3A
"Eccentric but fun" service contributes much to the *"olde
worlde charm"* of this *"favourite"* Theatreland fish parlour; for
best results, stick to simple dishes and sit downstairs.
/ 11.30 pm, Cabin Room 10.30 pm; closed Sun L; pre-th. £24(FP).

Mao Tai SW6 £36 ②②②

58 New King's Rd (020) 7731 2520 10–1B
It may be *"less personal since it doubled in size"*, but *"you
can't really fault"* this long-running Parson's Green success
story; it's *"always full"*, thanks to its *"delicious"* Chinese
cooking, *"immaculate"* service and *"fun"* atmosphere.
/ 11.30 pm; no smoking area.

Marché Mövenpick SW1 £21 ④④④

Bressenden Pl (020) 7630 1733 2–4B
You get *"lots of choice"* at this large Swiss *"canteen"* near
Victoria; it fills a gap in a thin area and is *"fine for kids"*, but
otherwise reactions are very mixed. / 11 pm; no smoking area.

Maremma N1 £33 ③②③

11 Theberton St (020) 7226 9400 8–3D
"Authentic", *"moderately priced"* Italian cooking and
"courteous service" have already won quite a following for this
Islington newcomer; it can seem *"a little lacking in
atmosphere"*, though, and a significant minority reports
"all-round disappointment". / 11 pm; closed Mon.

Marine Ices NW3 £23 ④③③

8 Haverstock HI (020) 7482 9003 8–2B
"Kids delight" at this *"long-standing pasta/pizza/ice cream
place"* in Chalk Farm; *"the ice cream is to die for"*, but the
other fare is *"not so hot"*. / 11 pm; no Amex; no smoking area.

Maroush £35 ②④④

I) 21 Edgware Rd, W2 (020) 7723 0773 6–1D
II) 38 Beauchamp Pl, SW3 (020) 7581 5434 5–1C
III) 62 Seymour St, W1 (020) 7724 5024 2–2A
Swanky Lebanese outfits where *"everything is incredibly fresh"*;
the snack bars (at nos I and II) are *"classic"* late-night
destinations, while the restaurants at all three are *"expensive
but good overall"*; no I is *"good for a party night out"* (after
10.30pm music and dancing – minimum charge £48). / W1
1 am - W2 1.30 am - SW3 5 am.

The Marquis W1   £ 33   ❸❷④

121a Mount St   (020) 7499 1256   3–3B

With its "attentive service", "fine food" and "very fair prices for the heart of Mayfair", this agreeable modern British restaurant is certainly "good for lunch"; lack of passing evening traffic can make it "empty at dinner". / 10.45 pm; closed Sat L & Sun; smart casual.

Mas Café W11   £ 30   ④④❷

6-8 All Saints Rd   (020) 7243 0969   6–1B

"Young and hip" Notting Hill "hang-out"; it's especially "buzzy" at weekends, when the "great brunch" is the star feature. / 11.30 pm; D only, Sat & Sun open brunch & D; no Amex; no brunch bookings.

Mash W1   £ 40   ⑤⑤④

19-21 Gt Portland St   (020) 7637 5555   3–1C

"Style police" bar the uncool from this "would-be trendy" spot, just north of Oxford Street; those who make it past the rope report a "pretentious" place, where "arrogant" staff dish up "bland" and "overpriced" cooking; it's "fine for a drink". / 11.30 pm.

The Mason's Arms SW8   £ 25   ❷④❷

169 Battersea Park Rd   (020) 7622 2007   10–1C

"Great pub food" – from a "superb" and "frequently changing" menu – makes it "worth the wait for a table" at this "trendy" Battersea boozer. / 10.20 pm.

Matsuri SW1   £ 48   ❶❷❸

15 Bury St   (020) 7839 1101   3–3D

The "best all-round Japanese in the West End"; despite an ambience some find a mite elusive, this smart St James's teppan-yaki and sushi restaurant provides an "excellent experience", with "wonderful" food and "attentive" service. / 10.30 pm; closed Sun; no Switch.

Maxwell's   £ 25   ⑤④④

8-9 James St, WC2   (020) 7836 0303   4–2D
76 Heath St, NW3   (020) 7794 5450   8–1A

"Old haunts that don't improve much"; the chief virtue of these "American-type" burger stalwarts is that they "are enjoyed by younger members of the family". / Midnight; no smoking area.

Mediterraneo W11   £ 31   ❷❶❷

37 Kensington Park Rd   (020) 7792 3131   6–1A

"A top package" of "affordable" and "well prepared" Italian cooking, "great" service and a "top people-watching environment" ("was it the setting for 'Notting Hill'?") are making Osteria Basilico's upstart offspring even more popular than its parent. / 11.30 pm.

Mekong SW1   £19   ❸④④
46 Churton St   (020) 7630 9568   2–4B
*"Fragrant food" in a culinary desert makes it worth
remembering this "reasonably priced" Pimlico Vietnamese.
/ 11.30 pm; no Amex.*

Melati W1   £23   ❷④④
21 Great Windmill St   (020) 7437 2745   3–2D
*"Basic but satisfying" canteen, near Piccadilly Circus, whose
"very authentic" Indonesian cooking makes it a consistently
"good-value" (and "busy") West End refuge. / 11.30 pm, Fri & Sat
12.30 am; no Switch.*

Memories of India SW7   £22   ❷❷❸
18 Gloucester Rd   (020) 7589 6450   5–1B
*It's a bit "dull", but "efficient service and a general air of
cleanliness" help make this South Kensington subcontinental a
popular local; the cooking is "not the best, but well-priced".
/ 11.15 pm.*

Le Mercury N1   £20   ④④❸
140a Upper St   (020) 7354 4088   8–3D
*This "dated" budget bistro may indeed be "very cheap" and
have a "great location" (near Islington's Almeida Theatre), but
the cooking is "iffy" and service "erratic". / 1 am, Sun 11.30 pm;
no Amex; no smoking area.*

Mesclun N16   £25   ❶❶❸
24 Stoke Newington Ch St   (020) 7249 5029   1–1C
*It's "a real surprise" to discover this Stoke Newington venture
– it's "so welcoming", and its modern British menu is
"beautifully prepared" and "excellent value"; "the
atmosphere's much better since redecoration". / 11 pm; D only;
no Amex.*

Meson don Felipe SE1   £24   ❸❸❶
53 The Cut   (020) 7928 3237   9–4A
*"Playing sardines" only "adds to the atmosphere" at this
"genuine", "always crowded" tapas bar near the Old Vic; so
does the "wacky guitarist". / 11 pm; closed Sun; no Amex; book pre
7.30 pm only.*

Le Metro SW3   £25   ❸❸❷
28 Basil St   (020) 7589 6286   5–1D
*"A good stop-off point", near Harrods; this "reliable and
relaxing" basement wine bar may be "too cramped", but it
delivers a dependable (if "limited") menu, and a "great
selection of wines by the glass". / 10.30 pm; closed Sun; no booking
at L.*

Metrogusto SW8   £28   ❷❷❸
153 Battersea Park Rd   (020) 7720 0204   10–1C
*"It's worth a visit to this out-of-the-way location", 100 yards
west of Battersea Dogs' Home – a striking, new
pub-conversion, with "really good" Italian cooking. / 11 pm;
closed Sun D; no Amex; no smoking area.*

Mezzanine SE1 £ 29 ④❸④

National Theatre, South Bank (020) 7452 3600 2–3D
*The RNT's in-house restaurant is "very convenient" for all the
South Bank's cultural attractions, with suitably "fast" service;
some find the performance "better than you might expect",
but others just think it's "awful". / 11 pm; closed Sun;
no smoking area.*

Mezzo W1 £ 42 ⑤⑤⑤

100 Wardour St (020) 7314 4000 3–2D
*"Too big, too loud, too full of itself"; Conran's Soho behemoth
offers a lethal cocktail of "limp" and "overpriced" modern
British cooking and "really shoddy" and "inefficient" service.
/ Mon-Wed midnight, Thu-Sat 1 am (crustacea till 3 am); closed Sat L; pre-th.
£27(FP).*

Mezzonine W1 £ 33 ⑤⑤⑤

100 Wardour St (020) 7314 4000 3–2D
*Cooking that "lacks care", staff who "treat customers with
disdain", and a "dull" setting where "you all sit on top of one
another" – such are the attractions of Mezzo's "very pricey"
ground floor oriental canteen. / Mon-Thu 12.45 am, Fri-Sat 2.45 am;
closed Sun; pre-th. £22(FP).*

Midi EC1 £ 24 ④❷❷

140-142 St John St (020) 7250 0025 9–1A
*Bright, modish Smithfield yearling, with an unusually well
spaced, airy setting and "welcoming", "professional" service;
the middle Eastern/Mediterranean menu promises a mite
more than it delivers. / Midnight; closed Sun.*

Mildreds W1 £ 20 ❸④④

58 Greek St (020) 7494 1634 4–2A
*It's "way too cramped", but this "trendy" and "cheap 'n'
cheerful" Soho café is "one of the most reliable veggie options
in town". / 11 pm; closed Sun D; no credit cards; no smoking; no booking.*

Mimmo d'Ischia SW1 £ 48 ④❸❷

61 Elizabeth St (020) 7730 5406 2–4A
*"Mimmo's the man", say fans of this "impressive" but "fun"
Belgravian, which offers "great food coupled with the usual
flamboyant Italian style"; many, though, find the place "poor,
considering the price", and dismiss the whole approach as
"Jurassic". / 11.30 pm; closed Sun D; smart casual.*

Mims EN4 £ 30 ❸⑤⑤

63 East Barnet Rd (020) 8449 2974 1–1B
*The "adventurous", slightly wacky Anglo-French cooking at this
"ordinary-looking" Barnet spot is "variable" but "can be very
good"; the décor ("plastic") and service ("slow" or "curt") do it
few favours. / 11 pm; closed Mon; no Amex & no Switch; no smoking area;
set Sun L £20(FP).*

Min's Bar SW3 £ 39 ④❸❷

31 Beauchamp Pl (020) 7589 5080 5–1C
"Cosy", "chic" and "upmarket" (read 'Eurotrashy')
Knightsbridge townhouse bar/restaurant; it's more a place to
hang out at than eat, but some think it a "wonderful" lunch
spot. / 11 pm; closed Sun D.

MIRABELLE W1 £ 48 ❷❷❷

56 Curzon St (020) 7499 4636 3–4B
A "fantastic all-rounder"; with its "excellent" modern French
cooking, "James Bond" setting and "choreographed" service –
not to mention a "vast" wine list, with interest "at all prices" –
MPW's Mayfair "classic" has quickly become a top choice for
practically any occasion. / Midnight; no smoking area; set Sun L £31(FP).

The Mission SW6 £ 25 ❸❷❸

116 Wandsworth Br Rd (020) 7736 3322 10–1B
"Undiscovered" Sands End spot whose fans unanimously laud
the "unusual" modern British menu; on our visit, the soothing
décor was a greater attraction. / 11.15 pm; D only, Sat & Sun L & D;
no Amex; no smoking area.

Mitsukoshi SW1 £ 60 ❶❷⑤

14-16 Regent St (020) 7930 0317 3–3D
This "very Japanese" establishment in the basement of the
eponymous department store is, for some, "the best in town";
it's rather a dry experience, though. / 9.30 pm; closed Sun.

Miyama W1 £ 53 ❷❸⑤

38 Clarges St (020) 7499 2443 3–4B
"Top sushi" helps distinguish this Mayfair oriental, but the
atmosphere is very "Japanese businessy". / 10.30 pm; closed Sat L
& Sun L; smart casual.

Mohsen W14 £ 17 ❷④⑤

152 Warwick Rd (020) 7602 9888 7–2D
This Olympia pit stop, with its fine Sainsbury's Homebase
vista, serves enormous portions of good Persian grub, dirt
cheap; arrive early for a seat (but, even then, you may have to
re-jig at the whim of the staff); BYO. / 11.30 pm; no credit cards;
no booking.

Momo W1 £ 38 ④④❶

25 Heddon St (020) 7434 4040 3–2C
"High on fashion and style, not content", this "cool"
Moroccan, just off Regent Street, has a "delicious setting" and
"great atmosphere" – shame about the "indifferent" food and
"arrogant" service. / 10.30 pm.

Mon Plaisir WC2   £ 34   ②❶❶

21 Monmouth St   (020) 7836 7243   4–2B

"Thank heavens it's open again"; this "delightful", old bistro – "an oasis of resolute Frenchmen", in the heart of Theatreland – "still has the same high standards after the fire", not least of "honest-to-goodness" cooking; there is a particularly "good pre-theatre dinner" (and bargain set lunch). / 11.15 pm; closed Sat L & Sun; pre-th. £15(FP).

Mona Lisa SW10   £ 13   ❸❸④

417 King's Rd   (020) 7376 5447   5–3B

"A great way to 'slum it' with character", this "friendly" Chelsea greasy spoon offers "the cheapest home Italian cooking around", not to mention "the best fry-ups". / 11 pm; closed Sun D; no credit cards.

Mongolian Barbecue   £ 23   ⑤⑤⑤

12 Maiden Ln, WC2   (020) 7379 7722   4–3D
61 Gloucester Rd, SW7   (020) 7581 8747   5–2B
1-3 Acton Ln, W4   (020) 8995 0575   7–2A

"Mediocre expectations are fulfilled" at these pick-your-own stir-fry joints; "never again". / 11 pm; D only.

Monkeys SW3   £ 47   ❶❶❷

1 Cale St   (020) 7352 4711   5–2C

"Outstanding" old-school establishment, on Chelsea Green, whose "friendly" staff help create a "very agreeable" atmosphere; "delicious game, in season" is the highlight, complemented by a "spectacular" wine list. / 10.30 pm; closed Sat & Sun; no Amex.

Monsieur Max TW12   £ 34   ❶❷❸

133 High St, Hampton Hl   (020) 8979 5546   1–4A

"Correct cuisine du terroir", "scandalously cheap", ensures a diverse fan club for this "superb local restaurant" in Hampton Hill (nearest BR, Fulwell); "Max is a great character". / 9.30 pm; closed Sat L.

Montana SW6   £ 36   ❸❸❷

125-129 Dawes Rd   (020) 7385 9500   10–1B

"Always a fabulous, relaxing meal", say the many fans of this deepest-Fulham jazz bar/restaurant, cradle of the eponymous group; it's still the best of the bunch (especially for a "great brunch"), but – as at its siblings – the southwest USA fare is increasingly "hit-and-miss". / 11 pm, Fri & Sat 11.30 pm; closed Mon-Thu L; set weekday L £22(FP).

Montpeliano SW7   £ 46   ④❸❸

13 Montpelier St   (020) 7589 0032   5–1C

"Fun" and "slick" trattoria, near Harrods, where the "well presented but expensive" food is "very average". / Midnight; set weekday L £27(FP).

Monza SW3 £36 ❸②②

6 Yeoman's Rw (020) 7591 0210 5–2C
*"London needs more Italians like" this "compact"
Knightsbridge back street yearling, with its "great" specials,
"friendly" service and "sensible" prices.* / 11.30 pm; closed Mon L.

Moorgate Oriental EC2 £24 ④❸④

45 London Wall (020) 7638 2288 9–2C
*Oriental Restaurants group makeover of the brash City
bar/restaurant which formerly traded as Coates (RIP); only the
food has really changed (and not much for the better).* / 9 pm;
closed Sat & Sun.

Moro EC1 £32 ❶②②

34-36 Exmouth Mkt (020) 7833 8336 8–4D
*"Innovative Moorish cooking" – "a treat to find something so
different" – of "consistently high quality" has put this
"laid-back and cool" Clerkenwell two-year old firmly on the
map; service is "professional and unobtrusive".* / 10.30 pm;
closed Sat & Sun.

The Mortimer W1 £26 ❷④④

37-40 Berners St (020) 7436 0451 2–1B
*It's a pity this modern gastropub, with its "massive glass
frontage" (not far from Charlotte Street), isn't a bit more
atmospheric; it offers "better than expected" modern British
scoff at fair prices.* / 10 pm; closed Sun.

Morton's W1 £48 ②②②

28 Berkeley Sq (020) 7493 7171 3–3B
*"Stylish", dining room on the first floor of a fashionable
Mayfair club, whose recent opening to the public has been
well received; chef Gary Holihead left in mid-1999, and it's too
early to say whether the new régime is keeping up his
standards.* / 11.30 pm; closed Sat L & Sun.

Moshi Moshi Sushi £19 ❷❸❸

2nd Fl, Cabot Pl East, Canary Wf, E14 (020) 7513 1900 1–3D
Unit 24, Liverpool St Station, EC2 (020) 7247 3227 9–2D
7-8 Limeburner Ln, EC4 (020) 7248 1808 9–2A
*"Excellent, cheap sushi" creates "long queues" for these
"efficient" City conveyor-belt cafés.* / 9 pm; closed Sat & Sun;
no Amex and no Switch; EC2 no smoking - EC4 no smoking area; no booking.

Motcombs SW1 £38 ❸②②

26 Motcomb St (020) 7235 9170 2–4A
*"Clubby" Belgravia basement, which "makes the locals go
back time after time"; it's no surprise that the English cooking
is "rather expensive", but it is pretty consistent; "get a corner
table if you can".* / 11 pm; closed Sun D; smart casual; set weekday L
£25(FP).

Moxon's SW4 £ 32 ②②④
14 Clapham Park Rd   (020) 7627 2468   10–2D
"Fabulous fish" and *"obliging service"* are making this
"up-and-coming" Clapham yearling a big hit – *"locals no
longer live 'near the common', they live 'near Moxons'".*
/ 11.15 pm; D only; no Amex.

Mr Chow SW1 £ 44 ③③④
151 Knightsbridge   (020) 7589 7347   5–1D
Discreet Knightsbridge *"oriental with a difference"* that retains
its chicly *"'60s feel"*; it's *"expensive"* (except for the *"great set
lunch"*), but devotees still feel it's just about worth it. / Midnight;
set weekday L £26(FP).

Mr Kong WC2 £ 21 ②③④
21 Lisle St   (020) 7437 7341   4–3A
"Excellent Chinatown eatery" whose *"generous"* portions of
"inexpensive" but *"high quality"* Cantonese fare – *"be brave,
go for the specials!"* – are *"consistently excellent"*; *"downstairs
is not nice".* / 2.45 am.

Mr Wing SW5 £ 41 ②②❶
242-244 Old Brompton Rd   (020) 7370 4450   5–2A
"Great for a rumble in the jungle!" – but it's not just the *"fun"*
setting (complete with foliage and fish tanks) which makes this
"romantic" and *"upmarket"* Earl's Court Chinese *"simply the
best"*; *"the food's pretty good, too".* / Midnight.

Le Muscadet W1 £ 37 ④④④
25 Paddington St   (020) 7935 2883   2–1A
"Genuine, if slightly pricey" Gallic restaurant of long standing,
just off Baker Street; it retains a loyal fan club, but lack of
ingredient 'X' seems to discourage a wider following. / 10.45 pm,
Sat 10 pm; closed Sat L & Sun; smart casual.

Mustards Brasserie EC1 £ 28 ④④⑤
60 Long Ln   (020) 7796 4920   9–1B
"Convenient but uninspiring" Smithfield stand-by – *"a
post-work destination serving adequate food reasonably".*
/ 11 pm; closed Sat & Sun.

mychi WC1 £ 33 ④❸⑤
myhotel, 11-13 Bayley St   (020) 7667 6000   2–1C
"Oh dear"; who cares if Feng Shui witch doctors have blessed
this new Bloomsbury boutique hotel? – reporters dismiss the
brasserie as a *"rather clinical"* place whose simple cooking
(*"not so much fusion as confusion"*) too often disappoints.
/ 11 pm; closed Sun.

Naked Turtle SW14 £ 31 ❸②②
505 Upper Richmond Rd   (020) 8878 1995   10–2A
"Superb singing waitresses" and *"interesting food, like
crocodile and kangaroo"* are among the attractions of this
"lively" and *"entertaining"* East Sheen wine bar; it's *"good with
children"* and for parties. / 11 pm; closed L, Mon-Wed; no smoking area.

Nam Long SW5 £ 32 ④④❷
159 Old Brompton Rd (020) 7373 1926 5–2B
"Killer cocktails" (at exorbitant prices) keep this majorly Eurotrashy South Kensington bar/restaurant abuzz; the Vietnamese cooking is "fine". / 11.30 pm; closed Sat L & Sun.

Nancy Lam's Enak Enak SW11 £ 29 ❸⑤④
56 Lavender Hl (020) 7924 3148 10–1C
Combative TV chef Nancy Lam cooks for you at her tiny Clapham café; her fans think it's "great for a laugh", but "don't expect any of the TV-pyrotechnics from the cooking" – "I've had spicier food from Tesco". / 9 pm; D only; closed Sun-Tue; no Switch; no smoking.

Nanking W6 £ 28 ❷❷❸
332 King St (020) 8748 7604 7–2B
"Food and service give a refreshed impression" at this "cheap and reliable Chinese" – Hammersmith's best. / 11.30 pm.

Nautilus NW6 £ 21 ❶❸④
27–29 Fortune Gn Rd (020) 7435 2532 1–1B
"The best fish and chips" (fried in matzo-meal) in "good portions" make this West Hampstead fixture one of London's best chippies; "take away" is safest, though – some think the interior's "horrible". / 10 pm; closed Sun; no credit cards; no booking.

Navajo Joe WC2 £ 29 ⑤⑤❸
34 King St (020) 7240 4008 4–3C
It's "fantastic, if you love tequilas", but give the "expensive" southern American cooking a wide berth if you visit this huge, "fun and buzzing" Covent Garden bar/restaurant. / Midnight; closed Sun; pre-th. £18(FP).

Nayab SW6 £ 26 ❷❸⑤
309 New King's Rd (020) 7731 6993 10–1B
Parson's Green's "top local Indian" is a "friendly" and "solid" performer; the décor's "not great" – but you can always take away. / Midnight; smart casual.

Neal Street WC2 £ 54 ❸④④
26 Neal St (020) 7836 8368 4–2C
For his fans, TV-chef Antonio Carluccio's table-walking "makes you forget how overpriced the menu is" at his long-established Covent Garden Italian; the place is "badly in need of a revamp", though – and especially those who encounter "wildly unfriendly" service find it "a terrible let-down". / 11 pm; closed Sun; smart casual.

Neal's Yard Dining Rooms WC2 £ 12 ❸❷④
14 Neal's Yd (020) 7379 0298 4–2C
For a quick cheap bite in Covent Garden, this cheerful, first-floor 'world café' makes a particularly nice sunny day choice; BYO. / L only (open until 5 pm); closed Sun; no Amex; no smoking; no booking.

New Culture Revolution £ 21 ④❸④
305 King's Rd, SW3 (020) 7352 9281 5–3C
157-159 Notting Hl Gt, W11 (020) 7313 9688 6–2B
42 Duncan St, N1 (020) 7833 9083 8–3D
43 Parkway, NW1 (020) 7267 2700 8–3B
*"Cheap and filling" Asian grub in a "communist canteen"
setting makes this noodle chain a useful "alternative to
Wagamama". / 11 pm; no Amex; no smoking area; to book need 4+ .*

New Mayflower W1 £ 27 ❷④④
68-70 Shaftesbury Ave (020) 7734 9207 4–3A
*"There are so many restaurants to choose from in Chinatown
– this one is that little bit better", especially if you go for the
less standard items on the menu. / 3.45 am; D only.*

New World W1 £ 24 ❸④❸
Gerrard Pl (020) 7734 0677 4–3A
*"Trolley service of dim sum at lunchtime is fun and cheap" at
this enormous but otherwise undistinguished Chinatown
landmark; "rude staff – but we love it". / 11.45 pm;
no smoking area; no booking Sun L.*

Newton's £ 28 ⑤④④
175 New King's Rd, SW6 (020) 7731 6404 10–1B
33 Abbeville Rd, SW4 (020) 8673 0977 10–2D
*"Erratic depending on the cook and mood of staff on duty",
these local diners in Clapham and (now) Parson's Green
"should concentrate on quality, not quantity". / SW6 11 pm - SW4
11.30 pm; SW6 closed Sun & Mon - SW4 closed Sun; set weekday L £17(FP).*

Nico Central W1 £ 39 ❸④⑤
35 Great Portland St (020) 7436 8846 3–1C
*Nico's name guarantees little at this "cramped" and "formal"
Gallic restaurant north of Oxford Street; some do find it "a
good, safe choice", but others report "remarkably poor"
experiences. / 11 pm; closed Sat L & Sun; smart casual.*

Nicole's W1 £ 42 ❸❸❸
158 New Bond St (020) 7499 8408 3–3C
*"Ladies-who-lunch" basement of this "stylish" Mayfair fashion
emporium, which "pleasantly surprises" with its "expensive
but good" modern British cooking; evenings attract little
commentary. / 10.45 pm; closed Sat D & Sun; no smoking area.*

Nikita's SW10 £ 35 ⑤④④
65 Ifield Rd (020) 7352 6326 5–3B
*"Fortunately, the vodka is fine" at this "dated", "decadent"
and "discreetly boothed" Russian basement, on the fringe of
Chelsea. / 11.30 pm; D only; closed Sun.*

NOBU W1 £ 53 ❶❷❷

Metropolitan Hotel, Old Park Ln (020) 7447 4747 3–4A

"Sensational and original" cooking and "amazing people-watching" make this "wickedly expensive but wickedly good" Japanese/South American, NYC-to-Mayfair import "far and away the best" of London's trendiest dining rooms. / 10.15 pm, Sat 11.15 pm; closed Sat L & Sun; no smoking area; set weekday L £34(FP).

Noho £ 22 ④④④

32 Charlotte St, W1 (020) 7636 4445 2–1C

O2 Centre, 255 Finchley Rd, NW3 (020) 7794 5616 8–2A

"Quick and reasonably priced noodles" make these "modern, fast Asians" useful pit stops; "noise levels can become exhausting". / 11.30 pm.

Noor Jahan SW5 £ 28 ❷❷④

2a Bina Gdns (020) 7373 6522 5–2B

"Reliably good, reasonably priced" South Kensington curry house – a "local favourite" currently on "very consistent" form. / 11.30 pm; no Switch.

The North Pole SE10 £ 28 ④④❸

131 Greenwich High Rd (020) 8853 3020 1–3D

It may be "good for the area", but the modern British cooking "doesn't get it quite right" at this Greenwich pub yearling; indeed, the whole approach – including "farmhouse furniture in a 'modern' setting" – is rather "messy". / 10.15 pm; closed Mon.

Noto £ 22 ❸❸④

2-3 Bassishaw Highwalk, EC2 (020) 7256 9433 9–3B

7 Bread St, EC4 (020) 7329 8056 9–2C

"Manic" City Japaneses, whose "comforting bowls of cheap noodles" are "good for budget lunches". / EC2 10.15 pm - EC4 8.45 pm; closed Sat & Sun; EC2 no Amex – EC4 no credit cards; EC2 no smoking at L; EC2 no booking for L - EC4 no bookings.

Novelli EC1 EC1 £ 42 ④④⑤

30 Clerkenwell Gn (020) 7251 6606 9–1A

"Standards are slipping" at J-C Novelli's "bland" Gallic bistro in Clerkenwell; it's now "nothing special" to a rather pronounced degree. / 11 pm; closed Sat L & Sun.

Novelli W8 W8 £ 39 ④④⑤

122 Palace Gardens Terrace (020) 7229 4024 6–2B

"Sitting in your neighbour's lap" is not a great start to a meal at this overcrowded Kensington bistro (which many enter with "high expectations" on account of its owner's celeb status); things don't generally pick up. / 11 pm, Fri & Sat midnight, Sun 10 pm; closed Mon L & Sun.

O'Conor Don W1 £ 31 ④❸❸

88 Marylebone Ln (020) 7935 9311 3–1A

"Great oysters and Guinness" in the bar and "good Irish stew" (and so on) in the dining room above still win praise for this family-run Marylebone boozer; it's "not as good" as it was, though. / 10 pm; closed Sat & Sun; smart casual.

**Oak Room Marco Pierre White
Hotel Meridien W1**   £105   ❷④④

21 Piccadilly   (020) 7437 0202   3–3D

*"Silly" prices (half the reporters who mention this place do so
as their 'most overpriced' nomination) sour appreciation of the
often "superb" cooking at MPW's grand chandeliered
chamber; the "arrogant" service and the "stiff" atmosphere
also do it few favours.* / 11.15 pm; closed Sat L & Sun; set weekday L
£58(FP).

Oceana W1   £32   ④❸④

Jason's Ct, 76 Wigmore St   (020) 7224 2992   3–1A

*The cooking (now North African-slanted) and service may be
"fine", but this "variable" basement, near the Wigmore Hall,
has never built enough buzz to overcome its obscure location
and curiously "dubious" atmosphere; it "keeps on trying".*
/ 11.15 pm; closed Sat L & Sun.

L'Odéon W1   £50   ⑤⑤④

65 Regent St   (020) 7287 1400   3–3D

*"Unimaginative" cooking at "extortionate" prices, "dreadful"
service and an "impersonal" atmosphere leave this large
first-floor restaurant, near Piccadilly Circus, badly "in need of a
revamp".* / 11.30 pm; closed Sun; no smoking area at L.

Odette's NW1   £38   ❷❷❶

130 Regent's Pk Rd   (020) 7586 5486   8–3B

*A "marvellous", "so romantic" dining room (mirrors
everywhere) combines with "lovely" modern British cooking
and "courteous" service to maintain this Primrose Hill
veteran's standing as north London's top all-rounder.* / 11 pm;
closed Sat L & Sun; set weekday L £20(FP).

Odin's W1   £38   ❸❶❶

27 Devonshire St   (020) 7935 7296   2–1A

*"It's a bit dated, but so what?"; "everybody loves" this
"beautiful", "solid" and "comfortable" Marylebone dining
room; it's the "calm and efficient" service and "beautiful"
art-filled setting which make the place.* / 11 pm; closed Sat & Sun;
smart casual.

Offshore W11   £43   ❷❸④

148 Holland Park Ave   (020) 7221 6090   6–2A

*"You can smell the sea", say fans of the "brilliantly flavoured"
fish at this new Holland Park sibling to Jason's and Chez Liline;
the setting is a mite "chilling", however, and a number dismiss
upbeat opening reviews (our own included) as "way over the
top".* / 11 pm; set weekday L £27(FP).

The Old School Thai SW11   £24   ❷❶❸

147 Lavender Hl   (020) 7228 2345   10–1C

*It's "a better-than-average local", insist the many (local) fans
of this Battersea Thai, which offers "tasty" food and
"excellent" service.* / 11 pm; closed Sun L; no smoking area;
booking: evenings only.

Ye Olde Cheshire Cheese EC4 £ 32 ④❸❷
145 Fleet St (020) 7353 6170 9–2A
Though it reeks of history, this splendid ancient tavern has avoided becoming a touristy anachronism; its "very cosy and calm" dining room is no gastronomic temple, but serves some decent, solid "traditional" fare. / 9.30 pm; closed Sat & Sun.

Olio & Farina SW3 £ 27 ④④❸
4 Sydney St (020) 7352 3433 5–2C
Simple quality – of salads, salami and so on – is the apparent aim of this "fashionable" Chelsea 'rosticceria'; it's an aspiration that is only intermittently achieved. / 11 pm; no credit cards; no smoking area.

Oliveto SW1 £ 30 ❸❸④
49 Elizabeth St (020) 7730 0074 2–4A
Anywhere "not too expensive, for the area" is worth knowing about in Belgravia, and "fantastic pizzas" and "good modern Italian food" make this modishly decorated spot one to remember. / 11.30 pm.

Olivo SW1 £ 37 ❸❸④
21 Eccleston St (020) 7730 2505 2–4B
"Flavoursome" and "uncomplicated" cooking still wins bouquets at this "lively" and "cheerful" (but "too crowded") modern Italian, near Victoria; let-downs are getting more common, though, as are gripes of "skimpy portions". / 11 pm; closed Sat L & Sun L.

1 Lombard Street EC3 £ 46 ❸❸❷
1 Lombard St (020) 7929 6611 9–3C
"This is what the City needed", say supporters of Herbert Berger's "professional" modern British yearling, near the Bank of England; "get a table upstairs" (rather than in the cheaper brasserie in the converted banking hall downstairs) to avoid the noise of the "wide-boy" bar. / 10 pm; closed Sat & Sun; bookings: max 6 (7 in restaurant).

192 W11 £ 36 ④④❸
192 Kensington Pk Rd (020) 7229 0482 6–1A
"Still cool after all these years", Notting Hill's original hip bar/restaurant is "always seriously crowded" and offers "great people-watching"; the cooking is now "average", though, and "badly served". / 11 pm; no smoking area; set Sun L £24(FP).

Opus 70 W1 £ 41 ④❸④
70 Stratton St (020) 7344 7070 3–3C
"I don't understand its deletion", fumes a reporter about last year's omission of this "airy" and modern Mayfair dining room; as hotels go, it could certainly be worse, but, with its "airy and well spaced tables", it's primarily a "business" venue. / 11 pm; closed Sat L; no smoking area.

L'Oranger SW1   £ 49   ❸❸❸

5 St James's St   (020) 7839 3774   3–4D
It's "not quite the same, since last year's debacle" (involving the acrimonious departure of many of the staff), but after some rocky months there is a feeling that this agreeable modern French dining room in St James's "has started to climb back" towards its previous heights. / 11.15 pm; closed Sat L & Sun.

Oriel SW1   £ 30   ⑤⑤❷

50-51 Sloane Sq   (020) 7730 2804   5–2D
It's as a "buzzy hangout at weekends" that this prominently sited brasserie wins its spurs; foodwise it's "very disappointing for the price" and service is "slapdash". / 10.45 pm;
no smoking area; need 6+ to book; no w/e bookings.

Oriental City Food Court NW9   £ 16   ④④⑤

399 Edgware Rd   (020) 8200 0009   1–1A
"For a touch of Hong Kong street ambience" head down to the chaotic ("wild!") food court at this quirky Colindale shopping mall; all kinds of oriental cuisine come very cheaply.
/ 11 pm; no Amex.

Orrery W1   £ 50   ④❸④

55 Marylebone High St   (020) 7616 8000   2–1A
"Lovely", "light" and "slick" modern French Conran venture in Marylebone, which undercuts support with "way OTT prices"; it has quite a business following, in spite of tables being "too small and close together". / 10.30 pm.

Orsino W11   £ 42   ④④❷

119 Portland Rd   (020) 7221 3299   6–2A
It's a real shame that the "pricey" and "dull" food and the "haphazard" service has never lived up to the "cool" and "sophisticated" setting of this discreet Holland Park Italian.
/ 11.30 pm; no smoking area; set weekday L £24(FP).

Orso WC2   £ 39   ④④❸

27 Wellington St   (020) 7240 5269   4–3D
"An old favourite that's gone off" is how we have come to think of this once-fashionable Theatreland basement Italian; there have been fewer recent reports, though, of "flabby standards" – you never know, "it could rise again!" / Midnight;
no smoking area; pre-th. £23(FP).

Oslo Court NW8   £ 39   ❶❶❸

Prince Albert Rd   (020) 7722 8795   8–3A
"Faultless – so long as you don't mind eating with your grandparents' generation", this "cosseting" Regent's Park institution (at the foot of an apartment block) offers "delicious", unreformed International cooking and "incredibly attentive but not suffocating" service. / 11 pm; closed Sun;
smart casual.

Osteria Antica Bologna SW11   **£ 28**   ③④②
23 Northcote Rd   (020) 7978 4771   10–2C
*"Authentic" cooking from an "interesting" menu has long
made this "rustic and candlelit" Italian one of Battersea's best
known places; as always, some people find it rather "tired".*
/ 11 pm, Fri & Sat 11.30 pm.

Osteria Basilico W11   **£ 31**   ②③①
29 Kensington Pk Rd   (020) 7727 9957   6–1A
*"Who cares if you eat cheek by jowl" – Notting Hill trendies
will endure much for their Italian favourite, with its "bustling",
and "fun" atmosphere and "wonderful", "authentic
home-cooking"; consequently, it's "annoyingly hard to get into".*
/ 11 pm; no booking Sat L.

OXO TOWER SE1   **£ 43**   ④④②
Barge House St   (020) 7803 3888   9–3A
*"With views like this, the food's a bit irrelevant" at the survey's
most mentioned place – "just as well", as the "expensive"
modern British grub at the brasserie of this eighth-floor South
Bank landmark is "rather disappointing", and service decidedly
"second rate"; the adjoining restaurant is even pricier.*
/ 11.15 pm; set weekday L £23(FP).

Pacific Oriental EC2   **£ 45**   ④④③
1 Bishopsgate   (020) 7621 9988   9–2C
*Big and brassy, new City "fusion" bar/restaurant; we agree
with those who say it's "horrendously expensive", and that
sticking to the cheaper downstairs brasserie is the better bet.*
/ 9 pm; closed Sat & Sun.

Pacific Spice EC1   **£ 29**   ④④②
42 Northampton Rd   (020) 7278 9983   9–1A
*"Pricey and unimaginative" cooking is killing off support for
this atmospheric Clerkenwell pub-conversion yearling (an
offshoot of the Silks & Spices chain).* / 11 pm; no smoking area.

Le Palais du Jardin WC2   **£ 35**   ③④②
136 Long Acre   (020) 7379 5353   4–3C
*This "bright and buzzy" Covent Garden mega-brasserie is
something of a surprise – "given its scale, it still manages to
deliver"; that said, today's performance pales in comparison to
a few years ago.* / Midnight.

Palatino W4   **£ 30**   ③③④
6 Turnham Green Terrace   (020) 8994 0086   7–2A
*Many locals regard this "tasty" Turnham Green Tuscan, with
its "pretty patio garden", as a pretty much perfect
neighbourhood spot; the doubters, though, who are almost as
numerous, say it "always falls just short of expectations".*
/ 11 pm; no smoking area.

Palio W11 £31 ⑤⑤④
175 Westbourne Grove   (020) 7221 6624   6–1B
"Once very good Notting Hill hangout", where most now deprecate the *"dark"*, *"loud"* and *"cheesy"* setting, and *"poor"* cooking. / 11.30 pm.

La Pampa SW11 £34 ❷❸❷
60 Battersea Rise   (020) 7924 4774   10–2C
"Excellent steaks imported from Argentina" (and *"very good chips"*, too) are the highlights at this new rustic Battersea grill; when the place is busy, some find the ambience *"fantastic"*.
/ 11 pm; D only; no Amex.

Paparazzi Café £33 ④④❸
9 Hanover St, W1   (020) 7355 3337   3–2C
58 Fulham Rd, SW3   (020) 7589 0876   5–2C
"Huge fun, if you're not shy", maybe, but these *"loud"* and *"Eurotrashy"* pizzerias are *"definitely not the place for food or a tête-à-tête"*. / SW3 1 am - W1 5 am; W1 closed Sun.

The Papaya Tree W8 £26 ❸④❸
209 Kensington High St   (020) 7937 2260   7–1D
With its *"clean, simple décor"*, decent cooking and *"welcoming"* approach, this basement off Kensington High Street is a *"great Thai local"*. / 11 pm; no smoking area.

Paris-London Café N19 £22 ④❷❸
3-5 Junction Rd   (020) 7561 0330   8–1C
"A French oasis in polluted Archway", say fans of this *"little café with very good prices"*, near the tube; some think it has *"lost its way"* of late. / 11 pm.

The Park NW6 £27 ❸④❷
105 Salusbury Rd   (020) 7372 8882   1–2B
"In an area that needed a decent eatery", this large, *"trendy"* Queen's Park bar/restaurant is deservedly making a big splash; it's a pity that mean portions and off-hand service detract from the experience. / 11 pm; no smoking area.

The Park
Mandarin Oriental Hyde Park SW1 £46 ❸❸④
66 Knightsbridge   (020) 7235 2000   2–3A
Despite a prospect of the park, and *"plenty of space"* – not to mention sometimes *"noteworthy"* modern French cooking – this relaunched Knightsbridge dining room is *"just too lofty for real intimacy"*, and *"lacks atmosphere"*. / 10.30 pm; smart casual.

Pasha SW7 £40 ④❸❶
1 Gloucester Rd   (020) 7589 7969   5–1B
The *"exotic, cosy and different"* atmosphere of this trendy South Kensington Moroccan (*"like a secret meeting place for trysts and affairs"*) continues to bewitch the *"beautiful set"* – well it can't be the *"consistently bad food"*. / 11.30 pm; closed Sun L.

Pasha N1 £ 24 ④❶❷

301 Upper St (020) 7226 1454 8–3D

*"Wonderfully welcoming" staff and a "lively" feel make this
large Islington Turk a big hit locally; some wax lyrical over its
"reliable", "well priced" fare – others, who've fared "better at
M&S", advocate the budget set menus as the best option.*
/ 11.30 pm, Fri & Sat midnight; no Switch; set weekday L £15(FP).

Passione W1 £ 32 ❷❷❸

10 Charlotte St (020) 7636 2833 2–1C

*"Worthwhile" newcomer, whose "very good" (if sometimes
"hit-and-miss") Italian cooking and "friendly" service have
already won its "tiny" Fitzrovia premises a following; "the front
room is better than the back".* / 10.30 pm; closed Sat L & Sun.

Patio W12 £ 19 ④❸❷

5 Goldhawk Rd (020) 8743 5194 7–1C

*"If you like this sort of thing" – "Polish hospitality",
"overwhelming portions", "the free vodka of your choice",
"ordered chaos" – you'll love this festive Shepherd's Bush dive;
if not, you'll judge the food "dreary", and find yourself
serenaded by an "intolerable gypsy band".* / Midnight; closed Sat L
& Sun L; no smoking area.

Pâtisserie Valerie £ 20 ❷❷❷

105 Marylebone High St, W1 (020) 7935 6240 2–1A
44 Old Compton St, W1 (020) 7437 3466 4–2A
RIBA Centre, 66 Portland Pl, W1 (020) 7631 0467 2–1B
8 Russell St, WC2 (020) 7240 0064 4–3D
215 Brompton Rd, SW3 (020) 7823 9971 5–2C

*"Comforting" Gallic cafés, universally popular for their
"delicious breakfasts" and "some of the best pastries and
croissants in town"; the large Brompton Road branch has a
broader-than-average menu, and is a hugely popular
rendezvous.* / 6 pm-8 pm, Sun earlier; Portland Pl, closed Sun;
no smoking area; no booking.

Paulo's W6 £ 25 ❸❷④

30 Greyhound Rd (020) 7385 9264 7–2C

*"Relaxed buffet-style" Brazilian, in the front room of the home
of the jovial Paulo and his wife (by Charing Cross Hospital);
the eat-all-you-can formula makes for a "different" experience.*
/ 10.30 pm; D only, Sun open L only, closed Mon; no credit cards.

The Peasant EC1 £ 32 ❸❸④

240 St John St (020) 7336 7726 8–3D

*"Above-average food, for a pub" – both at the bar and in the
"attractive" upstairs room – make this converted Clerkenwell
boozer a useful standby, even if some find the ambience
"a little dead".* / 11 pm; closed Sat L & Sun.

Pelham Street SW7 £ 30 ④❸⑤
93 Pelham St (020) 7584 4788 5–2C
*Perhaps this "sterile" year-old modern British brasserie,
near Brompton Cross, will find more favour in its revised, l
ess ambitious format; it's potentially a useful place. / 11 pm;
closed Sun D.*

The Pen SW6 £ 32 ❸❸❸
51 Parson's Green Ln (020) 7371 8517 10–1B
*"Intimate" dining room over a done-up pub (opposite
Parson's Green tube); the modern British cooking is "variable",
but mostly "good quality, at the price". / 11 pm; no Amex.*

The People's Palace SE1 £ 38 ④❸④
South Bank Centre (020) 7928 9999 2–3D
*The "great view" and, to a lesser extent, "good set menus"
are the saving graces of the Festival Hall's cavernous
Thames-side dining room; the modern British cooking is
generally "average" and "overpriced". / 11 pm.*

Pepe Nero SW11 £ 27 ④④④
133 Lavender Hl (020) 7978 4863 10–1C
*The positive press for this Battersea Italian newcomer
bemuses us – it seems just like the humdrum local (Bucci) it
replaced; reporters – kinder folk – note "some teething
problems". / 11.30 pm; closed Sat L & Sun; no Amex.*

The Pepper Tree SW4 £ 17 ❷❷❸
19 Clapham Common S'side (020) 7622 1758 10–2D
*It's "always worth queueing" for the "very reliable cheap, fast,
good food" at this "friendly and popular", refectory-style
Clapham Thai. / 11 pm, Mon and Sun 10.30 pm; no Amex;
no smoking area; no D bookings.*

Perla £ 25 ❸❷❸
28 Maiden Ln, WC2 (020) 7240 7400 4–4D
803 Fulham Rd, SW6 (020) 7471 4895 10–1B
*"Noisy" central cantina with "well-prepared" Mexican grub
and "great staff"; it now has a cousin in Fulham. / WC2
11.45 pm - SW6 11 pm; SW6 D only, except weekends when L & D.*

Le P'tit Normand SW18 £ 27 ❸❷④
185 Merton Rd (020) 8871 0233 10–2B
*"Traditional French cuisine" in "enormous" portions
(particularly the "splendid cheeseboard") and a "charming"
welcome draw pilgrims to this "surprisingly genuine"
("authentically naff") small restaurant, next to a Southfields
bus stop. / 10 pm, Fri & Sat 11 pm; closed Sat L; set weekday L £17(FP).*

Pétrus SW1   £ 43   ❶❷❸
33 St James's St   (020) 7930 4272   3–4C
Marcus Wareing's "excellent" (and "good-value") modern French cuisine makes this St James's newcomer "a serious place for serious eating"; some find the service a little "overbearing", but most seem to like it that way, the somewhat "stilted" décor is the chief drawback. / 10.45 pm; closed Sat L & Sun; booking, max 6.

Pharmacy W11   £ 42   ⑤④④
150 Notting Hl Gt   (020) 7221 2442   6–2B
"Very hit-or-miss food", poor service and general "absence of substance" win few friends for this "pretentious" Notting Hill yearling – "they should give you anti-depressants with the bill". / 10.45 pm.

Philip Owens at The ICA SW1   £ 21   ④④❸
The Mall   (020) 7930 8619   3–4D
We are bemused by the hype surrounding the new café at this well known Mall-side institute; it's an OK place to eat if you're going there anyway; er, that's it. / 11 pm, Mon 10.30 pm; no smoking area; no booking.

Phoenicia W8   £ 34   ❸❷④
11-13 Abingdon Rd   (020) 7937 0120   5–1A
It "looks a bit like a hotel lobby", but this "friendly" Lebanese, off Kensington High Street, provides "reliable" cooking, and its "all-you-can-eat lunch" is "wonderful value". / 11.45 pm.

Phoenix Bar & Grill SW15   £ 30   ❷❷❸
Pentlow St   (020) 8780 3131   10–1A
Some consider it "oddly short of atmosphere", but this "light, airy and friendly" Putney "sister to Sonny's" is generally well liked for its "professional" approach and "consistent" seafood and grills. / 11.30 pm, Sun 10 pm; closed Sat L.

Phuket SW11   £ 19   ❸❷④
246 Battersea Pk Rd   (020) 7223 5924   10–1C
"Very cheap" Battersea Thai with "friendly owners"; there ain't much atmosphere, but you can take away. / 11.30 pm; D only.

Picasso SW3   £ 24   ④④❸
127 King's Rd   (020) 7352 4921   5–3C
The food may be "at the transport café level", but this long-established Chelsea coffee shop offers great weekend posing and hanging-out opportunities. / 11.15 pm.

PIED À TERRE W1   £ 55   ❶❷❸
34 Charlotte St   (020) 7636 1178   2–1C
"Brilliant", "cutting-edge" modern French cuisine makes this "serious" (but "not too formal") Fitzrovian one of London's shrinking field of places with real, first-rank culinary ambitions; some think it feels a mite "dead". / 10.45 pm; closed Sat L & Sun; smart casual.

Pimlico Tandoori SW1 £18 ❸❷❸
38 Moreton St (off Belgrave Rd) (020) 7834 3375 2–4C
*It may look like a "typical curry shop", but this "poky" Indian
is warmly applauded for its "decent food in charming
surroundings". / 11.30 pm.*

La Piragua N1 £19 ❷④❸
176 Upper St (020) 7354 2843 8–2D
*"The steaks are unbelievable value" at this lively, cramped
Islington Latin American, which makes a great choice for a
"cheap and cheerful" night out. / Midnight; no credit cards.*

Pitcher & Piano £23 ④④❷
1 Dover St, W1 (020) 7495 8904 3–3C
10 Pollen St, W1 (020) 7629 9581 3–2C
69-70 Dean St, W1 (020) 7434 3585 4–2A
40-42 King William IV St, WC2 (020) 7240 6180 4–4C
42 Kingsway, WC2 (020) 7404 8510 2–2D
214 Fulham Rd, SW10 (020) 7352 9234 5–3B
316-318 King's Rd, SW3 (020) 7352 0025 5–3C
871-873 Fulham Rd, SW6 (020) 7736 3910 10–1B
18-20 Chiswick High Rd, W4 (020) 8742 7731 7–2B
69 Upper St, N1 (020) 7704 9974 8–3D
94 Northcote Rd, SW11 (020) 7738 9781 10–2C
8 Balham Hl, SW12 (020) 8673 1107 10–2C
11 Bellevue Rd, SW17 (020) 8767 6982 10–2C
194-200 Bishopsgate, EC3 (020) 7929 5914 9–2D
28 Cornhill, EC3 (020) 7929 3989 9–2C
The Arches, 9 Crutched Friars, EC3 (020) 7480 6818 9–3D
*Large, "buzzy" bars, "good for drinks after work", where
eager twentysomethings exchange charged glances over
indifferent plates of nachos and the like. / 10 pm - 11 pm; W1, EC3
& EC2 closed Sun.*

Pizza Metro SW11 £25 ❶❷❸
64 Battersea Rise (020) 7228 3812 10–2C
*"Outstanding pizza" (sold by the metre) means this
"cramped" and "fun" Battersea spot – beloved of Italian
expats – is usually "frantic". / 11 pm; closed Mon & Tue L-Fri L.*

Pizza On The Park SW1 £24 ④❸❷
11 Knightsbridge (020) 7235 5273 2–3A
*"Upscale", very "'70s" PizzaExpress-in-disguise, whose airy
setting makes "a good place for lunch prior to a walk in Hyde
Park" (or breakfast, for that matter); the basement is a
well-known jazz venue (significant entry charge). / Midnight;
no smoking area; no booking.*

Pizza Pomodoro £ 23 ④④❷

125 Gt Titchfield St, W1 (020) 7636 1995 2–1B
51 Beauchamp Pl, SW3 (020) 7589 1278 5–1C
7 Steward St, E1 (020) 7377 6186 9–1D
"Noisy, crowded and squashed" it may be, but the "brilliant atmosphere for late-night pizza" (and "great music") at the Knightsbridge original has long made it a popular dive; the comparatively new offshoots are useful stand-bys – nothing more. / SW3 1 am – E1 midnight; E1 closed Sat & Sun; E1 no booking after 7.30 pm.

Pizza the Action SW6 £ 20 ④❸④

678–680 Fulham Rd (020) 7736 2716 10–1B
"Efficient" Fulham diner, whose "tasty pizzas" (and a "good variety of other dishes") attract a "strong local following". / Midnight.

PizzaExpress £ 19 ❸❸❸

154 Victoria St, SW1 (020) 7828 1477 2–4B
46 Moreton St, SW1 (020) 7592 9488 2–4B
10 Dean St, W1 (020) 7437 9595 3–1D
133 Baker St, W1 (020) 7486 0888 2–1A
20 Greek St, W1 (020) 7734 7430 4–2A
21-22 Barrett St, W1 (020) 7629 1001 3–1A
23 Bruton Pl, W1 (020) 7495 1411 3–2B
29 Wardour St, W1 (020) 7437 7215 4–3A
6 Upper St James St, W1 (020) 7437 4550 3–2D
7-9 Charlotte St, W1 (020) 7580 1110 2–1C
30 Coptic St, WC1 (020) 7636 3232 2–1C
80-81 St Martins Ln, WC2 (020) 7836 8001 4–3B
9-12 Bow St, WC2 (020) 7240 3443 4–2D
363 Fulham Rd, SW10 (020) 7352 5300 5–3B
6-7 Beauchamp Pl, SW3 (020) 7589 2355 5–1C
150-152 King's Rd, SW3 (020) 7351 5031 5–3C
895 Fulham Rd, SW6 (020) 7731 3117 10–1B
137 Notting Hl Gt, W11 (020) 7229 6000 6–2B
7 Rockley Rd, W14 (020) 8749 8582 7–1C
26 Porchester Rd, W2 (020) 7229 7784 6–1C
252 Chiswick High Rd, W4 (020) 8747 0193 7–2A
35 Earl's Ct Rd, W8 (020) 7937 0761 5–1A
335 Upper St, N1 (020) 7226 9542 8–3D
30 Highgate High St, N6 (020) 8341 3434 8–1B
187 Kentish Town Rd, NW1 (020) 7267 0101 8–2B
85-87 Parkway, NW1 (020) 7267 2600 8–3B
194 Haverstock Hl, NW3 (020) 7794 6777 8–2A
70 Heath St, NW3 (020) 7433 1600 8–1A
39-39a Abbey Rd, NW8 (020) 7624 5577 8–3A
4 Borough High St, SE1 (020) 7407 2995 9–3C
Cardomom Bldg, Shad Thames, SE1 (020) 7403 8484 9–4D
230 Lavender Hl, SW11 (020) 7223 5677 10–2C
46 Battersea Br Rd, SW11 (020) 7924 2774 5–4C
305 Up Richmond Rd W, SW14 (020) 8878 6833 10–2A
144 Up Richmond Rd, SW15 (020) 8789 1948 10–2B
539 Old York Rd, SW18 (020) 8877 9812 10–2B

PizzaExpress (continued)

43 Abbeville Rd, SW4   (020) 8673 8878   10–2D
125 London Wall, EC2   (020) 7600 8880   9–2B
7-9 St Brides St, EC4   (020) 7583 5126   9–2A

"Still the best" is still the verdict on this 'benchmark', chain whose *"surprising consistency"* makes it a 'default choice' for all kinds of Londoners; *"service varies from branch to branch"*. / 11 pm-midnight - Greek St Wed-Sat 1 am - Chapter Hs L only - St Bride's St 10 pm - London Wall Sat & Sun 8.30 pm; Chapter Hs, St Bride's St, Upper James Street & Bruton Pl closed Sat & Sun (Chapter Hs open Sat in summer); not all branches take bookings.

Pizzeria Castello SE1   £ 19   ❷❸❸

20 Walworth Rd   (020) 7703 2556   1–3C

"Amazing value, well worth going to the Elephant & Castle for" ensures there's often a queue for this *"always buzzing"* pizzeria; *"park in a well-lit area"*. / 11 pm, Fri & Sat 11.30 pm; closed Sat L & Sun; smart casual.

Pizzeria Condotti W1   £ 24   ❸❷❷

4 Mill St   (020) 7499 1308   3–2C

Disguised Mayfair PizzaExpress, where *"attractive"* décor, *"good"* service and *"competent"* pizzas have long proven a fruitful formula. / Midnight; closed Sun.

PJ's   £ 36   ④④❸

30 Wellington St, WC2   (020) 7240 7529   4–3D
52 Fulham Rd, SW3   (020) 7581 0025   5–2C
82 Hampstead High St, NW3   (020) 7435 3608   8–2A

"Fun" American bar/restaurants whose *"bustling"* South Kensington branch, in particular, has a *"great location and crowd"*, and serves a *"good brunch"*; the food is otherwise *"dire"*. / Midnight - SW3, 11.45 pm; WC2 closed Sun L.

The Place Below EC2   £ 20   ❷④❸

St Mary-le-Bow, Cheapside   (020) 7329 0789   9–2C

"Arrive early to avoid queues" for the *"great vegetarian lunches"* in the crypt of this impressive City church; *"the menu changes daily"*. / L only; closed Sat & Sun; no Amex; no smoking; no booking.

Planet Hollywood W1   £ 34   ⑤④❷

13 Coventry St   (020) 7287 1000   4–4A

"Great place, shame about the food" is still the story at this larger-than-life West End theme-joint; there's *"plenty to keep kids occupied"*, but otherwise it's *"suitable only for tourists who don't mind being ripped off"*. / 1 am; no smoking area; no booking for Sat D.

Plummers WC2   £ 26   – – –

33 King St   (020) 7240 2534   4–3C

How will this Covent Garden old-timer emerge from its post-fire refurb?; will it go stark and trendy (unlikely), or will the provincial time-warp décor be lovingly restored for its theatre-going regulars? / 11.30 pm; pre-th. £18(FP).

The Poet EC3   £ 32   ④❸④
20 Creechurch Ln   (020) 7623 2020   9–2D
"Very bad acoustics" set a discordant tone at this large, bright
City gastropub, where *"good after-work bar snacks"* are a
greater attraction than a full meal. / *L only (bar meals until 9 pm);
closed Sat & Sun.*

Poissonnerie de l'Avenue SW3   £ 49   ❷❷❸
82 Sloane Ave   (020) 7589 2457   5–2C
"They know how to cook their fish" at this *"expensive but
good"* Brompton Cross seafood parlour; to some its
"old-fashioned" setting can seem *"stuffy"* and rather
"cramped". / *11.30 pm; closed Sun; smart casual.*

The Polish Club SW7   £ 27   ④❷❷
55 Prince's Gt, Exhibition Rd   (020) 7589 4635   5–1C
"Quirky" dining room of a South Kensington émigrés club,
with an *"elegant"* – but *"relaxed"* and *"cheery"* – *"pre-war"*
ambience (and a great outside terrace in summer); the
"hearty" food is usually *"average"*. / *11 pm; smart casual;
set D £15(FP).*

Pollo W1   £ 14   ④④❸
20 Old Compton St   (020) 7734 5917   4–2A
"You can't argue with a bowl of pasta for £3.50", so this
studenty (*"scummy"*), '60s Soho institution still *"squeezes"*
'em in. / *Midnight; no credit cards; no booking.*

Polygon Bar & Grill SW4   £ 32   ④❷❸
4 The Polygon, Clapham Old Town   (020) 7622 1199   10–2D
It *"would be much pricier in the West End"*, say fans of this
"buzzy" and *"trendy"* Clapham venture, (where *"great Sunday
brunch"* is a highlight); those who think it *"fails to live up to
expectations"*, however, are becoming much more vociferous.
/ *11 pm; Mon-Thu L only, Fri-Sun open L & D.*

Pomegranates SW1   £ 36   ④④④
94 Grosvenor Rd   (020) 7828 6560   2–4C
A *"funny place"*, where satisfaction depends largely on
whether you find Patrick Wynn-Jones an *"amusing"* host, and
take to his Pimlico basement's *"eclectic and eccentric"* style;
doubters find prices *"high"*, and results from the proto-modern
British menu *"poor"*. / *11.15 pm; closed Sat L & Sun.*

LE PONT DE LA TOUR SE1   £ 60   ④④❷
36d Shad Thames   (020) 7403 8403   9–4D
Fans still applaud the Tower Bridge-side 'flagship' of the
Conran empire for its *"impressive setting"* (*"especially if you
get an outside table"*) and *"fine cuisine"*; food that is merely
"OK", though, and *"slow"* service are leading more and more
people to conclude that it *"no longer justifies its prices"*.
/ *11.30 pm; closed Sat L.*

Le Pont de la Tour Bar & Grill SE1   £ 38   ②③②
36d Shad Thames   (020) 7403 8403   9–4D
It's easy to "love the view" at this steak and seafood bar
adjoining the famed restaurant, and its scaled-down package is
much better overall value. / 11.30 pm; no booking.

Poons WC2   £ 20   ③⑤⑤
4 Leicester St   (020) 7437 1528   4–3A
This Chinatown-fringe canteen – once a very popular
West End budget choice – still offers OK value, but "seems
to have lost its way"; "very bad" service and "variable
cooking" are to blame. / 11.30 pm.

Poons, Lisle Street WC2   £ 21   ③④⑤
27 Lisle St   (020) 7437 4549   4–3B
"Still my favourite of the Poons, however primitive it is" –
the "reliable" original offers "very cheap and cheerful"
cooking, "without frills"; "service can be 'off'". / 11.30 pm;
no Amex.

Popeseye   £ 29   ②②⑤
108 Blythe Rd, W14   (020) 7610 4578   7–1C
277 Upper Richmond Rd, SW15   (020) 8788 7733   10–2A
A "simple, reliable formula" that "hits the spot" – terrific
steak", a good list of clarets, and that's about it; the new
Putney branch is "exactly the same as the Olympia original",
with décor "basic" to a fault. / 10.30 pm; D only; closed Sun;
no credit cards.

Porchetta Pizzeria N4   £ 17   ②③②
147 Stroud Green Rd   (020) 7281 2892   8–1D
"Like Naples" – this "noisy and chaotic" Finsbury Park
phenomenon attracts regular queues for its "massive pizzas"
and other "hearty, authentic" dishes; look out for a new
Islington branch, coming soon. / Midnight; N4 closed Mon L - Fri L;
no Amex.

La Porte des Indes W1   £ 43   ③③②
32 Bryanston St   (020) 7224 0055   2–2A
The "lavish" décor at this "spectacular" Indian "behind
Marble Arch" is at last being matched by some "interesting"
Indian/French cooking; some still think it "overpriced", but
this sibling to the Blue Elephant is finally showing its pedigree.
/ Midnight, Sun 10.30 pm; closed Sat L; smart casual; set Sun L £26(FP).

Porters WC2   £ 21   ④②④
17 Henrietta St   (020) 7836 6466   4–3D
Long pilloried for producing "allegedly English food for
tourists", this Covent Garden pie house has suddenly picked up
its act (particularly on the service front); that said, the menu
that often "fails to deliver" still needs work. / 11.30 pm.

Il Portico W8 £ 36 ④❷❸

277 Kensington High St (020) 7602 6262 7–1D
*"A good, old-fashioned reliable bet", say fans of this
"convenient" Italian, next to the Kensington Odeon; its
welcome may be "friendly", but the cooking's "rather
standard".* / 11.15 pm; closed Sun.

La Poule au Pot SW1 £ 39 ❸❸❶

231 Ebury St (020) 7730 7763 5–2D
*With its "many nooks and crannies" and the "Gallic attitude"
of the waiters – their "rudeness actually adds to the
ambience" – this Pimlico stalwart has always "dripped with
romance"; its sometimes "delicious", rustic French cuisine is
currently finding renewed favour.* / 11.15 pm; set weekday L £25(FP).

Prego TW9 £ 37 ④❸④

106 Kew Rd (020) 8948 8508 1–4A
*The burghers of Richmond are cross with their favourite Italian
– it's "too big, since it moved site" (in mid-1999), and the
already "overrated" cooking has not improved.* / 11 pm, Fri & Sat
11.30 pm; no smoking area.

Pret A Manger £ 8 ❸❶❸

12 Kingsgate Pd, Victoria St, SW1 (020) 7828 1559
75b Victoria St, SW1 (020) 7222 1020
100 Tottenham Court Rd, W1 (020) 7631 0014
120 Baker St, W1 (020) 7486 2264
163 Piccadilly, W1 (020) 7629 5044
173 Wardour St, W1 (020) 7434 0373
18 Hanover St, W1 (020) 7491 7701
298 Regents St, W1 (020) 7637 3836
41 Piccadilly, W1 (020) 7287 2706
54-56 Oxford St, W1 (020) 7636 5750
556 Oxford St, W1 (020) 7723 9004
63 Tottenham Court Rd, W1 (020) 7636 6904
7 Marylebone High St, W1 (020) 7935 0474
122 High Holborn, WC1 (020) 7430 2090
240-241 High Holborn, WC1 (020) 7404 2055
421 Strand, WC2 (020) 7240 5900
77-78 St Martins Ln, WC2 (020) 7379 5335
80 King's Rd, SW3 (020) 7225 0770
8-10 King St, W6 (020) 8563 1985
Kensington Arcade, W8 (020) 7938 1110
21 Islington High St, N1 (020) 7713 1371
157 Camden High St, NW1 (020) 7284 2240
10 Leather Ln, EC1 (020) 7831 7219
140 Bishopsgate, EC2 (020) 7377 9595
17 Eldon St, EC2 (020) 7628 9011
28 Fleet St, EC4 (020) 7353 2332
*Stainless steel-clad take-away supremos whose "tasty,
freshly-made sandwiches" (and other quick bites) present a
case study of "good, solid standards".* / 3.30 pm-11 pm; closed Sun
except some more central branches; no credit cards; no smoking area;
no booking.

The Prince Bonaparte W2   £ 24   ❷❸❷
80 Chepstow Rd   (020) 7313 9491   6–1B
"Loud", "smoky", "trendy" and "fun" Bayswater boozer, whose
"varied" grub gets surprisingly consistent praise; *"arrive early
for a table"*. / 10.20 pm; closed Tue L; no Amex; no booking.

Prism EC3   £ 42   ❷❸❸
147 Leadenhall St   (020) 7256 3888   9–2D
Harvey Nics's *"great new power-dining venue"* has made a
real splash in the City, thanks to its *"stylish"*, *"well spaced"*
setting, its *"attentive"* service and – most surprising of all –
its *"interesting"* modern British menu. / 10 pm; closed Sat & Sun.

prospectGrill WC2   £ 27   ❸❷❸
4-6 Garrick St   (020) 7379 0412   4–3C
Very reasonable prices help make this *"unpretentious"* new
Covent Garden grill an *"excellent find"*; it's a civilised one, too,
given its very central location. / Midnight; closed Sun.

Pucci Pizza SW3   £ 23   ❸④❶
205 King's Rd   (020) 7352 2134   5–3C
"A loud and young 'party' crowd is guaranteed", at this
Chelsea fixture, which is *"always fun"* and *"very good value"*.
/ 12.30 am; closed Sun L; no credit cards.

Pukkabar SE26   £ 23   ❸❷④
42 Sydenham Rd, Sydenham   (020) 8778 4629   1–4D
Three minutes from Sydenham BR, this cavernous dining room
at the back of the Two Halfs (sic) Bar has something of a local
reputation for its 'nouvelle Indian' grub; don't make a special
trip, though. / 10.45 pm.

Purple Sage W1   £ 31   ❸❸❸
90-92 Wigmore St   (020) 7486 1912   3–1A
"High ceilinged" and *"airy"* Italian (majoring in pizza) which is
"cheap, cheerful", and *"handily located for Oxford Street"*.
/ 10.30 pm; closed Sat L & Sun.

Putney Bridge SW15   £ 52   ❸❸❷
Embankment   (020) 8780 1811   10–1B
"The food has improved immeasurably" since the early-1999
relaunch of this striking riverside yearling; the modern French
set menus are undoubtedly *"expensive"*, but we are amongst
those who have encountered *"exceptional"* results of late.
/ 11 pm; closed Sun D; set Sun L £35(FP).

QUAGLINO'S SW1   £ 39   ④④④
16 Bury St   (020) 7930 6767   3–3D
"How the mighty have fallen"; the St James's mega-brasserie
which even Conran-phobes used to like is now *"so amateur"* in
all respects – an *"overpriced"* and *"noisy"* *"conveyor-belt"*,
delivering cooking *"with no soul"*. / Midnight, Fri & Sat 1 am, Sun
11 pm; set always available £26(FP).

The Quality Chop House EC1   £ 33   ❸❸④
94 Farringdon Rd   (020) 7837 5093   9–1A
*"God, the benches are awful" at this popular Farringdon
fixture (a restored 'Working Class Caterer') – many are willing
to suffer for the quality meat and fish dishes ("simple things
done well"), but results are "erratic".* / 11.30 pm; closed Sat L;
no Amex; no smoking area.

The Queen's NW1   £ 29   ❸④❷
49 Regents Park Rd   (020) 7586 0408   8–3B
*"Friendly and casual" Primrose Hill landmark (a trendified
Victorian pub) with a strong local following; results vary
between "interesting but not too ambitious" and "pretentious
and overpriced".* / 9.45 pm; no Amex; no booking.

Quilon SW1   £ 40   – – –
41 Buckingham Gt   (020) 7821 1899   2–4B
*Soon after we go to press, the Taj Hotels group is scheduled to
open this ambitious 100-seater south Indian – a brother to the
Bombay Brasserie – a few minutes' walk from Buck House.*
/ 11.30 pm; closed Sat L & Sun.

Quincy's NW2   £ 33   ❷❶❸
675 Finchley Rd   (020) 7794 8499   1–1B
*"Everything one could want in a small restaurant" – this
"cosy" and "cramped" spot, on the way to Golder's Green,
has "supreme" service and "excellent" French cooking.* / 11 pm;
D only.

Quo Vadis W1   £ 40   ❸④❸
26-29 Dean St   (020) 7437 4809   4–2A
*In mid-1999 (by which time it had become a "total disaster"),
Marco Pierre White re-relaunched this Soho classic; we
enjoyed a post- relaunch visit, finding the setting more
congenial and the modern Gallic cooking improved.* / 11.30 pm.

Radio Café WC2   £ 28   ⑤⑤④
29-30 Leicester Sq   (020) 7484 8888   4–4B
*"Good for teenagers", it may be, but grown-ups find the food
at this "noisy" West End theme diner a "let-down".* / Midnight;
no smoking area.

Ragam W1   £ 20   ❸❸⑤
57 Cleveland St   (020) 7636 9098   2–1B
*"Dingy" Telecom Tower-side "old faithful", where "charming"
staff serve "good" south Indian fare.* / 11.30 pm; no Switch.

Rain W10   £ 36   ④④❸
303 Portobello Rd   (020) 8968 2001   6–1A
*"Exceptional-looking staff and weird décor distract from the
so-so food" at this cramped and "very Notting Hill" fusion
restaurant.* / 10.30 pm; closed Mon L & Sun D; set weekday L £23(FP).

The Rainforest Cafe W1 £ 34 ⑤④❶

20 Shaftesbury Ave (020) 7434 3111 3–3D

"Great jungle scenery keeps the kids amused" – "they just love it" – at this Piccadilly Circus theme palace; it's "too expensive", though, and the food's "horrendous". / 10.30 pm, Fri & Sat 11.30 pm; no smoking.

Randall & Aubin W1 £ 28 ❸④❷

16 Brewer St (020) 7287 4447 3–2D

"Perfect for a glass of wine and a seafood snack", this "nice, informal" converted deli is a "fun place to eat" (and its location in the heart of Soho's sex-scene makes for "entertainment watching the world go by"). / 11 pm.

Rani N3 £ 24 ❸❷④

7 Long Ln (020) 8349 4386 1–1B

"Not as good as it used to be, but still better than average" – this once-excellent Finchley fixture still serves decent, south Indian veggie grub; no longer, however, does it "vaut le voyage". / 10.30 pm; D only; no smoking area.

Ranoush W2 £ 17 ❶④❸

43 Edgware Rd (020) 7723 5929 6–1D

"Kebabs which just don't get any better" and "exotic fruit juices" are among the culinary attractions of this "bustling" and "fun" late-night Bayswater Lebanese take-away; stop at a hole-in-the-wall first, it's 'cash only'. / 3 am; no credit cards.

Ransome's Dock SW11 £ 39 ❷❷❷

35 Parkgate Rd (020) 7223 1611 5–4C

This "thoughtful", "top class local", by the river in Battersea, provides "lovely" modern British cooking, "friendly" service, a "relaxed" setting and – last but not least – "a wide range of interesting and reasonably priced wines". / 11 pm; closed Sun D; smart casual.

Raoul's Café W9 £ 29 ❸④❸

13 Clifton Rd (020) 7289 7313 8–4A

"Still full of the Versace glasses and highlights crowd", this "reliable" Maida Vale café (with its "very good cappuccino and cakes") is "crowded at weekends", especially for brunch. / 10.30 pm; no Amex; no smoking area; book eve only.

Rapscallion SW4 £ 27 ❸❷❷

75 Venn St (020) 7787 6555 10–2D

"A fun, different and lively local", by Clapham's Picture House, which serves "interesting" food to a "trendy" crowd. / 11 pm.

Rasa £ 28 ❶❷❸
6 Dering St, W1 (020) 7629 1346 3–2B
55 Stoke Newington Ch St, N16 (020) 7249 0344 1–1C
"Awesome food" from a "genuinely different" vegetarian
Indian menu and "charming" service make this dynamic
Keralan duo a force to be reckoned with; the year-old Mayfair
branch ("now in its stride") is much larger than the Stoke
Newington original. / 11 pm; N16 closed Mon L-Thu L - both branches
closed Sun L; no smoking.

Rasa Samudra W1 £ 37 ❸❷④
5 Charlotte St (020) 7637 0222 2–1C
"Very imaginative" Indian fish and seafood is "served with real
attention to detail" at this Fitzrovia newcomer; we do agree
with those who think it's "too expensive", however, and the
building (formerly Interlude, RIP) seems inimical to the creation
of atmosphere. / Midnight; closed Sun L; no smoking area;
set weekday L £24(FP).

The Real Greek N1 £ 33 ❶❷❸
15 Hoxton Market (020) 7739 8212 9–1D
'True' Greek cuisine is apparently the inspiration, but
'modern British with a Greek twist' would perhaps more aptly
describe Theodore Kyriakou's modishly sparse new venture,
in über-trendy Hoxton; a very early visit found intriguing
cooking, as you would hope from the man who originated
the Livebait concept. / 10.30 pm.

Rebato's SW8 £ 24 ❸❷❷
169 South Lambeth Rd (020) 7735 6388 10–1D
"Like being on holiday in Spain"; "the bar tapas are great"
and the dining room "light and cheerful" at this "chaotic"
bar/restaurant, in unsunny Vauxhall. / 10.45 pm; closed Sat L & Sun.

Red Fort W1 £ 39 ❸❸④
77 Dean St (020) 7437 2525 4–2A
Well known, "traditional" Soho Indian where – as usual –
some wax lyrical about the "imaginative" and "authentic"
cooking, but others denounce "ordinary and overpriced" fare.
/ 11.30 pm; no smoking area; set weekday L £25(FP).

The Red Pepper W9 £ 28 ❷④❸
8 Formosa St (020) 7266 2708 8–4A
"Loud, hot and noisy", it may be, and service can be
"uncooperative", but "the pizzas are worth it" at this popular
Maida Vale spot (as are the other "really tasty and well
presented dishes"). / 10.45 pm; D only, Sat & Sun open L & D.

**The Red Room
Waterstones W1** £ 35 – – –
203-205 Piccadilly (020) 7851 2464 3–3D
Europe's largest bookshop opens as we go to press,
determined to be a major destination – let's hope that bodes
well for its modern British basement restaurant (and for its
fifth-floor 'Studio Lounge' – a tapas-type bar promising
impressive views).

Redmond's SW14   £ 35   ❷❷④
170 Upper R'mond Rd West   (020) 8878 1922   10–1A
"They make a real effort" at this ambitious Sheen local, where
many praise the *"enterprising"* modern British cooking; the
atmosphere, though, is rather *"flat and middle-aged"*.
/ 10.30 pm; closed Sat L & Sun D; no Amex.

Restaurant One-O-One SW1   £ 56   ❷❸❸
William St, 101 Knightsbridge   (020) 7290 7101   2–3A
"This man can cook!" – rare for an hotel – so it's worth
braving *"strangely dressed waiters"* and *"panoramic views of
passing 137 buses"* for the Gallic fish and seafood served at
this Knightsbridge *"goldfish bowl"*; *"not everything succeeds"*,
but the *"set menu is very good value"*. / 10.30 pm.

Retsina NW1   £ 12   ④❸④
83 Regent's Park Rd   (020) 7722 3194   8–3B
*"Cheap, authentic Greek which deserves its following more
than the neighbouring Lemonia"* – so say regulars at this
obscure but dependable Primrose Hill taverna. / 11 pm; D only;
no Switch.

Reubens W1   £ 40   ④④④
79 Baker St   (020) 7486 0035   2–1A
A *"good"* deli-style ground floor, contrasts with the
"outrageously priced" downstairs restaurant at this resurrected
yearling – the only Kosher place of any ambition near the
centre of town. / 10 pm; closed Fri D & Sat.

Reynier Wine Library EC3   £ 15   ④❷❶
43 Trinity Sq   (020) 7481 0415   9–3D
*"Wonderful, if a liquid lunch is in order and serious wine is
contemplated"* – book ahead for a seat in the *"finest wine
cellar in the City"* (whose merchant owners charge you retail
plus £2 corkage); your selection is complemented by a *"good,
cold buffet"*. / L only; closed Sat & Sun.

Rhodes in the Square SW1   £ 47   ❷❶❷
Dolphin Sq, Chichester St   (020) 7798 6767   2–4C
Gary Rhodes's *"awesome"* modern British cooking mostly wins
rave reviews for this *"relaxed but businesslike"* yearling –
a midnight blue *"cruise ship"* dining room, lost in the bowels
of a Pimlico apartment block; for a vociferous minority, though,
it's *"overhyped and overpriced"*. / 10 pm; closed Sat L & Sun D.

Rib Room & Oyster Bar
Hyatt Carlton Tower Hotel SW1   £ 53   – – –
2 Cadogan Pl   (020) 7858 7053   2–4A
This Belgravia grill room – long a popular business lunching
venue – is to be relaunched in September 1999 in a more
'with it' format, and with oysters co-starring with the beef for
which the place has long been known. / 11.15 pm; no Switch;
smart casual.

Riccardo's SW3 £ 26 ❸④❸

126 Fulham Rd   (020) 7370 6656   5–3B
"Bustling", "quick and cheap" (by Chelsea standards) Italian, offering "tasty" tapas-style dishes. / Midnight.

Richoux £ 27 ❸④❸

172 Piccadilly, W1   (020) 7493 2204   3–3D
41a South Audley St, W1   (020) 7629 5228   3–3A
86 Brompton Rd, SW3   (020) 7584 8300   5–1C
3 Circus Rd, NW3   (020) 7483 4001   8–3A
The "reliable" modernistic new 'Coffee Café' (next door to 172 Piccadilly) of this long-established upmarket coffee-shop chain is preferred to its stick-in-the-mud siblings; some do find them "so expensive". / W1 & NW8 11 pm, Sat 11.30 pm - SW3 8 pm; no smoking areas.

Riso W4 £ 32 – – –

76 South Parade   (020) 8742 2121   7–1A
First Tentazioni, then Grano… and hot on their heels this third member of the family is set to open as we go to press; like Grano, it's in Chiswick, but here more affordable prices are promised for the earthy Italian cooking.

Ristorante Italiano W1 £ 31 ④❸④

54 Curzon St   (020) 7629 2742   3–3B
Some still say "you can't go wrong" at this "old standby", long a haven of value near Shepherd Market; others, though, have found it "poor" of late. / 11.15 pm; closed Sat L & Sun; no smoking area.

The Ritz W1 £ 75 ④❷❶

150 Piccadilly   (020) 7493 8181   3–4C
What is "surely the most beautiful and romantic dining room in London" rarely stirs itself to produce cooking that's any more than "average" (or worse – "they can't even roast beef without destroying it!"). / 11 pm; jacket & tie; set Sun L £48(FP).

Riva SW13 £ 36 ❷❷④

169 Church Rd, Barnes   (020) 8748 0434   10–1A
For foodie fans, "superb" cooking and an "authentic feel" makes this "worth the drive" to this well known Barnes Italian; as ever, a few feel its lofty reputation is "unwarranted", especially given the slightly "gloomy" ambience. / 11 pm, Fri & Sat 11.30 pm, Sun 9.30 pm; closed Sat L; smart casual.

THE RIVER CAFÉ W6 £ 52 ❷❸❸

Thames Whf, Rainville Rd   (020) 7381 8824   7–2C
"Great", "simple" cooking using "fantastic ingredients" still makes this "difficult-to-find" Hammersmith luminary some folk's "best Italian"; however, "astronomical" prices (and, on occasion, "charmless" service) mean there are more people than ever who'd "prefer to stay at home with the cookbook". / 9.30 pm; closed Sun D.

RK Stanleys W1   £ 29   ④④④

6 Little Portland St   (020) 7462 0099   3–1C

It's an "excellent idea" – "great sausages with so many beers to choose from" – but the realisation is "not really good enough" at this year-old, retro-look diner, near Oxford Circus; can a banger really be such a great culinary challenge? / 11.30 pm; closed Sun; no smoking area.

Rôtisserie   £ 25   ❸❷④

56 Uxbridge Rd, W12   (020) 8743 3028   7–1C
134 Upper St, N1   (020) 7226 0122   8–3D

The "good unfussy formula" at this "cheap" and "reliable", small chain wins consistent praise – you get "good steak-frites" (and so on) and "slick" service. / 11 pm; W12 closed Sat L & Sun.

Rôtisserie Jules   £ 20   ❸❶⑤

338 King's Rd, SW3   (020) 7351 0041   5–3C
6-8 Bute St, SW7   (020) 7584 0600   5–2B
133 Notting Hl Gt, W11   (020) 7221 3331   6–2B

"Excellent staff" help make this "dependable" chain noteworthy, as do the "yummy" chicken 'n' chips "at prices rarely seen in these areas" (and the fact that you can BYO); now all they need to do is "spruce up the décor". / 11 pm.

Roussillon SW1   £ 42   ❷❸④

16 St Barnabas St   (020) 7730 5550   5–2D

"Promising" Gallic dining room whose cooking is "imaginative" and "beautifully presented", but rather "under-appreciated" (presumably as a result of its "obscure" Pimlico back street location); this "quiet" setting is romantic to some, "dull" to others. / 10.30 pm; closed Sat L & Sun; no smoking area; set weekday L £28(FP).

Rowley's SW1   £ 45   ⑤⑤④

113 Jermyn St   (020) 7930 2707   3–3D

"Expensive" steakhouse, not far from Piccadilly Circus, which trades on its location – "rushed" service delivers fare of "sub-airline" quality. / 11 pm; smart casual.

Royal China SW15   £ 29   ❷❷④

3 Chelverton Rd   (020) 8788 0907   10–2B

Putney oriental, whose formula is similar to its illustrious central namesakes; it's under different management, and a touch more "changeable". / 10.45 pm; no Visa, Mastercard or Switch; no booking for Sun L.

Royal China   £ 29   ❶④④

40 Baker St, W1   (020) 7487 4688   2–1A
13 Queensway, W2   (020) 7221 2535   6–2C
68 Queen's Grove, NW8   (020) 7586 4280   8–3A

"'Kick ass' dim sum" – "as good as Hong Kong" – help make this tacky trio (decked out like '70s discos) London's Chinese benchmark; branches are usually "crowded, noisy and chaotic". / 11 pm, Fri & Sat 11.30 pm.

RSJ SE1   **£ 30**   ②②③

13a Coin St   (020) 7928 4554   9–4A

*The atmosphere may be "quiet" and "rather dry", but
"for serious eating and drinking" this popular South Banker
is a foodie fave, thanks to its "great range of wines from the
Loire" and "good-value" modern British cooking. / 11 pm;
closed Sat L & Sun.*

Rudland & Stubbs EC1   **£ 33**   ④③④

35-37 Greenhill Rents, Cowcross St   (020) 7253 0148   9–1A

*"Solid" Smithfield fish parlour where some still praise the
"well prepared" food and "bustling old-fashioned" atmosphere;
too many, however, say it's gone "right off the boil" – "stick
to the simple dishes" seems to be good advice. / 10.45 pm;
closed Sat L & Sun.*

La Rueda   **£ 25**   ④③③

102 Wigmore St, W1   (020) 7486 1718   3–1A
642 King's Rd, SW6   (020) 7384 2684   5–4A
66-68 Clapham High St, SW4   (020) 7627 2173   10–2D

*"Noisy, crowded, 'garlicky' and fun", the atmospheric Clapham
original is still the most popular of this small Spanish chain
(but "stick to the tapas bar, rather than the restaurant"); the
others have less buzz, but marginally better grub. / 11.30 pm.*

Rules WC2   **£ 43**   ③③②

35 Maiden Ln   (020) 7836 5314   4–3D

*"Despite being a tourist magnet", London's oldest restaurant
(1798) is "good at what it does", with highlights including
"top game" and "the best Stilton in town"; the place remains
generally "safe", but satisfaction slipped somewhat this year.
/ 11.30 pm.*

Rupee Room EC2   **£ 24**   ③③④

10 Copthall Ave   (020) 7628 1555   9–2C

*"Cramped" City basement; it's perhaps "an overpriced choice
for a quick lunchtime curry", but fairly reliable. / 10.45 pm;
closed Sat & Sun.*

S&P   **£ 30**   ②③④

181 Fulham Rd, SW3   (020) 7351 5692   5–2C
9 Beauchamp Pl, SW3   (020) 7581 8820   5–1C

*"A cut above most Thais" – standards at these "easy" and
unpretentious Knightsbridge and South Kensington spots can
come as a "pleasant surprise". / 10.30 pm; no smoking areas.*

Sabai Sabai W6   **£ 24**   ②②④

270-272 King St   (020) 8748 7363   7–2B

*"Really tasty and well presented" food is served "quickly" at
this Hammersmith Thai, though its "naff" décor contributes to
a rather "soulless" atmosphere. / 11.30 pm; closed Sun L.*

Le Sacré-Coeur N1 £ 25 ❸❸❷

18 Theberton St (020) 7354 2618 8–3D

"Straight out of a Parisian back street", this "cosy" Islington bistro has a disproportionately large following for its "honest", "value-for-money" cooking; perhaps it has become too popular, as more people found it "disappointing" this year. / 11 pm; set weekday L £16(FP).

Saffron SW10 £ 25 ❸④④

306B Fulham Rd (020) 7565 8183 5–3B

"Small", brightly decorated, distant-Chelsea yearling, whose "diverse" Indian dishes generally find favour. / Midnight; D only .

Saigon Times EC3 £ 34 ❸❸④

Leadenhall Market (020) 7621 0022 9–2D

"Usually tasty French and Vietnamese fare" helps make this "eclectic" spot a popular City rendezvous. / 9.30 pm; closed Sat & Sun.

Saint WC2 £ 31 ⑤⑤❷

8 Great Newport St (020) 7240 1551 4–3B

"A great bar and club, but the food's a let down", at this "too trendy" and "too noisy" joint, near Leicester Square. / 11 pm; D only; closed Mon & Sun.

St John EC1 £ 37 ❸❸❸

26 St John St (020) 7251 0848 9–1B

"You need to know your guests' tastes before coming here", as "a strong stomach is needed" to enjoy the "great traditional meat dishes, with a twist" – that's offal, offal and more offal – at this uncompromising Smithfield spot; its popularity, however, continues to grow. / 11 pm; closed Sun.

St Moritz W1 £ 34 ❷❸❸

161 Wardour St (020) 7734 3324 3–1D

Don't be put off by its "touristy" exterior – "the best fondue" and "top-quality" meat and game are among the attractions of this "cramped" chalet, "a magic part of Switzerland, in Soho". / 11.30 pm; closed Sat L & Sun.

Sale e Pepe SW1 £ 36 ④❸❷

9-15 Pavilion Rd (020) 7235 0098 2–3A

"Mad" Knightsbridge Italian; it "gets ever noisier" and standards are "declining", but it's still "fun to visit every couple of years". / 11.30 pm; closed Sun.

Salloos SW1 £ 45 ❷❸④

62-64 Kinnerton St (020) 7235 4444 2–3A

The food's "worth the price" – no mean feat – at this discreet, "slightly odd" Pakistani "haven", long tucked away in a quiet Belgravia mews; you may wish to avail yourself of the "helpful menu guidance". / 11.15 pm; closed Sun; smart casual; set weekday L £27(FP).

The Salt House NW8   £ 26   ❷❷❸

63 Abbey Rd   (020) 7328 6626   8–3A
"Relaxed, friendly and with good food" – the team from
The Chiswick have worked wonders on this previously
lacklustre St John's Wood pub-conversion, which has a nice
outside terrace. / 10 pm; closed Mon L.

Sambuca SW3   £ 36   ④❷④

62-64 Lower Sloane St   (020) 7730 6571   5–2D
The "cramped" new home of this long-established Chelsea
trattoria is "not an improvement" on its characterful former
site; regulars still "always find a good welcome". / 11.30 pm;
closed Sun.

San Carlo N6   £ 37   ❸❷❸

2 Highgate High St   (020) 8340 5823   8–1B
"Well tuned in every department", this "airy" and "relaxed"
Highgate trattoria (long notable for its mediocrity) is at last
back on form – "nothing is too much trouble" for the staff,
and the cooking is "not cheap but reliable"; "lovely" garden.
/ 11 pm; closed Mon; no jeans; no smoking area.

San Daniele del Friuli N5   £ 28   ❸❷❸

72 Highbury Park   (020) 7359 0341   8–1D
The "best local Italian in town, or at least in Highbury!";
some think it "authentic", but we're with those who find it
a touch "routine". / 11 pm; closed Mon L & Sun; no Amex.

San Lorenzo SW3   £ 50   ⑤⑤❷

22 Beauchamp Pl   (020) 7584 1074   5–1C
"Why does anyone eat here?", is the eternal mystery
surrounding this celebrated Knightsbridge trattoria; it can't be
the "standard" cooking, the "'70s-tat" surroundings or the
"appalling" service ("if you're not an It-girl"), so it must be the
opportunity to gawp at the "rich and famous". / 11.30 pm;
closed Sun; no credit cards; smart casual.

San Martino SW3   £ 41   ④❸❸

101-105 Walton St   (020) 7589 3833   5–2C
"Nice" but "inconsistent" Knightsbridge trattoria of long
standing where "the bill adds up"; it used to have a buzz – it
could again if they shaved prices, and sharpened up their act.
/ 11.30 pm; no smoking area; set weekday L £25(FP).

Sandrini SW3   £ 37   ❸❸④

260 Brompton Rd   (020) 7584 1724   5–2C
That it's "a nice place to sit outside in summer" is the key
attraction at this "reliable", "old fashioned" Italian, by
Brompton Cross. / 11.30 pm.

Santa Fe N1 £ 24 ③②③
75 Upper St (020) 7288 2288 8–3D
*"Genuine" service is the highpoint at this large Islington Green
newcomer, which is already popular with an animated
twentysomething crowd; billed as southwest American, the
food – sort of souped up Tex-Mex – could be worse.* / 10.30 pm;
no smoking area; no booking.

Santini SW1 £ 53 ④④③
29 Ebury St (020) 7730 4094 2–4B
*Some do praise "perfect, plain Italian cooking" at this light
and stylish (but cramped and "cold") Belgravian; it's so
"expensive", though, that many dismiss it as a "rip-off".*
/ 11.30 pm; closed Sat L & Sun L; smart casual.

Sarastro WC2 £ 29 ⑤④❶
126 Drury Ln (020) 7836 0101 2–2D
*"Incredible… the first time"; the "unique", "OTT",
"junk-Baroque" setting of this Covent Garden phenomenon
certainly makes for an "entertaining" experience; the
"run-of-the-mill tourist food" has only a walk-on rôle.* / 11.30 pm.

Sarcan N1 £ 17 ③②②
4 Theberton St (020) 7226 5489 8–3D
*"Bustling but courteous" Turkish delight, just off Islington's
Upper Street, offering "wonderful grills" and "excellent-value
meze".* / Midnight; set weekday L £8(FP).

Sarkhel's SW18 £ 25 ❶②④
199 Replingham Rd (020) 8870 1483 10–2B
*"Enjoy it now, before people work out how to get there" –
ex-Bombay Brasserie chef Udit Sarkhel's Southfields
subcontinental may look undistinguished, but it "rightly gets
rave reviews" for its "fantastic cooking" and charming service.*
/ 10.30 pm; D only, except Sun when L & D, closed Mon; no Amex.

Sartoria W1 £ 52 ④③③
20 Savile Row (020) 7534 7000 3–2C
*By the standards of the Conran empire, this tailoring-themed
Mayfair spot is a good place – that is to say its "expensive"
Italian cooking is no worse than "run-of-the-mill", and its "dull"
setting is quite "comfortable".* / 11.15 pm; closed Sun D.

Satsuma W1 £ 23 ③③②
56 Wardour St (020) 7437 8338 3–2D
*"A formula product with style"; "interesting food served in
Bento boxes" makes this "plain" but "happy" Soho yearling a
"convenient rendezvous".* / 11 pm; no smoking; no booking.

Sauce NW1 £ 26 ❸❸❸

214 Camden High St (020) 7482 0777 8–2B
*"Funky decoration transforms an otherwise ordinary
basement" at this "pleasant" organic diner, near Camden
Market; fans praise the "interesting" and "well cooked" fare,
but it's "pricey" and some dishes are "standard".* / 11 pm;
closed Sun D; no Amex & no Switch; no smoking area; no booking (unless for
parties of 6+).

Savoy Grill WC2 £ 66 ❸❷❷

Strand (020) 7836 4343 4–3D
*With its elegant, "boardroom" ambience, and "effortlessly
smooth" service, this famous room remains a top "power
lunch" venue – it's "not so good in the evenings"; the cooking
is "always reliable, but unadventurous" and "not, at the price,
exceptional".* / 11.15 pm; closed Sat L & Sun; jacket & tie;
set post-th £32(FP).

Savoy River Restaurant WC2 £ 66 ④❷❷

Strand (020) 7420 2699 4–3D
*"Insipid" and "old-fashioned" cooking mars this classic
Thames-side dining room; it remains a "treat" for romance,
and "for a full English breakfast" it's sans pareil.* / 11.30 pm;
jacket & tie; set Brunch £42(FP).

Scalini SW3 £ 42 ❷❸❷

1-3 Walton St (020) 7225 2301 5–2C
*"Outrageously expensive but good quality" trattoria, not far
from Harrods; it's "fun", but "crowded" and "very noisy" –
"the food comes with a free headache!"* / Midnight; smart casual.

The Scarsdale W8 £ 26 ④④❷

23a Edwardes Sq (020) 7937 1811 7–1D
*"Quintessential English pub" whose major selling point is a
nice (but tiny) garden looking onto a "lovely square"; the food
is decidedly "average".* / 9.45 pm; smart casual.

Scoffers SW11 £ 27 ❸❸❷

6 Battersea Rs (020) 7978 5542 10–2C
*"Always full" – this Battersea bistro is "the perfect Battersea
local" according to its huge younger fan club.* / 11 pm.

Scott's W1 £ 48 ❸❸❸

20 Mount St (020) 7629 5248 3–3A
*"Spacious, comfortable and still with some cachet", this
re-launched Mayfair institution (now owned by Groupe Chez
Gérard) offers an "extensive" and quite "imaginative" choice
of fish and seafood; some feel it "lacks spark".* / 11 pm;
smart casual; no smoking area; set Brunch £31(FP).

Seafresh SW1 £ 20 ❷❸④

80-81 Wilton Rd (020) 7828 0747 2–4B
*"The fish and chips (and the mushy peas) are pretty good" at
this weather-beaten Pimlico veteran.* / 10.30 pm; closed Sun.

Searcy's Brasserie EC2 £ 38 ③③④

Level II, Barbican Centre (020) 7588 3008 9–1B

*The Barbican Centre's in-house restaurant is "quite good"
(even if "prices are too high"), and the lack of local choice
makes it a useful venue for business; some discern a
"mass-produced feel", however, "like an upmarket canteen".
/ 10.30 pm; Sun 7.30 pm; closed Sat L & Sun D; no smoking area.*

Seashell NW1 £ 23 ③④⑤

49 Lisson Grove (020) 7723 8703 8–4A

*Many still praise the "straight-up", "traditional" fish and chips
at this well-known, once-exemplary chippy, behind Marylebone
Station; it's "overrun by tourists, though", and more and more
people leave "unimpressed". / 10.30 pm; no smoking area; no booking;
pre-th. £16(FP).*

755 SW6 £ 39 ❶②④

755 Fulham Rd (020) 7371 0755 10–1B

*"A very pleasant surprise"; "varied and very good-quality"
modern British cooking wins high praise for this
unremarkable-looking Fulham spot; "if only it were
more lively!" / 11 pm; closed Sun D & Mon.*

Shakespeare's Globe SE1 £ 33 ④❸④

New Globe Walk (020) 7928 9444 9–3B

*"Ask for a window table" to enjoy the "good views" from the
elevated dining room of this year-old South Bank venue; the
"adequate" cooking promises more than it delivers. / 10.30 pm.*

Shampers W1 £ 28 ④❸❷

4 Kingly St (020) 7437 1692 3–2D

*"Friendly and unpretentious", this atmospheric "wine bar
from the old school" – with its "excellent" wine list and
"unassuming" French cooking – is a useful reminder that the
'70s had something going for them. / 11 pm; closed Sun (Aug also
Sat).*

Shanghai E8 £ 23 ❸❷❷

41 Kingsland High St (020) 7254 2878 1–1C

*"Particularly good dim sum" and "polite service" are two
reasons to seek out this Dalston Chinese; the impressive tiled
interior – previously a pre-eminent pie 'n' eel shop – is a third.
/ 11 pm; no Amex.*

J Sheekey WC2 £ 42 ❷❷❸

28-32 St Martins Ct (020) 7240 2565 4–3B

*The runes are still unclear about Messrs Corbin & King's
relaunch of this veteran Theatreland seafood parlour – though
some "wonderful" fish dishes win applause, "the atmosphere
hasn't gelled yet"; "unlike the Ivy, however, you can actually get
a table at reasonable notice". / Midnight; set Saturday lunch £26(FP).*

Shepherd's SW1 £ 35 ③②②
Marsham Ct, Marsham St (020) 7834 9552 2–4C
*With its "comfortable atmosphere", "crisp and helpful service"
and "reliable, if unspectacular, food", this "sensible" English
restaurant in Westminster makes a very useful "bolt hole" –
at least "it would be good if it weren't so full of politicians".*
/ 11 pm; closed Sat & Sun; no smoking area.

Shimla Pinks EC2 £ 27 ③①②
7-8 Bishopsgate Churchyard (020) 7628 7888 9–2D
*A new scion of the famous Brum curry house, in an interesting
City basement site, formerly Sri India (RIP); for fans, it's
"absolutely superb" all round – we're with those who say "the
cooking fails to live up to the high standard of service and
beautiful surroundings".* / 9.30 pm; closed Sat & Sun.

The Ship SW18 £ 24 ③④②
41 Jews Row (020) 8870 9667 10–2B
*The large terrace is "great when it's sunny", at this
Wandsworth riverside pub, and the summer barbecue and
other fare are "always of a good standard" – "once the nearby
building works are finished, the place will come into its own
again".* / 10.30 pm; no booking for Sun L.

Shoeless Joe's £ 32 ④④④
Temple Pl, WC2 (020) 7240 7865 2–2D
555 King's Rd, SW6 (020) 7610 9346 5–4B
*As sports bars go, these Fulham and (now) Temple spots are
fine "for a fun boozy evening"; some think the bar snacks and
restaurant cooking can be "very reasonable", too, but "for the
money, they should be better".* / 9 pm - SW6 10 pm Fri & Sat.

Shogun W1 £ 50 ①①③
Adam's Rw (020) 7493 1255 3–3A
*"Tokyo in W1" – "great teriyaki" and "very good sushi" win a
devoted following for this Mayfair stalwart, which, by Japanese
restaurant standards, has a "lovely ambience".* / 11 pm; D only;
closed Mon; no Switch.

Le Shop SW3 £ 22 ③③②
329 King's Rd (020) 7352 3891 5–3C
*"Delicious crêpes" and "nice" service win continued support
for this "cheerful" Chelsea café of long standing.* / Midnight;
no Switch.

Shoreditch Electricity Showrooms N1 £ 26 ④⑤⑤
39a Hoxton Sq (020) 7739 6934 9–1D
*"Better to lounge in the packed bar" at this buzzy
twentysomething Hoxton hangout than subject yourself to
"mammoth portions" of "not great" food.* / 10.30 pm; closed
Mon & Sun D; no Amex.

Shree Krishna SW17   **£ 18**   ❶④④
192-194 Tooting High St   (020) 8672 4250   10–2D
*"No change", in Tooting, at what many vote "the best
curry house in south London" (which is especially "good for
vegetarians"); "how do they make it so cheap?"* / 10.45 pm;
no Switch.

Signor Sassi SW1   **£ 43**   ❸②②
14 Knightsbridge Gn   (020) 7584 2277   5–1D
*"Mad, and not everyone's cup of espresso" – "bantering"
waiters deliver "satisfying, if not particularly original" fare at
this "entertaining" Knightsbridge Italian.* / 11.30 pm; closed Sun;
smart casual.

Silks & Spice   **£ 23**   ❸❸❸
23 Foley St, W1   (020) 7636 2718   2–1B
95 Chiswick High Rd, W4   (020) 8995 7991   7–2B
28 Chalk Farm Rd, NW1   (020) 7267 5751   8–2B
11 Queen Victoria St, EC4   (020) 7236 7222   9–2C
*"Nice, if not glamorous" small chain, with "cosy" premises and
"good" oriental cooking.* / 11 pm; W1 closed Sat L & Sun L; no smoking
areas.

Simply Nico   **£ 38**   ❸❸④
48a Rochester Rw, SW1   (020) 7630 8061   2–4C
London Bridge Hotel, SE1   (020) 7407 1717   9–4C
7 Goswell Rd, EC1   (020) 7336 7677   9–1B
*"Consistent-quality" cooking undoubtedly makes these
"professional" bourgeois restaurants useful, but they can be
"crowded", and lacking in atmosphere.* / 11 pm; SW10 closed
Mon L.

Simpson's of Cornhill EC3   **£ 21**   ❸②②
38 1/2 Cornhill   (020) 7626 9985   9–2C
*"Comforting, school-dinners fare" and a "brilliant" (which is to
say authentically gloomy) Dickensian setting make this back
alley chop-house "the best place in the City" for some
traditionalists.* / L only; closed Sat & Sun; no booking.

Simpsons-in-the-Strand WC2   **£ 46**   ④❸②
100 Strand   (020) 7836 9112   4–3D
*"It's always popular with visitors, as it has a traditional feel",
but this venerable institution's English cooking is "a flop"
(except at breakfast); the recent refurb may buck things up,
but our foray into the new, 'lighter' upstairs restaurant,
'Chequers', was hardly exciting.* / 11 pm, Sun 9 pm; closed Sat L;
jacket; pre-th. £31(FP).

Singapore Garden NW6   **£ 31**   ❸❸④
83-83a Fairfax Rd   (020) 7328 5314   8–2A
*"Reliable" food ensures this tacky but "good-value"
Swiss Cottage Chinese/Singaporean is "always packed".*
/ 10.45 pm, Fri & Sat 11.15 pm; set weekday L £19(FP).

Singapura £ 35 ③③④
78-79 Leadenhall St, EC3 (020) 7929 0089 9–2D
1-2 Limeburner Ln, EC4 (020) 7329 1133 9–2A
"Good, predictable, authentic food" makes these *"friendly"*
orientals popular City choices; they're slightly "characterless
business lunch places", though. / 9.30 pm; closed Sat & Sun;
smart casual.

6 Clarendon Rd W11 £ 32 ③④④
6 Clarendon Rd (020) 7727 3330 6–2A
Small, well-meaning, modern British newcomer in Holland
Park; it hasn't made much of a splash yet – well, there
aren't that many seats – but it may be one to watch. / 10 pm;
D only except Sun, when L & D; closed Mon; no Amex; no smoking area.

606 Club SW10 £ 35 ⑤④❷
90 Lots Rd (020) 7352 5953 5–4B
"If you like jazz, this is the place", but the food's *"not as good*
as it used to be" at this distant-Chelsea jazz club; it's entered
through a hole in the wall opposite the power station. / Mon-Thu
1.30 am, Fri & Sat 2 am, Sun 11.30 pm; D only; no Amex.

Sixty Two SE1 £ 29 ③③③
62 Southwark Bridge Rd (020) 7633 0831 9–4B
"Agreeable", *"off-the-beaten-track"* modern British bistro,
in Southwark, capable of some *"interesting"* dishes. / 10.30 pm;
closed Sat L & Sun; no smoking area.

Smiths of Smithfield EC1 £ 45 – – –
Smithfield Market (020) 7236 6666 9–1B
Two bars and two restaurants (one on the roof-top) are
among attractions billed at this November '99 Smithfield
mega-opening; it's backed by the Hopson Jones brothers (who
are taking a big leap from Clapham's Polygon), with John
Torode (ex Mezzo) as chef.

Smollensky's on the Strand WC2 £ 32 ④❸❸
105 Strand (020) 7497 2101 4–3D
"Kids love it" – especially at weekends, when there is
entertainment à go-go (face painting and so on) at this large
American-style diner; the food verges on *"awful"*. / 11.45 pm;
Thu-Sat 12.15 am; Sun 10.30 pm; no smoking area.

Snows on the Green W6 £ 34 ④④④
166 Shepherd's Bush Rd (020) 7603 2142 7–1C
Though some feel it has "improved", the consensus is that this
stark Brook Green Mediterranean delivers *"forgettable"*
modern British cooking that's "too clever by half".
/ 11 pm; closed Sat L.

Sofra £ 27 ④④④
1 St Christopher's Pl, W1 (020) 7224 4080 3–1A
18 Shepherd St, W1 (020) 7493 3320 3–4B
36 Tavistock St, WC2 (020) 7240 3773 4–3D
*"Crowded" and "basic" Turkish chain, long regarded as
"a good cheap stand-by"; there is a feeling that it's "taken a
turn for the worse", of late, and last year saw the closure of
the allied Café Sofra outlets.* / Midnight; set weekday L £17(FP).

Soho Soho W1 £ 28 ④④❸
11-13 Frith St (020) 7494 3491 4–2A
*Throbbing and "cramped" Soho brasserie; even those who
say it's a "reliable all-rounder" admit it's "overpriced", and to
others it's just plain "ordinary"; (there's a more expensive
restaurant upstairs).* / 12.45 am, Sun 10.30 pm; no smoking area L only.

Soho Spice W1 £ 26 ❸❸❷
124-126 Wardour St (020) 7434 0808 3–1D
*"Modern and bustling" Indian, whose colourful, stripped-down
premises offer some "well executed", slightly "different" dishes;
late opening (basement bar included), makes it a particular hit
with Soho trendies.* / 11.30 pm; 3 am Fri & Sat; no smoking area; need
4+ at L, 6+ at D to book.

Solly's Exclusive NW11 £ 30 ❸④❸
148 Golders Green Rd (020) 8455 0004 1–1B
*"Good atmosphere for a kosher restaurant" and "consistent",
"well cooked" food (and "plenty of it") win praise for this jolly,
"typically Israeli" Golders Green institution.* / 11.30 pm; closed Fri D
& Sat; no smoking area.

Sonny's SW13 £ 37 ❷❷❷
94 Church Rd (020) 8748 0393 10–1A
*This "newly revamped" Barnes star – long in the vanguard of
the "new breed of local modern British restaurant" – is a
"superb all rounder"; "definitely worth a trip, even if
Hammersmith Bridge is shut".* / 11 pm; closed Sun D; set Sun L
£25(FP).

Sotheby's Café W1 £ 32 ❷❶❷
34 New Bond St (020) 7293 5077 3–2C
*"A perfect setting in the heart of the auction house, for
lunch and a gossip" and "you overhear the most interesting
conversations"; the cooking is "simple, good, and light", the
wine list "impeccable" and service "exceptional".* / L only;
closed weekends, except May-Jul and Sep-Dec; no smoking.

Le Soufflé
Inter-Continental Hotel W1 £ 57 ❸❷④
1 Hamilton Pl (020) 7409 3131 3–4A
*"Smiling and attentive" staff and Peter Kromberg's "fresh"
and "generous" Gallic cuisine continue to win praise for this
Mayfair hotel dining room; the "staid", '70s setting, however,
has long been "due for a refit".* / 10.30 pm, Sat 11.15 pm; closed
Mon, Sat L & Sun D; smart casual; no smoking area.

Souk WC2 £ 23 ④④❷

27 Litchfield St   (020) 7240 1796   4–3B

"It feels like you're in the casbah", at this "fun" North African basement, near Cambridge Circus; its "lively" but cosy setting is as "suitable for large groups" as it is for a "romantic twosome", but this is "not a gastronomic experience". / 11.30 pm; no Amex.

Soulard N1 £ 26 ❷❶❶

113 Mortimer Rd   (020) 7254 1314   1–1C

"Cramped but welcoming" Islington-fringe bistro, which is "always a delight", thanks to its "authentic" cooking and the "wonderful" attentions of mein host, Philippe. / 10.30 pm; D only; closed Sun & Mon; no Amex & no Switch.

Soup Opera £ 9 ❷❷❸

2 Hanover St, W1   (020) 7629 0174   3–2C
Concourse Level, Cabot Pl East, Canary Wharf, E14
(020) 7513 0880   1–3D

"Fantastic, hearty soups" have brought immediate popularity to this bright new chain; will they have staying power, though? – a lot of people already find them "a bit overpriced". / W1 6 pm, Sat 5 pm - E14 4 pm; W1 closed Sun - E14 closed Sat & Sun; no credit cards; no smoking; no booking.

Soup Works £ 9 ❶❷⑤

15 Moor St, W1   (020) 7734 7687   4–2B
56 Goodge St, W1   (020) 7637 7687   2–1B
9 D'Arblay St, W1   (020) 7439 7687   3–1D
29 Monmouth St, WC2   (020) 7240 7687   4–2B

A "really delicious choice" – "every imaginable flavour, available in liquid form" – makes this new chain reporters top tip for the new soup craze; it's such a great formula – if only they could make it a touch less "uncomfortable". / 7 pm, Sat 5 pm - WC2 8 pm - Moor St 11 pm, Fri & Sat Midnight, Sun 6 pm; all except Moor St closed Sat D & Sun; credit cards taken at WC2 & D'Arblay St only; no smoking; no booking.

Southeast W9 £ 24 ❷❸❸

239 Elgin Ave   (020) 7328 8883   1–2B

"Fresh, quality cooking" makes this minimalist Maida Vale oriental an "excellent local". / 11 pm; no smoking area.

Spago SW7 £ 22 ❸④❸

6 Glendower Pl   (020) 7225 2407   5–2B

"Brilliant peasant pasta" and a "cheerful" atmosphere pack a "youngish crowd" into this "real" South Kensington local; the "basement is always full of Italians, watching the football". / 12.30 am; D only; no credit cards.

La Spiga W1 £ 30 ❸④④

84-86 Wardour St   (020) 7734 3444   3–2D

To its fans, this "fun", "hip" and "happening" Soho spot serves "the best pizza in the West End" (and "good pasta, salads and puddings", too); it is "ridiculously loud", though, and can – on all counts – "fail to live up to expectations". / 11 pm; Wed-Sat midnight.

La Spighetta W1   £ 30   ③④⑤
43 Blandford St   (020) 7486 7340   2–1A
The "tasty pizzas" get a good press at this "modern Italian", in a rather bleak Marylebone basement; "its acoustics spoil it", though, and service is "a question of luck". / 10.30 pm; closed Sun L; no smoking area.

Sporting Page SW10   £ 24   ④④❷
6 Camera Pl   (020) 7349 0455   5–3B
This "smart" Chelsea pub is a "pleasant" place for a pint (or a glass of champagne); its "good pub food" is not as good as it used to be. / 10 pm; no booking.

Springbok Café W4   £ 31   ❷❶❸
42 Devonshire Rd   (020) 8742 3149   7–2A
"True South African hospitality" and "very original" cooking (with "unusual" ingredients) are consistently praised at this "relaxed" but "spartan" Chiswick spot. / 11 pm; closed Sun; no Amex.

THE SQUARE W1   £ 60   ❶❷❸
6-10 Bruton St   (020) 7495 7100   3–2C
Phillip Howard's "excellent" modern French cooking continues to establish this grand and "professional" Mayfair venture in London's gastronomic vanguard; it gets flak for being "overpriced", however, and its style is perhaps a touch more "formal" than is necessary. / 10.45 pm; closed Sat L & Sun L; smart casual.

Sri Siam W1   £ 33   ❷❸④
16 Old Compton St   (020) 7434 3544   4–2A
"Superbly flavoured" cooking, served in "contemporary surroundings", makes this "consistently good" Soho fixture "a Thai to remember". / 11.15 pm; closed Sun L.

Sri Siam City EC2   £ 32   ❷❸④
85 London Wall   (020) 7628 5772   9–2C
It may be a "noisy barn", but this well known City basement Thai offers "reliably good" food and "fast" service. / 8.45 pm; closed Sat & Sun.

Sri Thai EC4   £ 30   ❸❸❸
3 Queen Victoria St   (020) 7827 0202   9–3C
"Consistent quality and service" make this large City Thai a "fail-safe" option (even if some do discern a "conveyor-belt" approach). / 8.30 pm; closed Sat & Sun.

The Stable SW13   £ 27   ❸④❸
39 Barnes High St   (020) 8876 1855   10–1A
"Good food" is let down by "poor" service in this cosy and unusual dining room, hidden behind Barnes's Bull's Head boozer. / Midnight; D only; closed Mon & Sun.

Standard Tandoori W2 £ 20 ❸④④
21-23 Westbourne Grove (020) 7229 0600 6–1C
A "classic stand-by", with "reasonable prices" and "solid cooking", whose large Bayswater premises live up to their name. / 11.45 pm; no smoking area.

Star Café W1 £ 20 ❸❸❸
22 Gt Chapel St (020) 7437 8778 3–1D
Soho-fringe diner whose cooked breakfast makes "a great way to start the day"; other grub is "dependable" and "filling".
/ 4 pm; closed Sat & Sun; no credit cards; no smoking area.

Star of India SW5 £ 36 ❷④❸
154 Old Brompton Rd (020) 7373 2901 5–2B
Famously "not your typical curry house", this "fun", long-established South Kensington subcontinental rejoices in striking and "amusing" (read 'camp') décor and an "eccentric" owner; the highlight, however, is the "interesting" menu realised to "above average" standards. / 11.45 pm.

Starbucks £ 8 ❸❷❷
137 Victoria St, SW1 (020) 7233 5170
27 Victoria St, SW1 (020) 7222 6298
1-2 Langham Pl, W1 (020) 7580 6199
111 Marylebone High St, W1 (020) 7486 9668
14 James St, W1 (020) 7495 6680
22-23 Princes St, W1 (020) 7491 7263
27 Berkeley St, W1 (020) 7629 5779
3 Grosvenor St, W1 (020) 7495 5534
34 Gt Marlborough St, W1 (020) 7434 0778
37-38 Golden Sq, W1 (020) 7434 1637
40-44 Dover St, W1 (020) 7495 5581
50 Shaftesbury Ave, W1 (020) 7439 1364
10 Russell St, WC2 (020) 7836 6231
28-29 Chancery Ln, WC2 (020) 7405 4774
357-359 The Strand, WC2 (020) 7836 5166
51-54 Long Acre, WC2 (020) 7836 2100
99 Kingsway, WC2 (020) 7404 9229
29-41 Earlham St, WC2 (020) 7836 3490
123a King's Rd, SW3 (020) 7376 4678
259 Old Brompton Rd, SW5 (020) 7370 6482
809 Fulham Rd, SW6 (020) 7371 9491
Unit 5, 17-35 Gloucester Rd, SW7 (020) 7581 2368
140 Notting Hl Gt, W11 (020) 7727 7890
227 Portobello Rd, W11 (020) 7727 5881
26 Pembridge Rd, W11 (020) 7243 4313
47-49 Queensway, W2 (020) 7243 1616
25a Kensington High St, W8 (020) 7937 5446
79 St John's Wood High St, NW8 (020) 7586 4365
33-38 Northcote Rd, SW11 (020) 7350 2887
39 Abbeville Rd, SW4 (020) 8673 4004
62 Exmouth Mkt, EC1 (020) 7278 0551
1 Poultry, EC2 (020) 7489 1994
18 Eldon St, EC2 (020) 7256 2144
90-94 Old Broad St, EC2 (020) 7588 4882

Starbucks (continued)
74 Cornhill, EC3   (020) 7283 1089
Peak House, 20 Eastcheap, EC3   (020) 7283 2466
10-15 Queen St, EC4   (020) 7489 1229
116 Cannon St, EC4   (020) 7929 4600
87 King William St, EC4   (020) 7929 4099
90 Fleet St, EC4   (020) 7936 3822
"It's overpriced, but I just love the Frappuccino!" – *"the food is not great and expensive but coffee and service are superb"* at this *"typically American"* import (which bought and last year re-branded the home-grown Seattle Coffee company).
/ 6 pm–11 pm; most City branches closed Sat and/or Sun; no smoking indoors; no booking.

Stargazer W1   £ 29   ④❸❸
11 Rathbone St   (020) 7636 1057   2–1C
"Slightly quirky" modern British bar/restaurant, near Charlotte Street; it generates little comment but is a useful rendezvous *"when you want to be able to hear yourself think"*. / 11 pm; closed Sat L & Sun.

Stephen Bull EC1   £ 33   ❸❸④
71 St John St   (020) 7490 1750   9–1A
The setting is *"a little harsh"* and *"cramped"*, but *"generally good"* modern British cooking makes Mr. Bull's Smithfield outpost a popular business lunch option. / 10.30 pm; closed Sat L & Sun; no smoking area.

Stephen Bull W1   £ 38   ❷❷❸
5-7 Blandford St   (020) 7486 9696   2–1A
"Dependably good" modern British cooking makes Mr Bull's original Marylebone HQ still the best of the bunch; like the others, it is *"a bit clinical"* and has *"zilch atmosphere when empty"*. / 10.30 pm; closed Sat L & Sun.

Stephen Bull WC2   £ 37   ❸❸⑤
12 Upper St Martin's Ln   (020) 7379 7811   4–3B
"Why aren't they full every night?", muses a fan of Bull's Theatreland branch's *"great cooking"*; it's *"a bit pricey"*, true, but the real villain of the piece is the *"lack of atmosphere"* and a *"sterile"* setting. / 11.30 pm; closed Sat L & Sun; pre-th. £24(FP).

The Stepping Stone SW8   £ 35   ❷❷❸
123 Queenstown Rd   (020) 7622 0555   10–1C
"All you could wish for in a neighbourhood restaurant" – this Battersea establishment combines *"gorgeous"* modern British cooking, *"calm and peaceful"* service and a convivially stylish setting. / 11 pm, Mon 10.30 pm; closed Sat L & Sun D; no smoking area.

Sticky Fingers W8   £ 24   ④❷❷
1a Phillimore Gdns   (020) 7938 5338   5–1A
"Burgers good, kids entertained" – what more could you ask of ex-Rolling Stone Bill Wyman's *"consistent"* American theme-restaurant, just off Kensington High Street? / 11.30 pm.

Stock Pot   **£ 14**   ④④④
40 Panton St, SW1   (020) 7839 5142   4–4A
18 Old Compton St, W1   (020) 7287 1066   4–2A
50 James St, W1   (020) 7486 9185   3–1A
273 King's Rd, SW3   (020) 7823 3175   5–3C
6 Basil St, SW3   (020) 7589 8627   5–1D
"Substantial portions" of "school dinners" fare at
bargain-basement prices ensure these useful bistros remain a
classic "cheap 'n' cheerful" choice. / 11 pm-Midnight; no credit cards;
some branches have no smoking areas; booking restricted at some times.

Stone Mason's Arms W6   **£ 25**   ❸④❸
54 Cambridge Grove   (020) 8748 1397   7–2C
"Good, cheap food from an ever-changing menu" ensures this
Hammersmith gastropub is often "heaving"; it can get "too
smoky", though, and service can be both "rude" and "slow".
/ 10.15 pm.

Stratford's W8   **£ 37**   ❸❸④
7 Stratford Rd   (020) 7937 6388   5–2A
"Consistent", "well prepared" and "good-value" Gallic fish and
seafood are the mainstay of this Kensington backwater spot,
whose "quiet" ambience some find "romantic". / 11 pm; set
weekday L £23(FP).

Street Hawker   **£ 19**   ❸❸❸
166 Randolph Ave, W9   (020) 7286 3869   8–3A
237 West End Ln, NW6   (020) 7431 7808   1–1B
Useful Maida Vale oriental providing "good value" cooking –
a "cosy blend of Thai, Chinese and Malaysian". / 11.15 pm.

Suan-Neo EC2   **£ 40**   ❸④⑤
31 Broadgate Circle   (020) 7256 5045   9–2D
With its "unusual" menu, the Singapura chain's year-old
Broadgate flagship offers sometimes "very good" oriental
dishes at quite stiff prices; its "well spaced" tables are
conducive to business", but the place can be "very quiet".
/ 9 pm; closed Sat & Sun.

The Sugar Club W1   **£ 43**   ❷❷❸
21 Warwick St   (020) 7437 7776   3–2D
It's a "real treat" – and a rare one – to find cooking as
"innovative" and "delicious" as Peter Gordon's fusion fare in
the heart of the West End; many applaud the "buzzy"
premises as "much improved on the Notting Hill original",
though they are a touch "echoey". / 11 pm; no smoking area.

The Sun & Doves SE5   **£ 26**   ❸❷❸
61 Coldharbour Ln   (020) 7733 1525   1–4C
"For Camberwell, a miracle" – this "light", "airy" and
"intriguingly decorated" pub is "very good all-round" (even if
the "occasional slip" is not unknown), it has a "great garden
in summer". / 10.30 pm.

Suntory SW1 £ 72 ③④④
72 St James's St   (020) 7409 0201   3–4D
"Mega-pricey", "all-suits" St James's veteran, which plutocratic reporters say is still "the best" for "high-quality Japanese food"; it is a "dry and dull" experience, though. / 10 pm; closed Sun L; smart casual; set weekday L £38(FP).

Le Suquet SW3 £ 41 ②③③
104 Draycott Ave   (020) 7581 1785   5–2C
"Super seafood" is the raison d'être of this "always crowded" Cannes-comes-to-Chelsea classic; the "very French" service is "precise" and "efficient" or "patronising" and "brusque", to taste. / 11.30 pm; set weekday L £24(FP).

Sushi Wong W8 £ 28 ③①⑤
38c Kensington Church St   (020) 7937 5007   5–1A
"If you like sushi" this small Japanese venture in Kensington can be "excellent"; "well-meaning service helps to undercut the zero atmosphere". / 10.30 pm; closed Sun L; pre-th. £18(FP).

Sushi-Say NW2 £ 30 ②③⑤
33b Walm Ln   (020) 8459 7512   1–1A
To say (as fans do) that this humble café in Willesden Green is "the most genuine Japanese in London", with "the best sushi and sashimi" overstates its case – but not by miles. / 11 pm; D only; closed Mon.

Sweetings EC4 £ 33 ②②①
39 Queen Victoria St   (020) 7248 3062   9–3B
"Time-warp bliss" – it may be a Victorian "dinosaur", but this "splendid" City seafood parlour "keeps up traditions", with "the freshest, simplest fish" served in a "basic" but "unique" and "timeless" setting. / L only; closed Sat & Sun; no credit cards; no booking.

Taberna Etrusca EC4 £ 37 ④⑤④
9 Bow Churchyard   (020) 7248 5552   9–2C
This popular City Italian is "open to the accusation of being bland", but it does have an "ideal location", near St Mary-le-Bow, and some "great" outside tables. / L only; closed Sat & Sun; no Switch.

Tajine W1 £ 26 ②③⑤
7a Dorset St   (020) 7935 1545   2–1A
Small Moroccan newcomer, hailed as the "best in town" by those who can forgive "dismal" décor for "delicious" cooking and "friendly" (if sometimes "slow") service; sceptics say it's "OK", but they've "had better". / 10.30 pm; closed Sat L & Sun; no Amex.

Tamarind W1 £41 ❶❷❷

20 Queen St (020) 7629 3561 3–3B
*"Lovely, fresh and original flavours" are winning a growing
reputation for this "unusual" and "excellent all round" Mayfair
"nouvelle-Indian"; it's now London's leading subcontinental
(with a Big Apple offshoot 'slated' for the 'fall'). / 11.30 pm;
closed Sat L.*

Tandoori Lane SW6 £23 ❷❶❸

131a Munster Rd (020) 7371 0440 10–1B
*"Seamless service" and "top-quality cooking" continue to win
praise for this "unchanging", "dark" and "intimate" Indian,
in deepest Fulham. / 11 pm; no Amex.*

Tandoori of Chelsea SW3 £40 ❷❷④

153 Fulham Rd (020) 7589 7749 5–2C
*"Reliable" Brompton Cross old trooper – given such "solid"
cooking, fans say it's "definitely under-rated". / Midnight.*

La Tante Claire
Berkeley Hotel SW1 £81 ❷❸④

Wilton Pl (020) 7823 2003 2–3A
*"Oh dear", Pierre Koffmann's move to Belgravia has, at a
stroke, reduced his restaurant – once London's greatest –
to also-ran status; there are still "fantastic" results, but for
too many they're just "mediocre", and the atmosphere seems
"wrong, cold and expensive". / 11 pm; closed Sat L & Sun; dinner,
jacket; set weekday L £42(FP).*

Tao EC4 £35 ④⑤❸

11 Bow Ln (020) 7248 5833 9–2C
*Flash ("fun and lively") City oriental, near St Mary-le-Bow,
better enjoyed as a bar than a restaurant. / 10 pm; closed Sat
& Sun.*

Tas SE1 £22 ❷❷❸

33 The Cut (020) 7928 2111 9–4A
*Large, bright and cheap – this Turkish newcomer near the
Old Vic, seemed, on our initial visit, to be a useful addition
to the South Bank. / 11.30 pm.*

Tate Gallery SW1 £43 ④❷❷

Millbank (020) 7887 8877 2–4C
*It's a mite better than it was, but, as ever, the "posh school
food" at the Tate's famous Whister-murralled dining room is
eclipsed by its "fabulous" and "very cheap" wine list (which
offers "a comprehensive selection from around the world").
/ L only; no smoking area.*

TATSUSO EC2 £65 ❶❸④

32 Broadgate Circle (020) 7638 5863 9–2D
*"Make sure someone else is paying" if you visit what many
hail as the "greatest Japanese in town"; it offers "perfect food
at unbelievably high prices", but the ambience – in both the
upstairs teppan-yaki and the basement restaurant – is "dull".
/ 9.45 pm; closed Sat & Sun; smart casual.*

Tawana W2   **£ 24**   ②④④
3 Westbourne Grove   (020) 7229 3785   6–1C
*"Good-value" Bayswater Thai; service is usually "friendly",
but not invariably so, and atmosphere can prove elusive.*
/ 11 pm.

Tbilisi N7   **£ 25**   ②③④
91 Holloway Rd   (020) 7607 2536   8–2D
*North Islington Georgian (ex USSR, not US); it's devoid of
atmosphere, but the simple cooking is satisfying, inexpensive
and 'different'.*

Teatro W1   **£ 46**   ③④④
93-107 Shaftesbury Ave   (020) 7494 3040   4–3A
*Opinions divide on this "smart" (and, on launch, rather
"overhyped") Theatreland yearling; while fans praise
"amazing" modern British cooking and a "chic" setting, others
say the place "is quite good, but just one among many".*
/ 11.45 pm; closed Sat L & Sun; pre-th. £31(FP).

Teca W1   **£ 43**   ③④⑤
54 Brooks Mews   (020) 7495 4774   3–2B
*"Cold" Mayfair mews yearling with all the atmosphere of
"a Milanese works canteen"; many do swear by the
"surprisingly good" modern Italian fare, but it's "very dear"
and "portions are very small". / 10.30 pm; closed Sun.*

10 EC2   **£ 39**   ③⑤⑤
10 Cutlers Gardens Arcade   (020) 7283 7888   9–2D
*Even if it's "very overpriced", this modishly styled basement,
near Liverpool Street, is potentially an "ideal business lunch
venue"; it "lacks atmosphere", though, and service is iffy.*
/ 11 pm; closed Sat & Sun.

Tentazioni SE1   **£ 40**   ②②⑤
2 Mill St   (020) 7237 1100   1–3D
*"Excellent" and "very imaginative" Italian cooking is "let down
by a grim setting" at this "out of the way" bar/restaurant, near
Tower Bridge, despite the efforts of the "charming" staff.*
/ 11 pm; closed Sat L & Sun.

The Tenth W8   **£ 46**   ③②②
Royal Garden Hotel, Ken' High St   (020) 7361 1910   5–1A
*"Stunning" views (over Kensington Gardens) and "attentive"
service make this tenth-floor dining room "worth a detour";
the modern British cooking is a touch "inconsistent", but
"generally good". / 11.30 pm; closed Sat L & Sun; no smoking area;
pre-th. £25(FP).*

The Terrace W8   **£ 40**   ②①②
33c Holland St   (020) 7937 3224   5–1A
*"Small but perfectly formed" yearling in a Kensington
"backwater", with "delicious" modern British cooking,
"personal and attentive" service and "romantic" atmosphere;
its "lovely terrace" is the icing on the cake. / 10.30 pm;
closed Sun D.*

Terrace W1   £39   ④❷❸

Le Meridien, 21 Piccadilly   (020) 7734 8000   3–3D
Star French chef Michel Rostang's new London outpost –
a relaunched conservatory dining-room above Piccadilly –
"doesn't hit quite the right note"; opinions on the food range
from "very good" to "ordinary", and on the setting from
"beautiful" to "antiseptic". / 11 pm; no smoking area.

Texas Embassy Cantina SW1   £28   ⑤⑤④

1 Cockspur St   (020) 7925 0077   2–2C
"Shockingly bad" Tex/Mex cavern, near Trafalgar Square;
"margaritas and tourists keep it alive". / 11 pm, Fri & Sat midnight.

Texas Lone Star SW7   £24   ⑤④④

154 Gloucester Rd   (020) 7370 5625   5–2B
"Lively" South Kensington veteran, whose attractions are now
restricted to "kids' entertainment" and "filling food on beery
Saturdays"; "you call this Mexican food? – I call it awful".
/ 11.30 pm; no booking.

TGI Friday's   £31   ④❸❸

25-29 Coventry St, W1   (020) 7839 6262   4–4A
6 Bedford St, WC2   (020) 7379 0585   4–4C
96-98 Bishops Bridge Rd, W2   (020) 7229 8600   6–1C
"The kids love them, who cares about the food?", is a common
parental view about these "fun" ("predictable") theme-diners;
some grown-ups, though, decry "overpriced American garbage
served in hellish surroundings". / Midnight, W2 11.30 pm;
smart casual; no smoking area; W1 & WC2, no booking Fri D-Sat L.

Thai Bistro W4   £24   ❷❷④

99 Chiswick High Rd   (020) 8995 5774   7–2B
"Great" Chiswick "local", where "very fresh", "tasty and
varied" dishes are "quickly" served at "simple bench-style
seating". / 11 pm; closed Tue L & Thu L; no Amex & no Switch; no smoking.

Thai Break W8   £27   ❷❸④

30 Uxbridge St   (020) 7229 4332   6–2B
"Consistently good" Thai, in a quiet backstreet near Notting
Hill Gate tube; tables are "too close together", though, and
"it could do with a face-lift". / 11 pm; closed Sun L.

Thai on the River SW10   £33   ❸❸❷

15 Lots Rd   (020) 7351 1151   5–4B
"If you sit with a view of the river", this hidden-away Chelsea
spot (near the power station) is a "super place", with some
"good" cooking. / 11 pm, Fri & Sat 11.30 pm; closed Sat L & Mon L.

Thai Pot   £26   ❸④④

5 Princes St, W1   (020) 7499 3333   3–1C
1 Bedfordbury, WC2   (020) 7379 4580   4–4C
148 Strand, WC2   (020) 7497 0904   2–2D
"Varied" menus of "good food at reasonable prices" underpin
the appeal of these rather anonymous orientals; service can
be "unsatisfactory". / 11.15 pm; closed Sun; no smoking areas,
W1 & Bedfordbury.

Thai Square SW1 £30 ③②④
21-24 Cockspur St   (020) 7839 4000   2–3C
By Trafalgar Square, the huge, percussive (ex-embassy)
premises of this new Thai Pot group offshoot are hardly
intimate, but were in impressively full swing on an early visit;
(there's a nightclub in the basement). / 1 am; set weekday L £12(FP).

Thailand SE14 £30 ②②④
15 Lewisham Way   (020) 8691 4040   1–3D
"Excellent" and "aromatic" cooking makes this tiny Lewisham
Thai "well worth checking out". / 10.30 pm; D only; closed Mon
& Sun; no Amex; no smoking.

The Thatched House W6 £22 ③②②
115 Dalling Rd   (020) 8748 6174   7–2B
Hammersmith is awash with trendified boozers, but this "airy"
newcomer is "the best example of a pub that's still a pub";
even those who acknowledge the food's "not as good as at its
rivals" revel in "the space and relative lack of smoke". / 10 pm;
no Amex; no booking.

Thierry's SW3 £33 ④④②
342 King's Rd   (020) 7352 3365   5–3C
It looks just like a "good neighbourhood French bistro",
so more's the pity that the cooking at this long-established
Chelsea joint is just "average" and "overpriced". / 10.45 pm.

Thon Buri EC2 £29 ③③⑤
9 Liverpool Arc   (020) 7623 5750   9–2D
The name's changed (from Inmala, RIP), but you'd be pressed
to spot much difference at this tackily dull Thai, near
Liverpool Street, offering tasty food at a fair price. / 9.30 pm;
closed Sat & Sun; no smoking area.

3 Monkeys SE24 £34 ②③③
136-140 Herne Hl   (020) 7738 5500   1–4C
It's "somewhat overpriced", but this "first-rate modern Indian",
with its "fresh" and "tasty" cooking, has been welcomed with
open arms in the barren wastes of Herne Hill; some think the
interior "stunning" – we thought it posey. / 11 pm; closed Mon;
no smoking area; set weekday L £21(FP).

Tibetan Restaurant WC2 £19 ④②③
17 Irving St   (020) 7839 2090   4–4B
The cooking is "lacklustre", but London's only Tibetan is not
expensive, and its first-floor location offers "a fantastic escape
from the bustle of Leicester Square", at modest cost. / 10.30 pm;
closed Wed L & Sun; no Amex & no Switch.

Tiger Lil's   £ 25   ⑤⑤④
500 King's Rd, SW3   (020) 7376 5003   5–3B
270 Upper St, N1   (020) 7226 1118   8–2D
15a Clapham Common S'side, SW4   (020) 7720 5433   10–2D
"Once the novelty's gone, it's not much fun", but these
"noisy, hot and chaotic" choose-your-own wok-joints are still
proclaimed *"good fun for groups"*, by some. / 11.30 pm, Fri & Sat
Midnight; SW10 closed Mon L-Fri L - SW4 & N1 closed Mon L-Thu L;
no Amex; no smoking areas; SW10 & SW4 max 30; N1 max 40.

Tiger Tiger SW1   £ 29   ⑤④❸
29 Haymarket   (020) 7930 1885   4–4A
"An awful, tacky zoo", it may be, but as London is ridiculously
short of places to drink, dine and dance, this West End
newcomer has its attractions – the *"eclectic"* cooking is not
one of them. / 3 am, Sun 10.30 pm.

Time SE10   £ 34   ❸❸❸
7a College Approach   (020) 8305 9767   1–3D
The bar below the mezzanine modern British restaurant at
this central Greenwich newcomer is undoubtedly a *"fantastic"*
space (if a *"deafening"* one at weekends); the restaurant is,
in all respects, more subdued. / 10.30 pm; closed Mon L.

Titanic W1   £ 38   ⑤⑤⑤
Regent Palace Hotel   (020) 7437 1912   3–3D
"It's great for a drink and people-watching", otherwise *"words
cannot describe"* this vast and *"electric"* 'teen-scene', off
Piccadilly Circus; some reporters did try – *"awful"*, *"disaster"*,
"dreadful", *"horrible"*, *"no imagination"*, *"overpriced"*, *"ugh!"*
/ 11.30 pm.

Toast NW3   £ 35   ④❸❸
50 Hampstead High St   (020) 7431 2244   8–1A
The tiny, rather *"precious"* menu and risible wine list disqualify
this newcomer above Hampstead tube from consideration
as a 'serious' restaurant; judged, though, as a stylish
thirtysomething 'scene', it's already quite a place. / Midnight.

Toff's N10   £ 26   ❶❷⑤
38 Muswell Hl Broadway   (020) 8883 8656   1–1B
"Unsurpassed, south of Watford", this celebrated Muswell Hill
chippy offers *"great fish and chips in massive portions"*.
/ 10 pm; closed Mon & Sun; no booking on Sat; set weekday L £15(FP).

Tokyo Diner WC2   £ 15   ④❷④
2 Newport Pl   (020) 7287 8777   4–3B
"OK for cheap Japanese"; this Chinatown café remains a
popular and *"friendly"* central *"stand-by"*, even if it's *"gone
downhill compared to the emerging competition"*. / Midnight;
no Amex; no smoking area; Fri & Sat no booking.

Tom's W10 £ 22 ③④③
226 Westbourne Grove (020) 7221 8818 6–1B
"Snazzy", "very Hugh Grant" Notting Hill deli whose
"memorable sandwiches", "superb eggs" and other "high
quality" snacks ensure "you often have to queue" (especially
at brunch); "go just to see the beautiful people"; BYO. / 10 pm;
closed Sat D & Sun D; no smoking; no booking.

Tootsies £ 22 ④③③
35 James St, W1 (020) 7486 1611 3–1A
177 New King's Rd, SW6 (020) 7736 4023 10–1B
107 Old Brompton Rd, SW7 (020) 7581 8942 5–2B
120 Holland Pk Ave, W11 (020) 7229 8567 6–2A
148 Chiswick High Rd, W4 (020) 8747 1869 7–2A
198 Haverstock Hl, NW3 (020) 7431 7609 8–2A
147 Church Rd, SW13 (020) 8748 3630 10–1A
"Consistently good burgers" and a "very child-friendly" attitude
mean these popular diners "always make a great stand-by".
/ 11 pm-11.30 pm, Fri & Sat Midnight; no smoking areas at SW19, W11
& W4; no booking.

Topsy-Tasty W4 £ 20 ③④⑤
5 Station Parade (020) 8995 3407 1–3A
The '50s tea room setting is "dismal", but you still get "tasty"
Thai cooking "at low prices" at this café by Chiswick BR; BYO.
/ 10.30 pm; D only; closed Sun; no credit cards.

Toto's SW1 £ 40 ②②②
Lennox Gardens Mews (020) 7589 0075 5–2D
"Wonderful, traditional Italian" behind Harrods – "a great
all-rounder" with a "comfortable" and "romantic" setting,
"lovely" service and "reliable" cooking. / 11.30 pm; smart casual.

Townhouse Brasserie WC1 £ 25 ③②④
24 Coptic St (020) 7636 2731 2–1C
"Why is it so often empty?", ask fans of this cosy townhouse,
near the British Museum, which is praised for its affordable
modern British cooking. / 11 pm; no smoking area; pre-th. £16(FP).

Troika NW1 £ 20 ④③③
101 Regents Pk Rd (020) 7483 3765 8–2B
"Mouthwatering blinis" are the high point at this "relaxed",
cheap and "different" Russian café on Primrose Hill (where
you can BYO); "enormous English breakfasts" are also
appreciated. / 10.30 pm; no Amex; no smoking area.

Troubadour SW5 £ 27 ③④❶
265 Old Brompton Rd (020) 7370 1434 5–3A
"A great place to linger and relax" – the "fabulous",
"Bohemian" atmosphere has survived a change of ownership
at this quirky Earl's Court coffee house; "delicious all-day
breakfasts" remain a feature, but evenings are now quite busy,
too. / 11 pm; no credit cards; no smoking area; no booking.

Tuba SW4   £ 28   ❷❸❸
4 Clapham Common Southside   (020) 7978 3333   10–2D
"Cool", younger-scene bar/restaurant, by Clapham Common tube, providing unexpectedly good pasta and light Italian dishes. / 11.15 pm; closed Mon.

Tui SW7   £ 29   ❶❸④
19 Exhibition Rd   (020) 7584 8359   5–2C
"Exceptional", fiery cooking has regained its former reliability at this "authentic" South Kensington Thai; post-refurbishment, the setting is still "cramped" and "cold". / 10.45 pm; smart casual.

Tuk Tuk N1   £ 23   ④④❸
330 Upper St   (020) 7226 0837   8–3D
"Once-good" Islington Thai, whose cooking is now "average" at best (ditto service); "it fills a hole", though, and it's "cheap". / 11 pm; closed Sat L & Sun L.

Turner's SW3   £ 57   ❸❸④
87-89 Walton St   (020) 7584 6711   5–2C
TV chef Brian Turner's "rather old-fashioned" (and chi-chi) Knightsbridge spot remains many people's favourite, thanks to its consistently "well prepared" French cuisine; increasingly, though, people note that it's a "shame about the prices". / 11 pm; closed Sun; smart casual; set weekday L £28(FP).

Two Brothers N3   £ 24   ❷❷④
297-303 Regent's Pk Rd   (020) 8346 0469   1–1B
"Excellent fish" ("peripherals are so-so") ensure that this "noisy" Finchley chippy is always "full of happy diners". / 10.15 pm; closed Mon & Sun; no smoking area; book L only.

The Union Café W1   £ 34   ④④④
96 Marylebone Ln   (020) 7486 4860   3–1A
Veteran Chelsea restaurateur John Brinkley now owns this "bright and airy" Marylebone café; its 'Californian' style is in sharp contrast to his other ventures, but otherwise it's very much a Brinkley baby, offering "amazing" wine bargains but "very ordinary" cooking. / 10.30 pm; closed Sun.

Uno SW1   £ 30   ❸❷④
1 Denbigh St   (020) 7834 1001   2–4B
For best results at this popular and noisy Pimlico trattoria, stick to the "really good pizzas" (other fare is "mediocre") and "sit upstairs". / 11.30 pm; closed Sun.

Upper Street Fish Shop N1   £ 19   ❷❸❸
324 Upper St   (020) 7359 1401   8–2D
"Fabulous food and eccentric service" make an "ever-reliable" combination at this "charming" Islington chippy; a "wide variety of delicious fish" (not all fried) is served in a bistro setting; BYO. / 10.15 pm; closed Mon L & Sun; no credit cards; no booking.

The Vale W9 £ 26 ❷❶④
99 Chippenham Rd (020) 7266 0990 1–2B
*Thanks to its "confidently executed" modern British cooking
and "attentive" service, this "spartan" but "good-value"
Maida Hill spot has made "a good start in a difficult area".*
/ 11.30 pm; closed Sat L; no Amex; no smoking area.

Vama SW10 £ 36 ❶❷❸
438 King's Rd (020) 7351 4118 5–3B
*"Wonderful, imaginative" cooking, delivered by "polite and
timely" staff is winning ever-greater recognition for this
"lovely", if cramped, World's End Indian.* / 11.30 pm; Sun 10 pm.

Vasco & Piero's Pavilion W1 £ 35 ❸❶④
15 Poland St (020) 7437 8774 3–1D
*"Regulars are treated like old friends" at this "genuine"
old-Soho Italian, and the cooking ("excellent set meals", in
particular) "can be really good"; they "should make the décor
cosier", though.* / 11 pm; closed Sat L & Sun; smart casual.

Veeraswamy W1 £ 36 ❸④④
Victory House, 99 Regent St (020) 7734 1401 3–3D
*Given the owners' track record at Chutney Mary, one could
have hoped for more from their year-old relaunch of London's
oldest Indian – the "colourful", modern décor is not to all
tastes and the "nouvelle Indian" cooking is rather "bland".*
/ 11.30 pm; pre-th. £25(FP).

Vegia Zena NW1 £ 28 ❷❷❸
17 Princess Rd (020) 7483 0192 8–3B
*"Superior" and "unusual" Genoese cooking makes this
"friendly", Primrose Hill Italian of some note; "the basement
is a bit grim".* / 11 pm; set weekday L £13(FP).

Vendôme W1 £ 38 ④❸❸
20 Dover St (020) 7629 5417 3–3C
*Intriguingly "louche" décor – not the "mediocre" and
"expensive" cooking – is the strength of this striking Mayfair
bar/restaurant.* / 11 pm; closed Sat & Sun.

Veronica's W2 £ 33 ❸❷❷
3 Hereford Rd (020) 7229 5079 6–1B
*"Interesting and very tasty", "good but strange" – such are the
typical reactions to the olde English recipes at this Bayswater
curiosity; some find its quiet atmosphere 'romantic'.* / 11.30 pm;
closed Sat L & Sun.

Le Versailles SW9 £ 30 ④④④
20 Trinity Gdns (020) 7326 0521 10–2D
*Gallic Brixton bistro that's "pleasant"-enough, but nothing to
set the world on fire.* / 10.30 pm, Fri & Sat 11 pm; closed Mon; no Amex;
no smoking area; set Dinner £20(FP).

Vic Naylors EC1 £ 27 ④④❸
38 & 40 St John St   (020) 7608 2181   9–1B
A "fun post-work hang-out" – this Smithfield wine bar trades
on its "good ambience", not its variable grub. / 11 pm; closed Sun.

Il Vicolo SW1 £ 31 ❷❷④
3-4 Crown Passage   (020) 7839 3960   3–4D
"Authentic" and "consistently good" cooking makes it worth
seeking out this "cramped" Italian "bargain", "tucked away"
in pricey St James's; downstairs, though, it can be "deadly".
/ 10 pm; closed Sat & Sun.

Vijay NW6 £ 20 ❷❷④
49 Willesden Ln   (020) 7328 1087   1–1B
"Very interesting food, especially the vegetarian options," wins
a dedicated following for this dowdy but "dead cheap" Kilburn
Indian. / 10.45 pm, Fri & Sat 11.45 pm; no Amex.

Villa Bianca NW3 £ 41 ④❷❷
1 Perrins Ct   (020) 7435 3131   8–2A
Chi-chi Hampstead Italian, which is "an old favourite, thanks
to its location" (in a cute cobbled lane, off the High Street),
rather than its "expensive" and "variable" cooking. / 11.30 pm;
set weekday L £25(FP).

Village Bistro N6 £ 38 ❸❸❷
38 Highgate High St   (020) 8340 5165   8–1B
"Eccentric" and "cramped" Highgate cottage, whose
necessarily "intimate" atmosphere many find "romantic";
fans differ as to whether the Gallic fare is "fabulous" or
rather "inconsistent". / 11 pm; set Sun L £24(FP).

Villandry Dining Rooms W1 £ 36 ❸⑤④
170 Gt Portland St   (020) 7631 3131   2–1B
"The slowest service in the world" "saps your patience" in the
"noisy" and "overcrowded" annexe of this large, "foodie"
Marylebone deli; the modern British fare is "not as good as
when it was on the original site", but it still has its moments.
/ 10 pm; closed Sun D; no smoking.

The Vine NW5 £ 31 ❸❸❸
86 Highgate Rd   (020) 7209 0038   8–1B
"A great neighbourhood star for Kentish Town", this "lovely",
"warm" gastropub (with its "great all-year garden") produces
"solid pub food with flair", and it's delivered by "friendly" staff.
/ 10 pm; closed Mon L; no smoking area.

Vingt-Quatre SW10 £ 26 ❸❷④
325 Fulham Rd   (020) 7376 7224   5–3B
"Always open and welcoming" Chelsea 'Beach' diner, with
"surprisingly good food"; it's "a nice place for brunch", but
"nothing beats a VQ burger at 3am". / open 24 hours; no booking.

VONG SW1 £ 42 ❷❸❸

Wilton Pl   (020) 7235 1010   2–3A
Fans rave over "brilliant" and "original" Thai/French cooking at the Belgravia outpost of top NYC chef Jean-Georges Vongerichten; the dining room is "smart", but a tad neutral, and some find the whole experience "pretentious". / 11.30 pm; no smoking area.

Vrisaki N22 £ 24 ❷❷❸

73 Myddleton Rd   (020) 8889 8760   1–1C
"Tons of food" – "the best value meze in London" – make it "worth the trip" to "huge buzzing Greek restaurant, hidden behind a Bounds Green kebab shop". / Midnight; closed Sun; no Amex.

Wagamama £ 16 ❸❸❸

101 Wigmore St, W1   (020) 7409 0111   3–1A
10a Lexington St, W1   (020) 7292 0990   3–2D
4a Streatham St, WC1   (020) 7323 9223   2–1C
26 Kensington High St, W8   (020) 7376 1717   5–1A
11 Jamestown Rd, NW1   (020) 7428 0800   8–3B
"I wish they were on every high street", say the many fans of these "extremely fast" and "loud" refectories and their "reasonably priced", "noodelicious" cuisine; the strains of growing the chain so fast, though, risk denting satisfaction. / 11 pm; no smoking; no booking.

Wakaba NW3 £ 38 ❷❸⑤

122a Finchley Rd   (020) 7586 7960   8–2A
It's "expensive", but the sushi "really is first-class" at this Nipponese café, opposite North Finchley tube; the ultra-stark setting may delight architecture students, but, let's be honest, it's a "lousy space". / 10.45 pm; D only; closed Sun.

The Waldorf Meridien WC2 £ 57 ④❸❷

Aldwych   (020) 7836 2400   2–2D
"The space and the atmosphere are the treat" in the Palm Court of this grand Covent Garden-fringe hotel; breakfast is "great", but the food "then goes downhill for the rest of the day" (though tea is a "lovely experience"). / 11.15 pm; closed Sat L; jacket & tie req'd for tea dances; no smoking area; pre-th. £34(FP).

The Waterloo Fire Station SE1 £ 29 ④④④

150 Waterloo Rd   (020) 7401 3267   9–4A
The modern British grub is "surprisingly adventurous" but rather "hit-and-miss" at this large South Bank bar/refectory; the space – "wonderful" and "attractive", to some – can seem "inhospitable" when the place is crowded. / 11 pm; Sun, 9.15 pm.

Weng Wah House NW3 £ 23 ❸❷❸

240 Haverstock Hl   (020) 7794 5123   8–2A
"Friendly" Belsize Park fixture whose "reliable" oriental standards and "middle-of-the-road charm" make it a "good local". / 11.30 pm; no Amex; set weekday L £15(FP).

The Westbourne W2   £24   ④⑤❶
101 Westbourne Park Villas   (020) 7221 1332   6–1B
*"Get there early" – especially on a sunny day – before the
food runs out at this "fun" but shambolic Bayswater boozer;
it's always "overcrowded" with trustafarian Hillbillies. / 10 pm;
closed Mon L; no Amex.*

White Cross Hotel TW9   £18   ④⑤❶
Water Ln   (020) 8940 6844   1–4A
*A "terrific, riverside, dog-friendly beer garden" is but one of
the attractions of this tremendous, traditional Young's pub,
near Richmond Bridge; it serves "cheap, good-quality" lunches.
/ L only; no Amex; no booking.*

The White Onion N1   £34   ❶❶❷
297 Upper St   (020) 7359 3533   8–3D
*"The star of Islington", on account of its "amazing" and
"interesting" modern British cooking and "attentive" service;
some find the understated setting "gloomy" – it's "nicer
upstairs". / 11 pm; closed L, Mon-Fri.*

Whittington's EC4   £44   ❸④④
21 College HI   (020) 7248 5855   9–3B
*"Interesting" specials sometimes "surprise" in the restaurant
attached to the wine bar in the cellar of Dick's old home,
near St Paul's. / L only; closed Sat & Sun.*

William IV NW10   £26   ❷❷❷
786 Harrow Rd   (020) 8969 5944   1–2B
*A "great Sunday pub lunch venue", this "out-of-the-way"
Kensal Green gastropub offers satisfying and "reasonably
priced" fare, and has an attractive courtyard garden. / 10.30 pm,
Fri & Sat 11 pm.*

Willie Gunn SW18   £26   ④❷❷
422 Garratt Ln   (020) 8946 7773   10–2B
*"The place to go" – in Earlsfield – this "really pleasant"
bar/restaurant is highly esteemed by locals for its "good meaty
hamburgers" and "hangover breakfasts"; avoid anything fancy.
/ 11 pm; no Amex.*

Wilson's W14   £32   ❸❶❸
236 Blythe Rd   (020) 7603 7267   7–1C
*"Devolution has not hurt" this "informal" and "very friendly"
Caledonian outpost in Shepherd's Bush – "the bagpipes are
less present, nowadays, but the menus are more interesting".
/ 10 pm; closed Sat L & Sun D; no Amex; set weekday L £20(FP).*

Wiltons SW1   £52   ❷❷❷
55 Jermyn St   (020) 7629 9955   3–3C
*Notoriously "pricey" St James's stalwart, famed for its oysters
and praised for its "always reliable" seafood, meat and game;
it's "too much like a gentlemen's club", for some tastes, but it
"can't be outdone for power lunches". / 10.30 pm; closed Sat;
jacket & tie; set Sun L £36(FP).*

Windows on the World
Park Lane Hilton Hotel W1   £ 70   ⑤④❶
22 Park Ln   (020) 7208 4021   3–4A
"Stunning view, but ouch!" – the cooking is "poor and very expensive" on the 28th floor of this Mayfair hotel; as an all-round experience, weekend brunches "take a lot of beating", and in the evening it's "romantic". / Mon-Thu 10.30 pm, Fri & Sat 11.30 pm; closed Sat L & Sun D; dinner, jacket & tie; set Brunch £48(FP).

Windsor Castle W8   £ 26   ❸④❶
114 Campden Hl Rd   (020) 7243 9551   6–2B
"A wonderful pub, inside and out"; thanks to its "good pub food" and "lovely garden", this old Kensington inn is often "overcrowded" – no excuse for sometimes "surly" service. / 10.30 pm; no smoking area (L only); no booking.

Wine Gallery SW10   £ 23   ④⑤❷
49 Hollywood Rd   (020) 7352 7572   5–3B
"Amazingly cheap wine" – and it's quality stuff, too – helps maintain the buzz at this "reliable" Chelsea "old favourite"; the grub is "nothing special", and the place is especially good "for parties" or for "sitting outside in summer". / 11.45 pm; no Amex.

Wiz W11   £ 27   ④❸❷
123a Clarendon Rd   (020) 7229 1500   6–2A
Fans of this "trendy" and "beautiful" Holland Park yearling delight in its "mixed culture" tapas concept; too many, though, dismiss it as a typical Anthony Worrall Thompson "gimmick", delivering "small" and "mainly indifferent" portions that score "four misses for every hit". / 11 pm; midnight, Fri & Sat.

Wódka W8   £ 33   ④④❸
12 St Alban's Grove   (020) 7937 6513   5–1B
"Good for drinks, not food" – the fare is "beside the point" at this discreetly located Kensington Pole, whose attraction is its "great vodkas", and the "exuberant" atmosphere they fuel. / 11.15 pm; closed Sat L & Sun L; smart casual; set weekday L £20(FP).

Wok Wok   £ 26   ④❸④
10 Frith St, W1   (020) 7437 7080   4–2A
140 Fulham Rd, SW10   (020) 7370 5355   5–3B
7 Kensington High St, W8   (020) 7938 1221   5–1A
67 Upper St, N1   (020) 7288 0333   8–3D
51-53 Northcote Rd, SW11   (020) 7978 7181   10–2C
"Noisy, young and fun" oriental noodle chain which may be "nothing special", but whose "light and airy" branches are "good for a quick, cheap meal". / W1 Mon-Wed 11 pm, Thu-Sat midnight, Sun 10.30 pm – SW10 11 pm, Fri midnight - SW11 & N1 11 pm; W1 closed Sun L; SW10 Sat & Sun no booking, Mon-Fri L only - W1 party bookings (8+) only for D.

Wolfe's WC2 £ 26 ③④④
30 Gt Queen St   (020) 7831 4442   4–1D
Homesick Yanks seek out this large, "very American" family restaurant in Covent Garden, known for its "great burgers"; the one behind Harrods has been knocked down. / 11.30 pm; closed Sun.

Wong Kei W1 £ 18 ④⑤④
41-43 Wardour St   (020) 7437 8408   4–3A
"Service is so bad, it's entertainment" at this infamous Chinatown phenomenon (whose "vicious waiters just love intimidating you"); "it's so cheap it doesn't matter", though, and there are those who've "not had a bad scoff in 25 years". / 11.30 pm; no credit cards; no booking.

Woodlands £ 24 ④③④
37 Panton St, SW1   (020) 7839 7258   4–4A
77 Marylebone Ln, W1   (020) 7486 3862   3–1A
"Cheap" and (reasonably) cheerful south Indian vegetarians, in Theatreland and Marylebone. / 10.30 pm.

Yas W14 £ 25 ③⑤④
7 Hammersmith Rd   (020) 7603 9148   7–1D
Useful, very late-night Iranian, near Olympia which "gets lively around 11pm"; meze are better than main courses. / 5 am; no Amex.

Yellow River Café E14 £ 20 – – –
10 Cabot Sq, North Colonnade, Canary Wharf   tel n/a   1–3D
The culinary badlands of Canary Wharf are the backdrop for the November opening of this new pan-Asian chain prototype in Canary Wharf – a marriage of the talents of The Oriental Restaurants Group (Sri Siam, and so on) and eminent chef Ken Hom.

Yima NW1 £ 13 ②③③
95 Parkway   (020) 7267 1097   8–3B
Moroccan Camden café newcomer – an inconspicuous basement offering an exotic environment in which to enjoy a top-quality light meal; shame there's no alcohol! / 10 pm; no credit cards; no smoking area.

Yo! Sushi W1 £ 24 ③②②
52-53 Poland St   (020) 7287 0443   3–1D
"Pricey, but a fun feed" – the "novelty" of this space-age Soho venture continues to appeal; the conveyor-belt sushi is "not bad at all, if you want it quick and easy". / Midnight; no smoking; no booking.

Yoshino W1 £ 27 ②③④
3 Piccadilly Pl   (020) 7287 6622   3–3D
"The best sushi" makes this small Japanese gem, near Piccadilly Circus, worth seeking out; "to get the best out of it, you need to go with a native speaker" – especially at lunch, when there's no menu in English! / 9 pm; closed Sun; no smoking area.

Yum Yum N16 £24 ❷❷❷
30 Stoke Newington Ch St (020) 7254 6751 1–1C
*"Always-good food and welcoming service" has long proved a
winning formula for this "crowded" Stoke Newington Thai.
/ 10.45 pm, Fri & Sat 11.15 pm.*

ZAFFERANO SW1 £44 ❶❶❷
16 Lowndes St (020) 7235 5800 2–4A
*"Fight to get in", if you want to enjoy the "awesome" cooking
at what is for many reporters "the best Italian in town"; only
the low-key décor of its Belgravia premises inspires anything
short of total adulation. / 11 pm; closed Sun.*

Zaika SW3 £35 ❶❷❸
257-259 Fulham Rd (020) 7351 7823 5–2C
*"The Indian Chelsea didn't know it needed"; Vineet Bhatia's
"exciting and different" cuisine, not to mention the supremely
well-oiled service and comfortably distinctive décor, have made
this newcomer (on the site of Chavot, RIP) an instant hit.
/ 10.45 pm; closed Sat L & Sun.*

Zamoyski NW3 £22 ④④❸
85 Fleet Rd (020) 7794 4792 8–2A
*"Go for the vodka" to this "squashed" but "charming"
Hampstead bar/restaurant; the "variable" cooking is
"Polish-basic". / 11 pm; D only; Sun open L & D; smart casual.*

Zen SW3 £44 ❷❸④
Chelsea Cloisters, Sloane Ave (020) 7589 1781 5–2C
*"Delicious food and courteous service, but a dingy room" is
the current state of the "comfortable" Chelsea cradle of this
Chinese dynasty. / 11.15 pm; no Amex; smart casual; set weekday L
£23(FP).*

Zen Central W1 £52 ❸④④
20-22 Queen St (020) 7629 8089 3–3B
*"Blandly decorated", "very, very, very expensive" Chinese in
Mayfair; many do feel the "well executed" cooking (including
"the best crispy duck") lives up, but others query why
"ordinary food comes at extraordinary prices". / 11.30 pm;
no Amex; smart casual; set weekday L £33(FP).*

Zen Garden W1 £45 ❸❸④
15-16 Berkeley St (020) 7493 1381 3–3C
*"Civilised", if rather "stuffy" Mayfair Chinese, with "reliable"
cooking, but where "bills can mount alarmingly"; new
management may shake the place up. / 11 pm; smart casual; set
weekday L £24(FP).*

ZeNW3 NW3 £35 ❷❷❸
83 Hampstead High St (020) 7794 7863 8–2A
*The "interesting", '80s design is still notable at this
impressively glazed Hampstead Chinese, as is the "good
but expensive" cooking. / 11.30 pm; smart casual.*

Ziani SW3 £ 35 ③③②

45-47 Radnor Wk   (020) 7352 2698   5–3C
"Happy and well priced", if "unbearably crowded" and
"hectic", Chelsea backstreet trattoria where service is "great if
you want to be quick, but not if you don't"; "they do rely a bit
on their reputation". / 11.30 pm; set Sun L £24(FP).

Zilli Fish W1 £ 43 ②③③

36-40 Brewer St   (020) 7734 8649   3–2D
Even fans admit its "a bit overpriced", but "excellent fresh
fish", "friendly" service and a "buzzy atmosphere" win many
more bouquets than brickbats for this trendy Soho corner site.
/ 11.45 pm; closed Sun.

Zinc W1 £ 30 ⑤⑤④

21 Heddon St   (020) 7255 8899   3–2C
"Possibly OK for a tourist", but who else would patronise this
"disappointing and typically Conran" establishment, where
"bland food" is served in "zero-ambience" surroundings at
"silly prices"? / 11 pm, Thu-Sat 11.30 pm; closed Sun.

Zoe W1 £ 39 ⑤④⑤

3-5 Barrett St   (020) 7224 1122   3–1A
Presumably, it's the "useful" location – not far from Selfridges,
and with some good outside tables – which enables this
"mediocre" modern British brasserie to soldier on. / 11.30 pm;
closed Sun; smart casual; no smoking area.

Zucca W11 £ 36 ④④④

188 Westbourne Grove   (020) 7727 0060   6–1B
A sense of promise unfulfilled hangs over this "clinical"
Notting Hill Italian, whose pizza-and-more cooking achieves
only "adequate" results. / 11 pm; no Amex; no sat lunch.

INDEXES

INDEXES

BIG GROUP BOOKINGS
(more expensive establishments which will contemplate large bookings in the main dining room – see also private rooms)

Central
Al Hamra *(25)*
Bam-Bou *(15)*
Bank *(14)*
Beotys *(20)*
Cave *(25)*
Claridges Restaurant *(20)*
Dorchester, Oriental *(16)*
Elena's L'Etoile *(30)*
L'Escargot *(20)*
L'Estaminet *(20)*
Manzi's *(50)*
Miyama *(16)*
Momo *(25)*
Mon Plaisir *(28)*
Motcombs *(14)*
L'Odéon *(30)*
Opus 70 *(14)*
La Poule au Pot *(20)*
Sale e Pepe *(14)*
Savoy River Restaurant *(35)*
Simpsons-in-the-Strand *(20)*
Le Soufflé *(25)*
La Spiga *(30)*
Stephen Bull *(15)*
Suntory *(50)*
Vendôme *(20)*
Windows on the World *(30)*

West
Bluebird *(22)*
The Canteen *(30)*
Chez Moi *(16)*
Chutney Mary *(60)*
The Collection *(30)*
Conrad Hotel *(25)*
Dakota *(16)*
English House *(15)*
La Famiglia *(14)*
Julie's Bar *(30)*
Ken Lo's Memories *(20)*
Kensington Place *(26)*
Scalini *(20)*

North
Frederick's *(60)*
Lemonia *(15)*

South
Blue Print Café *(14)*
Ransome's Dock *(14)*

BREAKFAST
(with opening times)

Central
Atrium *(8)*
Aurora *(8)*
Balans: *all branches (8)*
Bank *(7.30)*

Bar Italia *(7)*
Café Bohème *(8)*
Café Flo: *WC2 (10); SW1, Wardour St W1 (9); Thayer St W1 (9, Sat & Sun 10)*
Café Pasta: *both WC2 (9.30)*
Café Rouge: *all central branches (10)*
Caffè Nero: *Frith St W1 (7); Brewer St W1 (7, Sat & Sun 9); Tottenham Court Rd W1, Regent St W1, all in WC2 (7, Sat 8, Sun 9)*
Caffè Uno: *Argyll St W1 (10); Tottenham Court Rd W1, Binney St W1, Baker St W1 (9)*
Chez Gérard: *Chancery Ln WC2 (8, not Sat & Sun)*
Chunk *(7.30)*
Claridges Restaurant *(7)*
Coffee Republic: *Gt Marlborough St W1, South Molton St W1, Berwick St W1, all in WC2 (7); Wardour St W1 (8)*
Connaught *(7.30)*
Cranks: *Marshall St W1, Tottenham St W1 (8); Barrett St W1, Unit 11, 8 Adelaide St WC2 (8, Sat 9); Great Newport St WC2 (9)*
Dôme: *W1 (10); both WC2 (8)*
Dorchester Grill *(7, Sun 7.30)*
Eat: *W1, WC2 (7); both SW1 (7.30)*
1837 at Brown's Hotel *(7)*
Fifth Floor (Café) *(10)*
Food for Thought *(9.30)*
Giraffe: *(8, Sat & Sun, 9)*
Goring Hotel *(7)*
Grissini *(7, Sun 8)*
The Halkin *(7)*
Indigo *(6.30)*
Lanes *(7)*
The Lanesborough *(7)*
Maison Bertaux *(9)*
Mash *(8, Sat & Sun 11)*
Maxwell's: *WC2 (9.30)*
Nicole's *(10)*
Oriel *(8.30, Sun 9)*
The Park, Hyde Park Hotel *(7)*
Pâtisserie Valerie: *Old Compton St W1 (7.30, Sun 9); RIBA Centre, 66 Portland Pl W1 (8); Marylebone High St W1 (8, Sun 9); WC2 (9.30, Sun 9)*
Pizza On The Park *(8.15)*
Pret A Manger: *Tottenham Court Rd W1 (7.15); Victoria St SW1, Marylebone High St W1, High Holborn WC1 (7.30); Baker St W1 (7.45); Kingsgate Pd, Victoria St SW1, Regents St SW1, Oxford St W1, Wardour St W1, Hanover St W1, Piccadilly W1, Oxford St W1, Piccadilly W1, Tottenham Court Rd W1, High Holborn WC1, both WC2 (8)*
Restaurant One-O-One *(7)*
Richoux: *Piccadilly W1 (8); South Audley St W1 (8, Sun 9)*
The Ritz *(7)*
Savoy River Restaurant *(7)*
Simpsons-in-the-Strand *(Mon-Fri 7.30)*
Sotheby's Café *(9)*
Soup Opera: *all branches (7.30)*
Star Café *(7.30)*
Stock Pot: *SW1 (7); James St W1 (8)*
Terrace *(7)*

INDEXES

BRUNCH MENUS

South
Belair House
Blue Print Café
Butlers Wharf Chop-house
The County Hall
Lawn
Oxo Tower
Le Pont de la Tour
Putney Bridge
RSJ

East
The Big Chef
Bleeding Heart
Brasserie 24
Brasserie Rocque
Bubb's
Café du Marché
Caravaggio
City Brasserie
City Miyama
City Rhodes
Coq d'Argent
Dibbens
Gladwins
Imperial City
Luc's Brasserie
Moro
Novelli EC1
1 Lombard Street
Pacific Oriental
Prism
Singapura: *EC3*
Sri Siam City
Stephen Bull: *EC1*
Suan-Neo
Sweetings
Tatsuso
10
Whittington's

BYO
(Bring your own wine)

Central
Aurora
Food for Thought
Fryer's Delight
India Club
Neal's Yard

West
Adams Café
Alounak: *W14*
Bedlington Café
Blah! Blah! Blah!
Café 209
Chelsea Bun Diner
Fat Boy's
El Gaucho
Kalamaras
Mandola
Mohsen
Rôtisserie Jules: *SW7*
Tom's

Topsy-Tasty
Yas

North
Diwana B-P House
Troika
Upper St Fish Shop

South
Basilico: *SW11*
The Cook House
Eco Brixton
Escaped Cafe
Monsieur Max

East
Faulkner's
Lahore Kebab House

CHILDREN
(h – high or special chairs
m – children's menu
p – children's portions
e – weekend entertainments
o – other facilities)

Central
Al Bustan *(hp)*
Al Hamra *(p)*
Al Sultan *(h)*
Alastair Little *(hm)*
Alfred *(hp)*
Aroma II *(hme)*
Ask! Pizza: *all branches (hp)*
Axis *(m)*
Back to Basics *(p)*
Balans: *W1 (hp)*
Bank *(hp)*
Barra *(h)*
Belgo Centraal: *WC2 (hp)*
Benihana: *W1 (hm)*
Bice *(h)*
The Birdcage *(p)*
Blues *(o)*
Boudin Blanc *(h)*
Browns: *W1 (h); WC2 (hm)*
Café Emm *(h)*
Café Fish *(m)*
Café Flo: *all branches (h)*
Café Med: *W1 (hm)*
Café Pacifico *(m)*
Café Pasta: *W1 (h); both WC2 (hpo)*
Café Rouge: *Frith St W1, WC2 (hm)*
Caffè Uno: *all branches (hm)*
China City *(h)*
Chor Bizarre *(h)*
Chuen Cheng Ku *(h)*
Claridges Restaurant *(h)*
Como Lario *(h)*
Corney & Barrow: *all branches (hp)*
Cranks: *all central branches (h)*
The Criterion *(h)*
Deals: *W1 (hm)*
Dorchester Grill *(hm)*
Dorchester, Oriental *(h)*

INDEXES

ENTERTAINMENT
(Check times before you go)

Central

Pizza On The Park
(jazz, nightly)

Pizza Pomodoro: W1
(music, nightly)

PizzaExpress: *Dean St W1*
(jazz, nightly); Greek St W1
(jazz, Thu-Sat)

La Porte des Indes
(jazz, Sun brunch)

Quaglino's
(jazz, nightly in bar)

Radio Café
(resident DJ)

Rib Room
(pianist Mon-Sat eves)

The Ritz
(band, Fri & Sat)

La Rueda: *W1*
(Spanish music & dancing, Fri & Sat)

Saint
(DJ, nightly)

Sarastro
(opera, Mon; Turkish music, Sun)

Savoy River Restaurant
(dinner dance, nightly ex Sun)

Smollensky's
(music, nightly; dancing, Thu-Sat; jazz, Sun D)

Sofra: *WC2*
(music, Mon-Sat)

Le Soufflé
(string trio, Sun L)

Thai Square
(Thai music & dancing, nightly)

Tiger Tiger
(nightclub)

The Waldorf Meridien
(jazz, Sun brunch)

Windows on the World
(dinner dance, Fri & Sat; jazz, Sun brunch)

West

All Bar One: *W4*
(jazz, Sun pm)

Big Easy
(band, nightly)

Bombay Brasserie
(piano & singer nightly)

Brompton Bay
(jazz, Wed & Sat eves)

Cactus Blue
(jazz, Sat & Sun brunch)

Café Lazeez: *SW7*
(music, Wed, Fri & Sat)

Cambio de Tercio
(guitarist, Wed)

Chicago Rib Shack
(music, Wed, Thu & Fri)

Chutney Mary
(jazz, Sun L)

Conrad Hotel
(singer & pianist, nightly)

Da Mario
(disco, nightly ex Sun)

Floriana
(piano player nightly)

Havana: *SW6 (DJ &*
Latin dancing, nightly)

Maroush: *W2*
(music & dancing, nightly)

Mas Café
(bands & party nights)

Montana
(jazz, Wed-Sun)

Mr Wing
(jazz Thu-Sat)

Nikita's
(Russian music, weekends)

Palio
(jazz, Thu eves)

Paparazzi Café: *SW3 (music, nightly)*

Patio
(gypsy music, nightly)

The Pen
(jazz, Sun L)

Pizza Pomodoro: *SW3*
(music, nightly)

PizzaExpress: *W8 (jazz, Fri & Sat;*
W14 (jazz, Sat); Beauchamp Pl SW3
(jazz, Sat & Sun)

Shoeless Joe's: *SW6*
(video screens)

606 Club
(jazz, nightly)

Star of India
(music, Thu & Fri (winter only))

The Tenth
(pianist nightly; band nights)

Texas Lone Star
(music, 3 nights a week)

Troubadour
(poetry, Mon; comedy, Tue;
music, Thu-Sat)

William IV
(DJ, Fri & Sat)

Wilson's
(bagpipes most eves)

North

Angel of the North
(jazz)

Les Associés
(accordion 1st Fri of month)

Babe Ruth's: *NW3*
(basketball, video games)

La Brocca
(jazz, Thu)

Café Rouge: *NW3*
(jazz, Wed)

China Blues
(jazz, nightly)

Cuba Libre
(dancing, Fri & Sat)

Don Pepe
(singing & organist, nightly)

La Finca: *N1*
(rhumba & flamenco, Wed; salsa some Fri)

The Fox Reformed
(wine tastings, backgammon
tournaments, book club)

House on Rosslyn Hill
(karaoke, Mon; live music, Fri & Sat)

Idaho
(jazz, Wed-Sat eves)

The Landmark Hotel
(jazz, Sun L; band & dancing Sat D)

Lola's
(jazz, Sun L)

PizzaExpress: *Kentish Town Rd NW1*
(jazz, Tue & Thu eves)

Troika
(Russian music, Fri & Sat)

Villa Bianca
(guitar, twice weekly)

Weng Wah House
(karaoke, nightly)

Zamoyski
(Russian music, Fri & Sat)

South

Archduke Wine Bar
(jazz, nightly)

Bah Humbug
  (nightly, in adjacent Bug Bar)
Batt. Barge Bistro
  (guitarist, Thu-Sat)
La Bouffe
  (live music, Sun eve)
Café Rouge: *SW15*
  (jazz, Sat & Sun); SW11
  (pianist, Thur; clown, Sun)
La Finca: *SE11*
  (Latin music, Sat)
Ghillies: *SW17*
  (band, Sun eves)
Heather's
  (jazz, first Tue of month)
Hornimans
  (jazz, Sun)
Lawn
  (jazz, Sun pm)
La Mancha
  (guitar, nightly)
Meson don Felipe
  (flamenco guitar, nightly)
Naked Turtle
  (jazz, nightly & Sun L)
PizzaExpress: *SW18*
  (large sports TV)
Le Pont de la Tour Bar &
Grill
  (jazz, nightly)
Rebato's
  (music, Wed-Sat eves)
La Rueda: *SW4*
  (disco, Fri & Sat)
Sash Oriental Bar: *SW4*
  (jazz, nightly)
Tas
  (music, nightly)
Time
  (jazz, Sun & Wed eves)
Willie Gunn
  (jazz pianist, nightly in winter)

East

Al's
  (DJ, Thu-Sat)
Babe Ruth's: *E1*
  (basketball, games area)
Barcelona Tapas: *EC3*
  (magician, regularly; occasional flamenco)
Café du Marché
  (music, nightly)
Cantaloupe
  (DJ's Wed, & Fri-Sun pm)
Dibbens
  (pianist & singer, Fri eves)
Dôme: *EC1*
  (jazz, Fri)
Fuego
  (disco, Tue-Fri)
Pizza Pomodoro: *E1*
  (music, nightly)
Sri Siam City
  (music, Thu eves)
Sri Thai
  (music, Wed)

LATE

**(open till midnight or later as
shown; may be earlier Sunday)**

Central

a.k.a. *(1 am, 11.30 pm Tue-Thu,
  9.30 pm Sun)*

Atlantic Bar & Grill *(bar food until
  2.30 am)*
The Avenue *(midnight, 12.30am Fri
  & Sat, 10pm Sun)*
Balans: *W1 (Mon-Sat 5 am, Sun 1 am)*
Bar Italia *(4 am, Fri & Sat 24 hours)*
Beiteddine
Benihana: *(Fri & Sat only)*
Blues *(Thu-Sat only)*
Boulevard
Brahms
Browns: *WC2*
Café Bohème *(2.45 am, Thu-Sat
  open 24 hours)*
Café de Paris *(10.45 pm (bar 3 am))*
Café du Jardin
Café Emm *(Fri & Sat 12.30 am)*
Café Pasta: *W1*
Caffè Nero: *Frith St W1 (2 am; 4 am,
  Thu-Sun)*
Caffè Uno: *Tottenham Court Rd W1,
  Binney St W1, Argyll St W1, both WC2*
Le Caprice
China Jazz *(midnight, Sun 10 pm)*
Circus *(midnight, Fri & Sat 12.30 am)*
The Criterion *(not Sun)*
Deals: *W1 (Fri & Sat 1 am)*
Denim *(midnight, Sun 10 pm)*
Dover Street *(3 am)*
Ed's Easy Diner: *all central
  branches (midnight, Fri & Sat 1 am)*
Efes Kebab House: *Gt Portland St
  W1 (Fri & Sat 3 am)*
Fakhreldine
Garlic & Shots *(Fri & Sat 12.15 am)*
The Gaucho Grill: *W1 (not Sun)*
Golden Dragon *(Fri & Sat only)*
Goya *(11.30 pm, midnight for tapas)*
Hard Rock Café *(12.30 am, Fri
  & Sat 1 am)*
home (Between Six & Eight)
Hujo's
Ishbilia
The Ivy
Joe Allen *(12.45 am)*
Kettners
Kundan
The Lanesborough
Little Italy *(4 am, Sun midnight)*
Maroush: *W1 (1 am)*
Maxwell's: *WC2*
Melati *(Fri & Sat 12.30 am)*
Mezzo *(Mon-Wed midnight, Thu-Sat
  1 am (crustacea till 3 am))*
Mezzonine *(Mon-Thu 12.45 am, Fri-
  Sat 2.45 am)*
Mirabelle
Mr Chow
Mr Kong *(2.45 am)*
Navajo Joe
New Mayflower *(3.45 am)*
Orso
Le Palais du Jardin
Paparazzi Café: *W1 (5 am)*
Pitcher & Piano: *Dover St
  W1 (3 am, Thu-Sat)*
Pizza On The Park

INDEXES

OUTSIDE TABLES
(* particularly recommended)

INDEXES

Taberna Etrusca*
Tao*
Thon Buri

PRIVATE ROOMS

**(for the most comprehensive
listing of venues for functions –
from palaces to pubs – see
Harden's Mumm Millennium
Party Guide for London, available
in all good bookshops)
* particularly recommended**

Central

INDEXES

Le Pont de la Tour
Le Pont de la Tour B & G
Putney Bridge

East
Aquarium
Brasserie 24
Coq d'Argent
Searcy's Brasserie

VEGETARIAN

Central
Chiang Mai
Cranks
Dorchester Grill
Food for Thought
India Club
The Lanesborough
Malabar Junction
Mandeer
Mildreds
Museum St Café
Neal's Yard Dining Rooms
Ragam
Rasa
Savoy River Restaurant
Woodlands

West
Blah! Blah! Blah!
Blue Elephant
The Gate
Halcyon Hotel
Leith's

North
Chutneys
Diwana Bhel-Poori House
Geeta
Manna
Rani
Rasa
Vijay
Yum Yum

South
Bah Humbug
Escaped Cafe
Heather's
Kastoori
Le Pont de la Tour
Shree Krishna

East
Carnevale
Cranks
Futures *x 2*
The Place Below
Sri Siam City

NOTABLE WINE LISTS

Central
Alastair Little
Andrew Edmunds
Boisdale

Che
Cork & Bottle
1837 at Brown's Hotel
The Fifth Floor
Le Gavroche
Hardy's
Mirabelle
Sartoria
Shampers
The Square
La Tante Claire
Tate Gallery
Teca

West
Bibendum
Clarke's
The Crescent
Hilaire
Leith's
Le Metro
Monkeys
192

North
Odette's

South
Cantinetta Venegazzú
Enoteca Turi
Le Pont de la Tour
Ransome's Dock
RSJ

East
Bleeding Heart
Reynier

CUISINES

An asterisk (*) after an entry indicates exceptional or very good cooking.

BELGIAN

Central
Belgo Centraal *(WC2)*

West
Belgo Zuid *(W10)*

North
Belgo Noord *(NW1)*

East
Abbaye *(EC1)*

BRITISH, MODERN

Central
a.k.a. *(WC1)*
Alastair Little *(W1)*
Alfred *(WC2)*
All Bar One *(W1, WC1, WC2)*
Andrew Edmunds *(W1)*
Atlantic Bar & Grill *(W1)*
Atrium *(SW1)*
Aurora *(W1)*
The Avenue *(SW1)*
Axis *(WC2)*
Bank *(WC2)*
Blues *(W1)*
Boisdale *(SW1)*
Café de Paris *(W1)*
Café du Jardin *(WC2)*
Café Fish *(W1)*
Café Med *(W1)*
Le Caprice *(SW1)*
Che *(SW1)*
Circus *(W1)*
Coast *(W1)*
Cork & Bottle *(WC2)*
Corney & Barrow *(WC2)*
Drones *(SW1)*
Ebury Street Wine Bar *(SW1)*
The Fifth Floor *(SW1)*
French House *(W1)*
Giraffe *(W1)*
Goring Hotel *(SW1)*
Ha Ha *(W1)*
Hodgson's *(WC2)*
Indigo *(WC2)*
The Ivy *(WC2)*
The Lanesborough *(W1)*
Langan's Brasserie *(W1)*
Leith's Soho *(W1)*
The Lexington *(W1)*
Lindsay House *(W1)*
The Little Square *(W1)*
The Marquis *(W1)*
Mash *(W1)*

Mezzo *(W1)*
The Mortimer *(W1)*
Motcombs *(SW1)*
mychi *(WC1)*
Nicole's *(W1)*
Oceana *(W1)*
Opus 70 *(W1)*
Park, Hyde Park Hotel *(SW1)*
Plummers *(WC2)*
Quaglino's *(SW1)*
The Red Room
  Waterstones *(W1)*
Rhodes in the Sq *(SW1)*
Rowley's *(SW1)*
Saint *(WC2)*
Scott's *(W1)*
Shoeless Joe's *(WC2)*
Sotheby's Café *(W1)*
Star Café *(W1)*
Stargazer *(W1)*
Stephen Bull *(W1)*
Stephen Bull *(W1)*
The Sugar Club *(W1)*
Tate Gallery *(SW1)*
Teatro *(W1)*
Titanic *(W1)*
The Union Café *(W1)*
Zinc *(W1)*
Zoe *(W1)*

West
Admiral Codrington *(SW3)*
Alastair Little W11 *(W11)*
All Bar One *(SW10, SW6, SW7, W11, W2, W4)*
The Anglesea Arms *(W6)*
Arcadia *(W8)*
At Last *(SW10)*
Beach
  Blanket Babylon *(W11)*
Belvedere *(W8)*
Bistrot 190 *(SW7)*
Bluebird *(SW3)*
Blythe Road *(W14)*
The Brackenbury *(W6)*
Brinkley's *(SW10)*
Café Med *(SW10, W11, W6)*
The Canteen *(SW10)*
Charco's *(SW3)*
The Chelsea Ram *(SW10)*
Chinon *(W14)*
Chiswick *(W4)*
Clarke's *(W8)*
Coopers Arms *(SW3)*
The Cow *(W11)*
The Crescent *(SW3)*
The Crown *(SW3)*
Dan's *(SW3)*
Deco *(SW10)*
English Garden *(SW3)*

English House (SW3)
First Floor (W11)
The Good Cook (W11)
Goolies (W8)
Halcyon Hotel (W11)*
The Havelock Tavern (W14)*
Hilaire (SW7)*
Joe's Brasserie (SW6)
Joe's Café (SW3)
Julie's (W11)
Kensington Place (W8)
The Ladbroke Arms (W11)
Launceston Place (W8)*
Leith's (W11)*
Mas Café (W11)
Le Metro (SW3)
Min's Bar (SW3)
The Mission (SW6)
Nayab (SW6)*
Newton's (SW6)
192 (W11)
Patio (W12)
The Pen (SW6)
Pharmacy (W11)
The Prince Bonaparte (W2)*
Raoul's Café (W9)
755 (SW6)*
606 Club (SW10)
Snows on the Green (W6)
Stone Mason's Arms (W6)
The Tenth (W8)
The Terrace (W8)*
The Thatched House (W6)
The Vale (W9)*
Vingt-Quatre (SW10)
The Westbourne (W2)
William IV (NW10)*
Wilson's (W14)

North

All Bar One (N1, N6, NW3, NW8)
Blakes (NW1)*
Bradley's (NW3)*
Byron's (NW3)
Café Med (NW8)
The Chapel (NW1)*
Cucina (NW3)
The Duke of Cambridge (N1)
The Engineer (NW1)
Euphorium (N1)*
Frederick's (N1)*
Giraffe (NW3)*
Globe Restaurant (NW3)
Granita (N1)*
Gresslin's (NW3)
Ha Ha (NW1)
Hudson's (NW1)
Jindivick (N1)
Kavanagh's (N1)*
Lansdowne (NW1)

Lola's (N1)
The Lord Palmerston (N19)
Mango Room (NW1)*
Mesclun (N16)*
Odette's (NW1)*
The Queen's (NW1)
Quincy's (NW2)*
The Salt House (NW8)*
The Vine (NW5)

South

All Bar One (SE1, SW11, SW18)
The Apprentice (SE1)*
Archduke Wine Bar (SE1)
Bah Humbug (SW2)
Belair House (SE21)
Blue Print Café (SE1)
The Blue Pumpkin (SW15)
Buchan's (SW11)
Café Med (SW18)
Cantina Vinopolis (SE1)*
The Castle (SW8)
Chapter Two (SE3)
Chez Bruce (SW17)*
The Cook House (SW15)*
The County Hall (SE1)
The Depot (SW14)
Glaisters (SW11)
The Glasshouse (TW1)*
Helter Skelter (SW9)*
The Honest Cabbage (SE1)
Laughing Gravy (SE1)
Lavender (SE1, SE11, SW11, SW9)*
Lawn (SE3)
The Mason's Arms (SW8)*
Mezzanine (SE1)
Moxon's (SW4)*
Naked Turtle (SW14)
The North Pole (SE10)
Oxo Tower (SE1)
The People's Palace (SE1)
Phoenix (SW15)*
Le Pont de la Tour (SE1)
Ransome's Dock (SW11)*
Rapscallion (SW4)
Redmond's (SW14)*
RSJ (SE1)*
Scoffers (SW11)
Shakespeare's Globe (SE1)
Sixty Two (SE1)
Sonny's (SW13)*
The Stable (SW13)
The Stepping Stone (SW8)*
The Sun & Doves (SE5)
Time (SE10)
Waterloo Fire Station (SE1)
White Cross Hotel (TW9)
Willie Gunn (SW18)

East
Al's (EC1)
All Bar One (E14, EC1, EC2, EC3, EC4)
Bar Bourse (EC4)
The Big Chef (E14)
Café Med (EC1)
Cantaloupe (EC2)*
City Brasserie (EC3)
City Rhodes (EC4)*
Dibbens (EC1)
Frocks (E9)
Gladwins (EC3)*
Home (EC1)
1 Lombard Street (EC3)
The Peasant (EC1)
The Poet (EC3)
Prism (EC3)*
Quality Chop House (EC1)
St John (EC1)
Searcy's Brasserie (EC2)
Stephen Bull (EC1)
Vic Naylors (EC1)
Whittington's (EC4)

BRITISH, TRADITIONAL

Central
Claridges Restaurant (W1)
Connaught (W1)
Dorchester Grill (W1)*
Fryer's Delight (WC1)
Green's (SW1)
Greenhouse (W1)
Grenadier (SW1)
The Guinea (W1)*
Lanes (W1)
Odin's (W1)
Porters (WC2)
Rib Room (SW1)
The Ritz (W1)
RK Stanleys (W1)
Rules (WC2)
Savoy Grill (WC2)
Savoy River Restaurant (WC2)
Seafresh (SW1)*
Shepherd's (SW1)
Simpsons-in-the-Strand (WC2)
Star Café (W1)
Wiltons (SW1)*

West
Basil St Hotel (SW3)
Costa's Fish (W8)*
Fat Boy's (W4)
Ffiona's (W8)
Geale's (W8)
Maggie Jones's (W8)*
Monkeys (SW3)
Turner's (SW3)
Veronica's (W2)

Windsor Castle (W8)

North
Nautilus (NW6)*
Seashell (NW1)
Toff's (N10)*
Two Brothers (N3)*
Upper St Fish Shop (N1)*

South
Brady's (SW18)*
Butlers Wharf Chop-
house (SE1)

East
The Bow Wine Vaults (EC4)
Fox & Anchor (EC1)*
George & Vulture (EC3)
Hope & Sir Loin (EC1)*
Ye Olde Cheshire
Cheese (EC4)
Quality Chop House (EC1)
Reynier (EC3)
Simpson's of Cornhill (EC3)
10 (EC2)

DANISH

West
Lundum's (SW7)

EAST & CENTRAL EUROPEAN

Central
Gay Hussar (W1)
St Moritz (W1)*

North
Café Mozart (N6)
Troika (NW1)

EAST/WEST

Central
Asia de Cuba (WC2)
Bam-Bou (W1)
The Birdcage (W1)*
Nobu (W1)*
The Sugar Club (W1)*
Vong (SW1)*

West
Bali Sugar (W11)*
I Thai (W2)
Rain (W10)

FISH & SEAFOOD

Central
Back to Basics (W1)*
Bank (WC2)
Barra (W1)
Belgo Centraal (WC2)

Bentley's *(WI)*
Café Fish *(WI)*
Cave *(WI)**
Fung Shing *(WC2)**
Green's *(SWI)*
Livebait *(WC2)*
Manzi's *(WC2)**
Motcombs *(SWI)*
Le Palais du Jardin *(WC2)*
Quaglino's *(SWI)*
Scott's *(WI)*
J Sheekey *(WC2)**
Wiltons *(SWI)**
Zilli Fish *(WI)**

West
La Belle Epoque *(SW3)*
Bibendum Oyster Bar *(SW3)**
Big Easy *(SW3)*
La Dordogne *(W4)*
Ghillies *(SW6)*
Jason's *(W9)**
Lou Pescadou *(SW5)*
Mandarin Kitchen *(W2)**
Mediterraneo *(WII)**
Offshore *(WII)**
Poissonnerie de
   l'Avenue *(SW3)**
Stratford's *(W8)*
Le Suquet *(SW3)**

North
Belgo Noord *(NWI)*
Bradley's *(NW3)**
Chez Liline *(N4)**

South
Bah Humbug *(SW2)*
fish! *(SEI)**
Ghillies *(SW17)*
Livebait *(SEI)*
Lobster Pot *(SEII)**
Moxon's *(SW4)**
Polygon Bar & Grill *(SW4)*
Le Pont de la Tour Bar &
   Grill *(SEI)**

East
Aquarium *(EI)*
Gow's *(EC2)*
The Grapes *(EI4)*
Rudland & Stubbs *(ECI)*
Sweetings *(EC4)**

FRENCH

Central
L'Artiste Musclé *(WI)*
Beotys *(WC2)*
Boudin Blanc *(WI)*
Café Bohème *(WI)*
Café des Amis du Vin *(WC2)*

Café Flo *(SWI, WI, WC2)*
Café Rouge *(WI, WC2)*
Cave *(WI)**
Chez Gérard *(WI, WC2)*
Chez Nico *(WI)**
Claridges Restaurant *(WI)*
Connaught *(WI)*
The Criterion *(WI)*
1837 at Brown's Hotel *(WI)*
Elena's L'Etoile *(WI)*
L'Escargot *(WI)**
L'Estaminet *(WC2)*
Le Gavroche *(WI)**
Kaspia *(WI)*
Langan's Bistro *(WI)*
Magno's Brasserie *(WC2)*
Mirabelle *(WI)**
Mon Plaisir *(WC2)**
Morton's *(WI)**
Le Muscadet *(WI)*
Nico Central *(WI)*
Oak Room MPW *(WI)**
L'Odéon *(WI)*
Odin's *(WI)*
L'Oranger *(SWI)*
Orrery *(WI)*
Le Palais du Jardin *(WC2)*
Pétrus *(SWI)**
Pied à Terre *(WI)**
La Poule au Pot *(SWI)*
Quo Vadis *(WI)*
Randall & Aubin *(WI)*
Rest. One-O-One *(SWI)**
The Ritz *(WI)*
Roussillon *(SWI)**
Savoy River Restaurant *(WC2)*
Simply Nico *(SWI)*
Le Soufflé *(WI)*
The Square *(WI)**
La Tante Claire *(SWI)**
Terrace *(WI)*
Townhouse Brasserie *(WCI)*
Villandry *(WI)*
Windows on the World *(WI)*

West
The Abingdon *(W8)*
Amandier *(W2)*
Aubergine *(SW10)**
La Belle Epoque *(SW3)*
Bibendum *(SW3)*
La Bouchée *(SW7)*
Brass. du Marché *(W10)*
La Brasserie *(SW3)*
Brasserie St Quentin *(SW3)*
Café Flo *(SW3, SW6, SW7, W8)*
Café Rouge *(SW3, SW6, SW7, W11,
   W2, W4, W6, W8, W9)*
Capital Hotel *(SW3)*
Chez Gérard *(SW3)*

Chez Moi *(W11)*
Chezmax *(SW10)**
Chinon *(W14)**
Christian's *(W4)*
Le Colombier *(SW3)*
La Dordogne *(W4)*
Emile's *(SW6)*
Francofill *(SW7)*
Gordon Ramsay *(SW3)**
Icon *(SW3)*
Langan's Coq d'Or *(SW5)*
Lou Pescadou *(SW5)*
Monkeys *(SW3)**
Novelli W8 *(W8)*
Pelham Street *(SW7)*
Poissonnerie de
l'Avenue *(SW3)**
6 Clarendon Rd *(W11)*
Stratford's *(W8)*
Le Suquet *(SW3)**
Thierry's *(SW3)*
Turner's *(SW3)*

North
Les Associés *(N8)*
L'Aventure *(NW8)**
Café Delancey *(NW1)*
Café Flo *(N1, NW3)*
Café Rouge *(N6, NW1, NW3, NW8)*
La Cage Imaginaire *(NW3)*
Camden Brasserie *(NW1)*
Le Mercury *(N1)*
Mims *(EN4)*
Oslo Court *(NW8)**
Paris-London Café *(N19)*
Le Sacré-Coeur *(N1)*
Soulard *(N1)**
Village Bistro *(N6)*
The White Onion *(N1)**

South
Le Bouchon Bordelais *(SW11)*
La Bouffe *(SW11)*
Café de la Place *(SW11)*
Café Rouge *(SE1, SW11, SW14, SW15, SW4)*
Emile's *(SW15)*
Gastro *(SW4)*
Le Gothique *(SW18)*
Lobster Pot *(SE11)**
Monsieur Max *(TW12)**
Newton's *(SW4)*
Le P'tit Normand *(SW18)*
Putney Bridge *(SW15)*
Simply Nico *(SE1)*
Le Versailles *(SW9)*

East
Bleeding Heart *(EC1)**
Bubb's *(EC1)*
Café du Marché *(EC1)**
Café Flo *(EC4)*

Café Rouge *(E14, EC4)*
Chez Gérard *(EC1, EC2, EC3)*
Club Gascon *(EC1)**
Coq d'Argent *(EC3)*
Luc's Brasserie *(EC3)**
Maison Novelli *(EC1)*
Novelli EC1 *(EC1)*
Saigon Times *(EC3)*
Simply Nico *(EC1)*

GAME

Central
Dorchester Grill *(W1)**
The Marquis *(W1)*
Rules *(WC2)*
Wiltons *(SW1)**

West
Monkeys *(SW3)**

GREEK

Central
Beotys *(WC2)*
Jimmy's *(W1)*

West
Costa's Grill *(W8)*
Halepi *(W2)*
Kalamaras *(W2)*

North
Daphne *(NW1)*
Halepi *(NW3)*
Lemonia *(NW1)*
The Real Greek *(N1)**
Retsina *(NW1)*
Vrisaki *(N22)**

South
Beyoglu *(SW11)*

HUNGARIAN

Central
Gay Hussar *(W1)*

North
Café Mozart *(N6)*

ITALIAN

Central
Al Duca *(SW1)**
Bertorelli's *(W1, WC2)*
Bice *(W1)*
Buona Sera *(W1)*
Café Pasta *(W1, WC2)*
Caffè Uno *(W1, WC2)*
Caldesi *(W1)*
La Capannina *(W1)*
Caraffini *(SW1)**
Cecconi's *(W1)*

Como Lario *(SW1)*
Il Convivio *(SW1)*
Denim *(WC2)*
Diverso *(W1)**
La Fontana *(SW1)*
Grissini *(SW1)**
The Halkin *(SW1)*
Ibla *(W1)*
L'Incontro *(SW1)*
Isola *(SW1)*
Italian Kitchen *(WC1)*
Little Italy *(W1)*
Luigi's *(WC2)*
Luna Nuova *(WC2)*
Maggiore's *(WC2)*
Mimmo d'Ischia *(SW1)*
Neal Street *(WC2)*
Oliveto *(SW1)*
Olivo *(SW1)*
Orso *(WC2)*
Paparazzi Café *(W1)*
Passione *(W1)**
Pollo *(W1)*
Purple Sage *(W1)*
Ristorante Italiano *(W1)*
Sale e Pepe *(SW1)*
Santini *(SW1)*
Sartoria *(W1)*
Signor Sassi *(SW1)*
La Spiga *(W1)*
La Spighetta *(W1)*
Teca *(W1)*
Toto's *(SW1)**
Uno *(SW1)*
Vasco & Piero's Pavilion *(W1)*
Il Vicolo *(SW1)**
Zafferano *(SW1)**
Zilli Fish *(W1)**

West
L'Accento Italiano *(W2)*
Aglio e Olio *(SW10)**
Al San Vincenzo *(W2)**
Assaggi *(W2)**
Bersagliera *(SW3)*
Café Milan *(SW3)*
Café Pasta *(W4, W8)*
Caffè Uno *(SW6, W2, W4, W8)*
Calzone *(SW10, SW3, W11)*
La Candela *(W8)*
Cibo *(W14)**
Da Mario *(SW7)*
Daphne's *(SW3)*
De Cecco *(SW6)*
La Delizia *(SW3, SW5)*
Elistano *(SW3)**
Il Falconiere *(SW7)*
La Famiglia *(SW10)*
Floriana *(SW3)**
Formula Veneta *(SW10)*

Grano *(W4)**
The Green Olive *(W9)**
I Thai *(W2)*
King's Road Café *(SW3)*
Leonardo's *(SW10)*
Luigi's Delicatessen *(SW10)**
Made in Italy *(SW3)**
Mona Lisa *(SW10)*
Montpeliano *(SW7)*
Monza *(SW3)*
Olio & Farina *(SW3)*
Orsino *(W11)*
Osteria Basilico *(W11)**
Palatino *(W4)*
Palio *(W11)*
Paparazzi Café *(SW3)*
Picasso *(SW3)*
Il Portico *(W8)*
The Red Pepper *(W9)**
Riccardo's *(SW3)*
Riso *(W4)*
The River Café *(W6)**
Sambuca *(SW3)*
San Lorenzo *(SW3)*
San Martino *(SW3)*
Sandrini *(SW3)*
Scalini *(SW3)**
Spago *(SW7)*
Ziani *(SW3)*
Zucca *(W11)*

North
Artigiano *(NW3)*
The Black Truffle *(NW1)*
La Brocca *(NW6)*
Café Pasta *(N1, NW3)*
Caffè Uno *(N1, N6, NW1, NW8)*
Calzone *(N1, NW3)*
Cantina Italia *(N1)**
Casale Franco *(N1)*
Florians *(N8)*
Maremma *(N1)*
Marine Ices *(NW3)*
The Park *(NW6)*
La Porchetta Pizzeria *(N4)**
San Carlo *(N6)*
San Daniele *(N5)*
Vegia Zena *(NW1)**
Villa Bianca *(NW3)*

South
Antipasto & Pasta *(SW11)*
Arancia *(SE16)**
Bellinis *(W13)*
Buona Sera *(SW11)*
Café Pasta *(SW15)*
Caffè Uno *(SW13)*
Cantina del Ponte *(SE1)*
Cantinetta Venegazzú *(SW11)*
Del Buongustaio *(SW15)**
Eco *(SW4)**

Eco Brixton (SW9)*
Enoteca Turi (SW15)*
La Lanterna (SE1)
Metrogusto (SW8)*
Ost. Antica Bologna (SW11)
Pepe Nero (SW11)
Pizzeria Castello (SE1)*
Prego (TW9)
Riva (SW13)*
Tentazioni (SE1)*
Tuba (SW4)*

East
Alba (EC1)*
Caravaggio (EC3)
Gt Eastern Dining Rm (EC2)*
Taberna Etrusca (EC4)

IRISH

Central
O'Conor Don (W1)

MEDITERRANEAN

Central
Drones (SW1)
Fifth Floor (Café) (SW1)
Frith St (W1)
Hujo's (W1)
Indigo (W1)
Mezzonine (W1)
Soho Soho (W1)
Tiger Tiger (SW1)
Zoe (W1)

West
The Atlas (SW6)*
Brompton Bay (SW3)
Cross Keys (SW3)
Made in Italy (SW3)*
Mediterraneo (W11)*
Palio (W11)

North
Centuria (N1)

South
Newton's (SW4)
Oxo Tower (SE1)

East
The Eagle (EC1)*

ORGANIC

North
The Duke of Cambridge (N1)
Sauce (NW1)

POLISH

West
Daquise (SW7)
The Polish Club (SW7)
Wódka (W8)

North
Café Mozart (N6)
Zamoyski (NW3)

PORTUGESE

South
Café Portugal (SW8)*

RUSSIAN

Central
FireBird (W1)
Kaspia (W1)

West
Nikita's (SW10)

North
Troika (NW1)

SCANDINAVIAN

West
Lundum's (SW7)

North
Anna's Place (N1)

STEAKS & GRILLS

Central
Café Coq (WC2)
Chez Gérard (W1, WC2)
Christopher's (WC2)
The Gaucho Grill (W1)*
The Guinea (W1)*
Kettners (W1)
prospectGrill (WC2)
Quaglino's (SW1)
Rib Room (SW1)
Smollensky's (WC2)
Soho Soho (W1)
Wolfe's (WC2)

West
Chez Gérard (SW3)
El Gaucho (SW3)
Popeseye (W14)*
Rôtisserie (W12)
Rôtisserie Jules (SW3, SW7, W11)

North
Camden Brasserie (NW1)
Gaucho Grill (NW3)*
Rôtisserie (N1)

South
Polygon Bar & Grill (SW4)
Le Pont de la Tour Bar & Grill (SE1)*
Popeseye (SW15)*

East
Arkansas Café *(E1)*
Chez Gérard *(EC1, EC2)*
Fox & Anchor *(EC1)**
Gaucho Grill *(EC3)**
Hope & Sir Loin *(EC1)**
Simpson's of Cornhill *(EC3)*
Smiths of Smithfield *(EC1)*

SPANISH

Central
Goya *(SW1)*
La Rueda *(W1)*

West
Cambio de Tercio *(SW5)*
Galicia *(W10)*
Lomo *(SW10)*
La Rueda *(SW6)*

North
Bar Gansa *(NW1)**
Don Pepe *(NW8)*
La Finca *(N1)*

South
Barcelona Tapas *(SE22)*
don Fernando's *(TW9)*
La Finca *(SE11)*
La Mancha *(SW15)*
Meson don Felipe *(SE1)*
Rebato's *(SW8)*
La Rueda *(SW4)*

East
Barcelona Tapas *(E1, EC3)*
Fuego *(EC3)*
Gaudi *(EC1)*
Moro *(EC1)**

SWISS

Central
St Moritz *(W1)**

INTERNATIONAL

Central
Alphabet *(W1)**
Balans *(W1)*
Boulevard *(WC2)*
Brahms *(SW1)*
Browns *(W1, WC2)*
Café Emm *(W1)*
Deals *(W1)*
Dôme *(W1, WC2)*
Dover Street *(W1)*
Footstool *(SW1)*
Garlic & Shots *(W1)*
Gordon's Wine Bar *(WC2)*
Grumbles *(SW1)*
Hanover Square *(W1)*

Hardy's *(W1)**
Lanes *(W1)*
Lunch *(WC2)**
Marché Mövenpick *(SW1)*
Oriel *(SW1)*
Philip Owens *(SW1)*
Pitcher & Piano *(W1, WC2)*
PJ's *(WC2)*
Pomegranates *(SW1)*
Sarastro *(WC2)*
Shampers *(W1)*
Stock Pot *(SW1, W1)*
Vendôme *(W1)*
The Waldorf Meridien *(WC2)*

West
Balans *(SW3)*
Balans West *(SW5)*
Blakes Hotel *(SW7)*
Browns *(SW3)*
Café Grove *(W11)*
Café Laville *(W2)*
Chelsea Bun Diner *(SW10)*
Chelsea Kitchen *(SW3)*
The Collection *(SW3)*
Conrad Hotel *(SW10)**
Coopers Arms *(SW3)*
Deals *(SW10, W6)*
Dôme *(SW3, SW5, W8)*
The Enterprise *(SW3)*
Foxtrot Oscar *(SW3)*
Front Page *(SW3)*
The Gasworks *(SW6)*
Glaisters *(SW10)*
Julie's Bar *(W11)*
Mackintosh's Brasserie *(W4)*
Pitcher & Piano *(SW10, SW3, SW6, W4)*
PJ's *(SW3)*
The Scarsdale *(W8)*
Sporting Page *(SW10)*
Stock Pot *(SW3)*
Windsor Castle *(W8)*
Wine Gallery *(SW10)*
Wiz *(W11)*

North
Angel of the North *(N1)*
Banners *(N8)*
Dôme *(N1, NW3)*
The Fox Reformed *(N16)*
Hot John's *(N1)*
House on Rosslyn Hill *(NW3)*
The Landmark Hotel *(NW1)*
The Little Bay *(NW6)*
Pitcher & Piano *(N1)*
PJ's *(NW3)*
Sauce *(NW1)*
Shoreditch ES *(N1)*
Toast *(NW3)*

South

Alma *(SW18)*
Batt. Barge Bistro *(SW8)*
Delfina Studio Café *(SE1)*
Escaped Cafe *(SE10)*
Glaisters *(SW13)*
Heather's *(SE8)*
Hornimans *(SW4)*
Naked Turtle *(SW14)*
Pitcher & Piano *(SW11, SW12, SW17)*
The Ship *(SW18)*

East

Brasserie 24 *(EC2)*
Brasserie Rocque *(EC2)*
Dôme *(EC1, EC4)*
Lunch *(EC1)**
Mustards Brasserie *(EC1)*
Pitcher & Piano *(EC3)*

AFTERNOON TEA

Central

Aurora *(W1)*
Fifth Floor (Café) *(SW1)*
The Lanesborough *(W1)*
Park, Hyde Park Hotel *(SW1)*
Villandry *(W1)*
The Waldorf Meridien *(WC2)*

West

Basil St Hotel *(SW3)*
Daquise *(SW7)*
Julie's Bar *(W11)*

BURGERS, ETC

Central

Deals *(W1)*
Ed's Easy Diner *(W1)*
Hard Rock Café *(W1)*
Joe Allen *(WC2)*
Luigi Malones *(WC2)*
Planet Hollywood *(W1)*
Radio Café *(WC2)*
The Rainforest Cafe *(W1)*
Tootsies *(W1)*
Wolfe's *(WC2)*

West

Big Easy *(SW3)*
Deals *(SW10, W6)*
Ed's Easy Diner *(SW3)*
Foxtrot Oscar *(SW3)*
Luigi Malones *(SW7)*
Sticky Fingers *(W8)*
Tootsies *(SW6, SW7, W11, W4)*

North

Ed's Easy Diner *(NW3)*
Tootsies *(NW3)*

South

Tootsies *(SW13)*

East

Arkansas Café *(E1)*
Babe Ruth's *(E1)*

FISH & CHIPS

Central

Fryer's Delight *(WC1)*
Seafresh *(SW1)**

West

Costa's Fish *(W8)**
Geale's *(W8)*

North

Nautilus *(NW6)**
Seashell *(NW1)*
Toff's *(N10)**
Two Brothers *(N3)**
Upper St Fish Shop *(N1)**

South

Brady's *(SW18)**

East

Faulkner's *(E8)**

ICE CREAM

North

Marine Ices *(NW3)*

PIZZA

Central

Ask! Pizza *(SW1, W1)*
Buona Sera *(W1)*
Gourmet Pizza Co. *(W1)*
It's *(W1, WC1)*
Kettners *(W1)*
Luna Nuova *(WC2)*
Mash *(W1)*
Oliveto *(SW1)*
Paparazzi Café *(W1)*
Pizza On The Park *(SW1)*
Pizza Pomodoro *(W1)*
PizzaExpress *(SW1, W1, WC1, WC2)*
Pizzeria Condotti *(W1)*
La Spiga *(W1)*

West

Ask! Pizza *(SW6, SW7, W11, W2, W4, W8)*
Basilico *(SW6)**
Calzone *(SW10, SW3, W11)*
Da Mario *(SW7)*
La Delizia *(SW3, SW5)*
Friends *(SW10)*
It's *(W11, W2, W4)*
Paparazzi Café *(SW3)*
Pizza Pomodoro *(SW3)*

Pizza the Action (SW6)
PizzaExpress (SW10, SW3, SW6, WII, WI4, W2, W4, W8)
Pucci Pizza (SW3)
Spago (SW7)

North
Ask! Pizza (NI, NW3)
La Brocca (NW6)
Calzone (NI, NW3)
Cantina Italia (NI)*
Casale Franco (NI)
It's (NWI)
Marine Ices (NW3)
PizzaExpress (NI, N6, NWI, NW3, NW8)
La Porchetta Pizzeria (N4)*

South
Basilico (SWII)*
Bellinis (SWI3)
Buona Sera (SWII)
Eco (SW4)*
Eco Brixton (SW9)*
Gourmet Pizza Co. (SEI)
Pizza Metro (SWII)*
PizzaExpress (SEI, SWII, SWI4, SWI5, SWI8, SW4)
Pizzeria Castello (SEI)*

East
Ask! Pizza (ECI)
Gourmet Pizza Co. (EI4)
Pizza Pomodoro (EI)
PizzaExpress (EC2, EC4)

SANDWICHES, CAKES, ETC

Central
Bar Italia (WI)
Caffè Nero (WI, WC2)*
Chunk (WC2)
Coffee Republic (WI, WC2)
Eat (SWI, WI, WC2)
Maison Bertaux (WI)*
Pâtisserie Valerie (WI, WC2)*
Pret A Manger (SWI, WI, WCI, WC2)
Richoux (WI)
Starbucks (SWI, WI, WC2)

West
Café Grove (WII)
Caffè Nero (SW7, WII, W6)*
Coffee Republic (SW10, SW3, SW7, WII, W2, W4)
Coins (WII)
Fileric (SW7)
King's Road Café (SW3)
Lisboa Patisserie (WI0)*
Pâtisserie Valerie (SW3)*
Pret A Manger (SW3, W6, W8)
Richoux (SW3)
Le Shop (SW3)

Starbucks (SW3, SW5, SW6, SW7, WII, W2, W8)
Tom's (WI0)
Troubadour (SW5)

North
Caffè Nero (NWI, NW3)*
Pret A Manger (NI, NWI)
Richoux (NW3)
Starbucks (NW8)

South
Boiled Egg (SWII)
Fileric (SW8)
Starbucks (SWII, SW4)

East
Brick Lane Beigel Bake (EI)*
Caffè Nero (EC2)*
Coffee Republic (ECI, EC2, EC3, EC4)
Eat (EC2, EC3, EC4)*
Pret A Manger (ECI, EC2, EC4)
Starbucks (ECI, EC2, EC3, EC4)

SOUP

Central
Chunk (WC2)
Soup Opera (WI)*
Soup Works (WI, WC2)*

East
Soup Opera (EI4)*

VEGETARIAN

Central
Chiang Mai (WI)*
Cranks (WI, WC2)
Dorchester Grill (WI)*
Food for Thought (WC2)*
India Club (WC2)
The Lanesborough (WI)
Malabar Junction (WCI)*
Mandeer (WCI)
Mildreds (WI)
Neal's Yard (WC2)
Ragam (WI)
Rasa (WI)*
Savoy River Restaurant (WC2)
Woodlands (SWI, WI)

West
Blah! Blah! Blah! (WI2)*
Blue Elephant (SW6)*
The Gate (W6)*
Halcyon Hotel (WII)*
Leith's (WII)*

North
Chutneys *(NW1)*
Diwana B-P House *(NW1)**
Geeta *(NW6)**
Manna *(NW3)*
Rani *(N3)*
Rasa *(N16)**
Vijay *(NW6)**
Yum Yum *(N16)**

South
Bah Humbug *(SW2)*
Escaped Cafe *(SE10)*
Heather's *(SE8)*
Kastoori *(SW17)**
Le Pont de la Tour *(SE1)*
Shree Krishna *(SW17)**

East
Carnevale *(EC1)**
Cranks *(E14)*
Futures *(EC2)*
Futures *(EC3)**
The Place Below *(EC2)**
Sri Siam City *(EC2)**

AMERICAN

Central
Christopher's *(WC2)*
Joe Allen *(WC2)*
Maxwell's *(WC2)*
Navajo Joe *(WC2)*
Planet Hollywood *(W1)*
Smollensky's *(WC2)*
TGI Friday's *(W1, WC2)*

West
Big Easy *(SW3)*
Chicago Rib Shack *(SW7)*
Dakota *(W11)*
Montana *(SW6)*
Shoeless Joe's *(SW6)*
TGI Friday's *(W2)*

North
Babe Ruth's *(NW3)*
Idaho *(N6)*
Maxwell's *(NW3)*
Santa Fe *(N1)*

South
Canyon *(TW10)*

East
Arkansas Café *(E1)*
Babe Ruth's *(E1)*

ARGENTINIAN

Central
The Gaucho Grill *(W1)**

North
Gaucho Grill *(NW3)**

South
La Pampa *(SW11)**

BRAZILIAN

West
Paulo's *(W6)*

CUBAN

North
Cuba Libre *(N1)*

MEXICAN/TEXMEX

Central
Café Pacifico *(WC2)*
Down Mexico Way *(W1)*
La Perla *(WC2)*
Texas Embassy Cantina *(SW1)*

West
Coyote Café *(W4)*
La Perla *(SW6)*
Texas Lone Star *(SW7)*

South
Dixie's Bar & Grill *(SW11)*

East
Al's *(EC1)*

SOUTH AMERICAN

Central
Havana *(W1)*
Little Havana *(WC2)*

West
Cactus Blue *(SW3)*
El Gaucho *(SW3)*
Havana *(SW6)*

North
La Piragua *(N1)**

South
Fina Estampa *(SE1)*

AFRO-CARIBBEAN

Central
Calabash *(WC2)*

North
Cottons *(NW1)*
Mango Room *(NW1)**

NORTH AFRICAN

Central
Ayoush *(W1)*
Momo *(W1)*
Oceana *(W1)*
Souk *(WC2)*
Tajine *(W1)**

West
Adams Café *(W12)*
Pasha *(SW7)*

North
Angel of the North *(N1)*
Laurent *(NW2)**
Yima *(NW1)**

East
Moro *(EC1)**

SOUTH AFRICAN

West
Springbok Café *(W4)**

SUDANESE

West
Mandola *(W11)*

TUNISIAN

Central
Ayoush *(W1)*

West
Adams Café *(W12)*

North
Laurent *(NW2)**

ISRAELI

North
Solly's Exclusive *(NW11)*

KOSHER

Central
Reubens *(W1)*

North
Nautilus *(NW6)**
Solly's Exclusive *(NW11)*

LEBANESE

Central
Al Bustan *(SW1)*
Al Hamra *(W1)**
Al Sultan *(W1)**
Beiteddine *(SW1)*
Fairuz *(W1)**
Fakhreldine *(W1)*
Ishbilia *(SW1)*
Maroush *(W1)**

West
Beirut Express *(W2)**
Maroush *(SW3, W2)**
Phoenicia *(W8)*
Ranoush *(W2)**

MIDDLE EASTERN

East
Midi *(EC1)*
Moro *(EC1)**

PERSIAN

West
Alounak *(W14, W2)**
Mohsen *(W14)**
Yas *(W14)*

TURKISH

Central
Efes Kebab House *(W1)*
Sofra *(W1, WC2)*

North
Gallipoli *(N1)**
Istanbul Iskembecisi *(N16)**
Iznik *(N5)**
Pasha *(N1)*
Sarcan *(N1)*

South
Beyoglu *(SW11)*
Tas *(SE1)**

AFGHANI

Central
Caravan Serai *(W1)*

North
Afghan Kitchen *(N1)**

BURMESE

West
Mandalay *(W2)**

CHINESE

Central
Aroma II *(W1)*
China City *(WC2)*
China House *(W1)*
China Jazz *(W1)*
Chuen Cheng Ku *(W1)*
Dorchester, Oriental *(W1)*
Fung Shing *(WC2)**
Golden Dragon *(W1)**
Harbour City *(W1)**
Hunan *(SW1)**
Jenny Lo's *(SW1)*
Joy King Lau *(W1)**
Ken Lo's Memories *(SW1)**
Mekong *(SW1)*
Mr Chow *(SW1)*
Mr Kong *(WC2)**
New Mayflower *(W1)**

New World *(W1)*
Poons *(WC2)*
Poons, Lisle Street *(WC2)*
Royal China *(W1)**
Wong Kei *(W1)*
Zen Central *(W1)*
Zen Garden *(W1)*

West
Good Earth *(SW3)*
Ken Lo's Memories *(W8)**
Mandarin Kitchen *(W2)**
Mao Tai *(SW6)**
Mr Wing *(SW5)**
Nanking *(W6)**
New Culture Rev'n *(SW3, W11)*
Royal China *(W2)**
Zen *(SW3)**

North
Cheng Du *(NW1)*
China Blues *(NW1)*
Feng Shang *(NW1)**
Gung-Ho *(NW6)**
New Culture Rev'n *(N1, NW1)*
Royal China *(NW8)**
Singapore Garden *(NW6)*
Weng Wah House *(NW3)*
ZeNW3 *(NW3)**

South
Four Regions *(SE1)**
Royal China *(SW15)**

East
Imperial City *(EC3)*
Shanghai *(E8)*

CHINESE, DIM SUM

Central
Chuen Cheng Ku *(W1)*
Dorchester, Oriental *(W1)*
Golden Dragon *(W1)**
Harbour City *(W1)**
Joy King Lau *(W1)**
New World *(W1)*
Royal China *(W1)**
Zen Central *(W1)*
Zen Garden *(W1)*

West
Royal China *(W2)**
Zen *(SW3)**

North
Royal China *(NW8)**

South
Royal China *(SW15)**

East
Shanghai *(E8)*

FRENCH-VIETNAMESE

Central
Bam-Bou *(W1)*

GEORGIAN

North
Tbilisi *(N7)**

INDIAN

Central
Café Lazeez *(W1)*
Chor Bizarre *(W1)*
Gopal's of Soho *(W1)**
India Club *(WC2)*
Kundan *(SW1)**
Malabar Junction *(WC1)**
Mandeer *(WC1)*
Pimlico Tandoori *(SW1)*
La Porte des Indes *(W1)*
Quilon *(SW1)*
Ragam *(W1)*
Rasa *(W1)**
Rasa Samudra *(W1)*
Red Fort *(W1)*
Salloos *(SW1)**
Soho Spice *(W1)*
Tamarind *(W1)**
Veeraswamy *(W1)*
Woodlands *(SW1, W1)*

West
Anarkali *(W6)**
Bombay Brasserie *(SW7)**
Bombay Palace *(W2)**
Brilliant *(UB2)**
Café Lazeez *(SW7)*
Chutney Mary *(SW10)**
Khan's *(W2)*
Khan's of Kensington *(SW7)**
Khyber Pass *(SW7)**
Madhu's Brilliant *(UB1)**
Malabar *(W8)**
Memories of India *(SW7)**
Nayab *(SW6)**
Noor Jahan *(SW5)**
Saffron *(SW10)*
Standard Tandoori *(W2)*
Star of India *(SW5)**
Tandoori Lane *(SW6)**
Tandoori of Chelsea *(SW3)**
Vama *(SW10)**
Zaika *(SW3)**

North
Anglo Asian Tandoori *(N16)**
Chutneys *(NW1)*
Diwana B-P House *(NW1)**
Geeta *(NW6)**
Great Nepalese *(NW1)*

Rani *(N3)*
Rasa *(N16)**
Vijay *(NW6)**

South
Babur Brasserie *(SE23)**
Battersea Rickshaw *(SW11)*
Bengal Clipper *(SE1)**
Bombay Bicycle Club *(SW12)**
Café Spice Namaste *(SW11)**
Haweli *(SW13)**
Indian Ocean *(SW17)**
Kastoori *(SW17)**
Ma Goa *(SW15)**
Pukkabar *(SE26)*
Sarkhel's *(SW18)**
Shree Krishna *(SW17)**
3 Monkeys *(SE24)**

East
Café City Lazeez *(EC1)*
Café Indiya *(E1)**
Café Spice Namaste *(E1)**
Lahore Kebab House *(E1)**
Rupee Room *(EC2)*
Shimla Pinks *(EC2)*

INDIAN, SOUTHERN

Central
India Club *(WC2)*
Malabar Junction *(WC1)**
Mandeer *(WC1)*
Ragam *(W1)*
Woodlands *(SW1, W1)*

North
Chutneys *(NW1)*
Diwana B-P House *(NW1)**
Geeta *(NW6)**
Rani *(N3)*
Rasa *(N16)**
Vijay *(NW6)**

South
Kastoori *(SW17)**
Shree Krishna *(SW17)**

INDONESIAN

Central
Melati *(W1)**

South
Nancy Lam's Enak
 Enak *(SW11)*

JAPANESE

Central
Benihana *(W1)*
Defune *(W1)**
Gili Gulu *(WC2)*
Ikeda *(W1)**

Ikkyu *(W1, WC2)**
Japanese Canteen *(W1)*
Kulu Kulu *(W1)**
Matsuri *(SW1)**
Mitsukoshi *(SW1)**
Miyama *(W1)**
Nobu *(W1)**
Satsuma *(W1)*
Shogun *(W1)**
Suntory *(SW1)*
Tokyo Diner *(WC2)*
Wagamama *(W1, WC1)*
Yo! Sushi *(W1)*
Yoshino *(W1)**

West
Bar Japan *(SW5)*
Benihana *(SW3)*
Inaho *(W2)**
Itsu *(SW3)*
Japanese Canteen *(W10)*
Latitude *(SW3)*
Sushi Wong *(W8)*
Wagamama *(W8)*

North
Benihana *(NW3)*
Bu San *(N7)*
Café Japan *(NW11)**
Jin Kichi *(NW3)**
Sushi-Say *(NW2)**
Wagamama *(NW1)*
Wakaba *(NW3)**

East
Aykoku-Kaku *(EC4)*
City Miyama *(EC4)**
Japanese Canteen *(EC1)*
Moshi Moshi Sushi *(E14, EC2, EC4)**
Noto *(EC2, EC4)*
Tatsuso *(EC2)**

KOREAN

Central
Kaya Korean *(W1)*

North
Bu San *(N7)*

MALAYSIAN

Central
Melati *(W1)**

West
Street Hawker *(W9)*

North
Café de Maya *(NW3)*
Singapore Garden *(NW6)*
Street Hawker *(NW6)*

East
Café Spice Namaste (E1)*
Singapura (EC3, EC4)

PAN-ASIAN

Central
China House (W1)
home (Between Six
  & Eight) (W1)
Mezzonine (W1)
Mongolian Barbecue (WC2)
Wok Wok (W1)

West
Bonjour Vietnam (SW6)
Jim Thompson's (SW6)
Mongolian Barbecue (SW7, W4)
Sash (SW6)
Southeast (W9)*
Tiger Lil's (SW3)
Wok Wok (SW10, W8)

North
Oriental City (NW9)
Tiger Lil's (N1)
Wok Wok (N1)

South
Nancy Lam's Enak
  Enak (SW11)
Sash Oriental Bar (SW4)
Tiger Lil's (SW4)
Wok Wok (SW11)

East
Cicada (EC1)
East One (EC1)
Moorgate Oriental (EC2)
Pacific Oriental (EC2)
Pacific Spice (EC1)
Suan-Neo (EC2)
Tao (EC4)
Yellow River Café (E14)

THAI

Central
Bangkok Brasserie (SW1)
Blue Jade (SW1)
Chiang Mai (W1)*
Manorom (WC2)
Noho (W1)
Silks & Spice (W1)
Sri Siam (W1)*
Thai Pot (W1)
Thai Pot Express (WC2)
Thai Square (SW1)

West
Bangkok (SW7)*
Bedlington Café (W4)
Ben's Thai (W9)

Blue Elephant (SW6)*
Busabong Too (SW10)
Busabong Tree (SW10)*
Café 209 (SW6)
Churchill Arms (W8)*
Esarn Kheaw (W12)*
Fat Boy's (W4)
I Thai (W2)
Krungtap (SW10)
Latymers (W6)*
The Papaya Tree (W8)
S&P Patara (SW3)*
Sabai Sabai (W6)*
Sash (SW6)
Silks & Spice (W4)
Street Hawker (W9)
Tawana (W2)*
Thai Bistro (W4)*
Thai Break (W8)*
Thai on the River (SW10)
Topsy-Tasty (W4)
Tui (SW7)*

North
Café de Maya (NW3)
Noho (NW3)
Silks & Spice (NW1)
Street Hawker (NW6)
Tuk Tuk (N1)
Yum Yum (N16)*

South
Chada (SW11)*
Kwan Thai (SE1)
Newton's (SW4)
The Old School Thai (SW11)*
The Pepper Tree (SW4)*
Phuket (SW11)
Thailand (SE14)*

East
Silks & Spice (EC4)
Sri Siam City (EC2)*
Sri Thai (EC4)
Thon Buri (EC2)

TIBETAN

Central
Tibetan Restaurant (WC2)

VIETNAMESE

Central
Mekong (SW1)

West
Nam Long (SW5)

East
Saigon Times (EC3)

AREA OVERVIEWS

CENTRAL

Soho, Covent Garden & Bloomsbury
(Parts of W1, all WC2 and WC1)

£60+	Savoy Grill	British, Traditional	③②②
	Savoy River Restaurant	French	④②②
£50+	Café de Paris	British, Modern	⑤⑤④
	Asia de Cuba	East/West	③④❶
	Neal Street	Italian	③④④
	The Waldorf Meridien	Afternoon tea	④③②
£40+	Alastair Little	British, Modern	③③④
	Atlantic Bar & Grill	"	⑤⑤③
	Axis	"	③②③
	Bank	"	④④④
	Circus	"	④④④
	Indigo	"	③②③
	The Ivy	"	❷❶❶
	Leith's Soho	"	③③④
	Lindsay House	"	❶❶②
	Mezzo	"	⑤⑤⑤
	The Sugar Club	"	❷③③
	Teatro	"	③④④
	Rules	British, Traditional	③③②
	Simpsons-in-the-Strand	"	④③②
	Livebait	Fish & seafood	③④⑤
	J Sheekey	"	❷❷③
	Zilli Fish	"	❷③③
	Beotys	French	⑤③④
	The Criterion	"	③⑤❶
	L'Escargot	"	❷❷❷
	Quo Vadis	"	③④③
	Luigi's	Italian	④④④
	Christopher's	American	④③③
	Kaya Korean	Korean	④③⑤
	home (Btwn Six & Eight)	Pan-Asian	— — —
£35+	Café du Jardin	British, Modern	③④③
	Stephen Bull	"	③③⑤
	Titanic	"	⑤⑤⑤
	Manzi's	Fish & seafood	❷③③
	Café des Amis du Vin	French	④③③
	L'Estaminet	"	④④④
	Magno's Brasserie	"	⑤④④
	Le Palais du Jardin	"	③④②
	Denim	Italian	⑤④④
	Little Italy	"	④②②
	Orso	"	④④③

Vasco & Piero's Pavilion	Italian		③①④
Frith St	Mediterranean		③②③
PJ's	International		④④③
Red Fort	Indian		③③④
£30+	Belgo Centraal	Belgian	⑤④③
	a.k.a.	British, Modern	③②②
	Alfred	"	②③④
	Andrew Edmunds	"	③③①
	Blues	"	③③①
	French House	"	②②②
	Hodgson's	"	④③③
	The Lexington	"	④③③
	mychi	"	④③⑤
	Saint	"	⑤⑤②
	Shoeless Joe's	"	④④④
	Barra	Fish & seafood	③④④
	Chez Gérard	French	④③③
	Mon Plaisir	"	②①①
	Gay Hussar	Hungarian	④①②
	Bertorelli's	Italian	④③④
	La Capannina	"	④②④
	Luna Nuova	"	④③③
	Maggiore's	"	④④④
	St Moritz	Swiss	②③③
	Browns	International	④④③
	Planet Hollywood	Burgers, etc	⑤④②
	The Rainforest Cafe	"	⑤④①
	La Spiga	Pizza	③④④
	Corney & Barrow	British, Modern	③②③
	Joe Allen	American	④③②
	Smollensky's	"	④③③
	TGI Friday's	"	④③③
	Little Havana	South American	⑤⑤③
	Fung Shing	Chinese	①④⑤
	Café Lazeez	Indian	③③②
	Mezzonine	Pan-Asian	⑤⑤⑤
	Chiang Mai	Thai	①④⑤
	Sri Siam	"	②③④
£25+	All Bar One	British, Modern	④④④
	Aurora	"	④④③
	Café Med	"	④④③
	Cork & Bottle	"	④④②
	Plummers	"	— — —
	Café Bohème	French	④④①
	Café Flo	"	⑤⑤④
	Café Rouge	"	⑤⑤⑤
	Randall & Aubin	"	③④②
	Townhouse Brasserie	"	③②④

	Name	Cuisine	Ratings
	Buona Sera	Italian	③④②
	Italian Kitchen	"	③③③
	Hujo's	Mediterranean	④①④
	Indigo	"	③④③
	Soho Soho	"	④④③
	prospectGrill	Steaks & grills	③②③
	Alphabet	International	②④①
	Balans	"	④②②
	Boulevard	"	③③③
	Deals	"	⑤⑤⑤
	Garlic & Shots	"	④④③
	Sarastro	"	⑤④①
	Shampers	"	④③②
	Radio Café	Burgers, etc	⑤⑤④
	Wolfe's	"	③④④
	Maxwell's	American	⑤④④
	Navajo Joe	"	⑤⑤③
	Café Pacifico	Mexican/TexMex	④④③
	La Perla	"	③②③
	Sofra	Turkish	④④④
	Aroma II	Chinese	④③④
	China City	"	③④④
	Chuen Cheng Ku	"	③④④
	Harbour City	"	②⑤⑤
	New Mayflower	"	②④④
	Gopal's of Soho	Indian	②④④
	Malabar Junction	"	②③②
	Soho Spice	"	③③②
	Wok Wok	Pan-Asian	④③④
	Thai Pot	Thai	③④④
	Thai Pot Express	"	③④④
£20+	Luigi Malones	Burgers, etc	⑤④④
	Star Café	British, Modern	③③③
	Porters	British, Traditional	④②④
	Café Pasta	Italian	④③④
	Caffè Uno	"	⑤④④
	Café Coq	Steaks & grills	④④④
	Café Emm	International	③④③
	Dôme	"	⑤⑤③
	Pitcher & Piano	"	④④②
	Ed's Easy Diner	Burgers, etc	③③②
	Kettners	Pizza	⑤④②
	Pâtisserie Valerie	Sandwiches, cakes, etc	②②②
	Mildreds	Vegetarian	③④④
	Calabash	Afro-Caribbean	③④⑤
	Souk	North African	④④②
	Golden Dragon	Chinese	②④③
	Joy King Lau	"	②③④
	Mr Kong	"	②③④

			Ratings
	New World	*Chinese*	③④③
	Poons	"	③⑤⑤
	Poons, Lisle Street	"	③④⑤
	Ikkyu	*Japanese*	②③③
	Satsuma	"	③③②
	Yo! Sushi	"	③②②
	Melati	*Malaysian*	②④④
	Mongolian Barbecue	*Pan-Asian*	⑤⑤⑤
	Manorom	*Thai*	③③④
£15+	Jimmy's	*Greek*	④②③
	Gordon's Wine Bar	*International*	④②①
	Lunch	"	②②④
	It's	*Pizza*	③②③
	PizzaExpress	"	③③③
	Food for Thought	*Vegetarian*	②④③
	Wong Kei	*Chinese*	④⑤④
	India Club	*Indian*	③②④
	Gili Gulu	*Japanese*	⑤⑤④
	Kulu Kulu	"	②③④
	Tokyo Diner	"	④②④
	Wagamama	"	③③③
	Tibetan Restaurant	*Tibetan*	④②③
£10+	Pollo	*Italian*	④④③
	Stock Pot	*International*	④④④
	Caffè Nero	*Sandwiches, cakes, etc*	②③③
	Cranks	*Vegetarian*	④④④
	Neal's Yard	"	③②④
£5+	Fryer's Delight	*Fish & chips*	③③④
	Bar Italia	*Sandwiches, cakes, etc*	③③①
	Coffee Republic	"	③②②
	Eat	"	②③③
	Maison Bertaux	"	②③③
	Pret A Manger	"	③①③
	Starbucks	"	③②②
	Chunk	*Soup*	③③④
	Soup Works	"	①②⑤

Mayfair & St James's
(Parts of W1 and SW1)

£100+	Oak Room MPW	*French*	②④④
£90+	Le Gavroche	*French*	①①③
£80+	Chez Nico	*French*	②③④
£70+	Connaught	*British, Traditional*	③①②

	Claridges Restaurant	*French*	④❸❷
	1837 at Brown's Hotel	"	④④❸
	The Ritz	"	④❷❶
	Windows on the World	"	⑤④❶
	Dorchester, Oriental	*Chinese*	❸❷④
	Suntory	*Japanese*	❸④④
£60+	The Square	*French*	❶❷❸
	Cecconi's	*Italian*	⑤⑤⑤
	Mitsukoshi	*Japanese*	❶❷⑤
£50+	Che	*British, Modern*	④④④
	The Lanesborough	"	④❷❶
	Dorchester Grill	*British, Traditional*	❷❶❶
	Green's	"	④❸❸
	Wiltons	"	❷❷❷
	Nobu	*East/West*	❶❷❷
	Bentley's	*Fish & seafood*	❸④❸
	L'Odéon	*French*	⑤⑤④
	Le Soufflé	"	❸❷④
	Sartoria	*Italian*	④❸❸
	China Jazz	*Chinese*	⑤⑤⑤
	Zen Central	"	❸④④
	Ikeda	*Japanese*	❷❷④
	Miyama	"	❷❸⑤
	Shogun	"	❶❶❸
£40+	The Avenue	*British, Modern*	④④❸
	Le Caprice	"	❷❶❶
	Coast	"	④④④
	Langan's Brasserie	"	④❸❷
	Nicole's	"	❸❸❸
	Opus 70	"	④❸④
	Rhodes in the Sq	"	❷❶❷
	Rowley's	"	⑤⑤④
	Scott's	"	❸❸❸
	Greenhouse	*British, Traditional*	❸❷❷
	Cave	*French*	❷❸❸
	Mirabelle	"	❷❷❷
	Morton's	"	❷❷❷
	L'Oranger	"	❸❸❸
	Pétrus	"	❶❷❸
	Diverso	*Italian*	❷❸④
	Teca	"	❸④⑤
	FireBird	*Russian*	– – –
	Kaspia	"	❸❷❸
	The Guinea	*Steaks & grills*	❷④❸
	Dover Street	*International*	⑤⑤④
	Lanes	"	⑤④⑤

	Reubens	*Kosher*	④④④
	Zen Garden	*Chinese*	❸❸④
	Quilon	*Indian*	– – –
	Tamarind	*"*	❶❷❷
	Benihana	*Japanese*	❸❸❸
	Matsuri	*"*	❶❷❸
£35+	Quaglino's	*British, Modern*	④④④
	The Red Room	*"*	– – –
	Terrace	*French*	④❷❸
	Bice	*Italian*	④❸④
	The Gaucho Grill	*Steaks & grills*	❷④❸
	Vendôme	*International*	④❸❸
	Momo	*North African*	④④❶
	Al Hamra	*Lebanese*	❷④④
	Al Sultan	*"*	❷❷④
	Fakhreldine	*"*	❸❸④
	China House	*Chinese*	– – –
	Chor Bizarre	*Indian*	❸❷❷
	Veeraswamy	*"*	❸④④
£30+	The Marquis	*British, Modern*	❸❷④
	Sotheby's Café	*"*	❷❶❷
	Zinc	*"*	⑤⑤④
	Café Fish	*Fish & seafood*	❸❸④
	Boudin Blanc	*French*	– – –
	Chez Gérard	*"*	④❸❸
	Al Duca	*Italian*	❷❸❸
	Paparazzi Café	*"*	④④❸
	Ristorante Italiano	*"*	④❸④
	Il Vicolo	*"*	❷❷④
	Browns	*International*	④④❸
	Thai Square	*Thai*	❸❷④
£25+	All Bar One	*British, Modern*	④④④
	The Little Square	*"*	④❸④
	Café Flo	*French*	⑤⑤④
	Tiger Tiger	*Mediterranean*	⑤④❸
	Hanover Square	*International*	④④④
	Hard Rock Café	*Burgers, etc*	④❸❷
	Gourmet Pizza Co.	*Pizza*	❸④④
	Richoux	*Sandwiches, cakes, etc*	❸④❸
	Down Mexico Way	*Mexican/TexMex*	⑤④❶
	Havana	*South American*	⑤④❸
	Sofra	*Turkish*	④④④
	Rasa	*Indian*	❶❷❸
	Yoshino	*Japanese*	❷❸④
	Bangkok Brasserie	*Thai*	❸④❸
	Thai Pot	*"*	❸④④
£20+	L'Artiste Musclé	*French*	④❸❷

	Caffè Uno	*Italian*	⑤④④
	Pitcher & Piano	*International*	④④❷
	Ask! Pizza	*Pizza*	④❸❷
	Pizzeria Condotti	"	❸❷❷
	Woodlands	*Indian*	④❸④
£15+	It's	*Pizza*	❸❷❸
	PizzaExpress	"	❸❸❸
£10+	Stock Pot	*International*	④④④
£5+	Coffee Republic	*Sandwiches, cakes, etc*	❸❷❷
	Eat	"	❷❸❸
	Pret A Manger	"	❸❶❸
	Starbucks	"	❸❷❷
	Soup Opera	*Soup*	❷❷❸

Fitzrovia & Marylebone
(Part of W1)

£50+	The Birdcage	*East/West*	❷❸❶
	Orrery	*French*	④❸④
	Pied à Terre	"	❶❷❸
£40+	Mash	*British, Modern*	⑤⑤④
	Bam-Bou	*French-Vietnamese*	⑤④❸
	La Porte des Indes	*Indian*	❸❸❷
	Defune	*Japanese*	❷❸⑤
£35+	Stephen Bull	*British, Modern*	❷❷❸
	Zoe	"	⑤④⑤
	Back to Basics	*Fish & seafood*	❶❸⑤
	Elena's L'Etoile	*French*	❸❶❷
	Le Muscadet	"	④④④
	Nico Central	"	❸④⑤
	Odin's	"	❸❶❶
	Villandry	"	❸⑤④
	Ibla	*Italian*	❸④④
	Ayoush	*North African*	❸❸❷
	Maroush	*Lebanese*	❷④④
	Rasa Samudra	*Indian*	❸❷④
£30+	Oceana	*British, Modern*	④❸④
	The Union Café	"	④④④
	Langan's Bistro	*French*	④❸❸
	Bertorelli's	*Italian*	④❸④
	Caldesi	"	❸❷④
	Passione	"	❷❷❸
	Purple Sage	"	❸❸❸
	La Spighetta	"	❸④⑤

			Ratings
	O'Conor Don	Irish	④❸❸
	Hardy's	International	❷❷❸
	Fairuz	Lebanese	❷❸④
£25+	All Bar One	British, Modern	④④④
	Ha Ha	"	❸❸④
	The Mortimer	"	❷④④
	Stargazer	"	④❸❸
	RK Stanleys	British, Traditional	④④④
	Café Flo	French	⑤⑤④
	Café Rouge	"	⑤⑤⑤
	La Rueda	Spanish	④❸❸
	Tajine	North African	❷❸⑤
	Sofra	Turkish	④④④
	Caravan Serai	Afghani	④❸⑤
	Royal China	Chinese	❶④④
£20+	Giraffe	British, Modern	❷❷❶
	Caffè Uno	Italian	⑤④④
	Tootsies	Burgers, etc	④❸❸
	Ask! Pizza	Pizza	④❸❷
	Pizza Pomodoro	"	④④❷
	Pâtisserie Valerie	Sandwiches, cakes, etc	❷❷❷
	Efes Kebab House	Turkish	④❷❷
	Mandeer	Indian	❸④④
	Ragam	"	❸❸⑤
	Woodlands	"	④❸④
	Ikkyu	Japanese	❷❸❸
	Japanese Canteen	"	⑤⑤⑤
	Noho	Thai	④④④
	Silks & Spice	"	❸❸❸
£15+	PizzaExpress	Pizza	❸❸❸
	Wagamama	Japanese	❸❸❸
£10+	Stock Pot	International	④④④
	Caffè Nero	Sandwiches, cakes, etc	❷❸❸
	Cranks	Vegetarian	④④④
£5+	Pret A Manger	Sandwiches, cakes, etc	❸❶❸
	Starbucks	"	❸❷❷
	Soup Works	Soup	❶❷⑤

Belgravia, Victoria & Pimlico (SW1, except St James's)

£80+	La Tante Claire	French	❷❸④
£60+	The Halkin	Italian	❸④④
	Isola	"	— — —

Price	Restaurant	Cuisine	Ratings
£50+	The Fifth Floor	British, Modern	④❸❸
	Restaurant One-O-One	French	❷❸❸
	L'Incontro	Italian	④❸④
	Santini	''	④④❸
	Rib Room	Steaks & grills	— — —
£40+	Boisdale	British, Modern	❸❸❷
	Goring Hotel	''	④❶❷
	Tate Gallery	''	④❷❷
	Vong	East/West	❷❸❸
	Roussillon	French	❷❸④
	Il Convivio	Italian	— — —
	Grissini	''	❷❷❸
	Mimmo d'Ischia	''	④❸❷
	Signor Sassi	''	❸❷❷
	Toto's	''	❷❷❷
	Zafferano	''	❶❶❷
	Park, Hyde Pk Hotel	Afternoon tea	❸❸④
	Al Bustan	Lebanese	❸❷④
	Ken Lo's Memories	Chinese	❷❷④
	Mr Chow	''	❸❸④
	Salloos	Indian	❷❸④
£35+	Atrium	British, Modern	⑤⑤④
	Drones	''	④❸④
	Motcombs	''	❸❷❷
	Grenadier	British, Traditional	❸④❷
	Shepherd's	''	❸❷❷
	La Poule au Pot	French	❸❸❶
	Simply Nico	''	❸❸④
	Como Lario	Italian	④❸❸
	La Fontana	''	❸❷❸
	Olivo	''	❸❸④
	Sale e Pepe	''	④❸❷
	Fifth Floor (Café)	Mediterranean	❸❸❷
	Pomegranates	International	④④④
£30+	Ebury Street Wine Bar	British, Modern	④❸❸
	Caraffini	Italian	❷❶❷
	Uno	''	❸❷④
	Goya	Spanish	④④❷
	Footstool	International	⑤④❸
	Oriel	''	⑤⑤❷
	Oliveto	Pizza	❸❸④
	Beiteddine	Lebanese	❸❸④
	Kundan	Indian	❷❷⑤
£25+	Grumbles	International	⑤④④
	Texas Embassy Cantina	Mexican/TexMex	⑤⑤④
	Ishbilia	Lebanese	❸❷④
	Hunan	Chinese	❶❷④

£20+	Marché Mövenpick	*International*	④④④
	Philip Owens	*"*	④④❸
	Seafresh	*Fish & chips*	❷❸④
	Ask! Pizza	*Pizza*	④❸❷
	Pizza On The Park	*"*	④❸❷
	Blue Jade	*Thai*	❸❸④
£15+	Brahms	*International*	❸④④
	PizzaExpress	*Pizza*	❸❸❸
	Jenny Lo's	*Chinese*	❸❷④
	Pimlico Tandoori	*Indian*	❸❷❸
	Mekong	*Vietnamese*	❸④④
£5+	Pret A Manger	*Sandwiches, cakes, etc*	❸❶❸
	Starbucks	*"*	❸❷❷

WEST

**Chelsea, South Kensington,
Kensington, Earl's Court & Fulham
(SW3, SW5, SW6, SW7, SW10 & W8)**

£80+	Blakes Hotel	International	4 4 1
£70+	Capital Hotel	French	3 2 3
£60+	Gordon Ramsay	"	1 2 3
£50+	Hilaire	British, Modern	2 2 2
	Aubergine	French	1 1 2
	Bibendum	"	3 3 2
	Turner's	"	3 3 4
	Floriana	Italian	2 4 3
	San Lorenzo	"	5 5 2
£40+	Belvedere	British, Modern	3 3 2
	Bluebird	"	5 4 3
	Clarke's	"	1 1 2
	English Garden	"	3 1 2
	English House	"	5 3 3
	Joe's Café	"	3 3 2
	Launceston Place	"	2 1 1
	The Tenth	"	3 2 2
	The Terrace	"	2 1 2
	Poissonnerie de l'Avenue	Fish & seafood	2 2 3
	La Belle Epoque	French	5 5 5
	Chezmax	"	1 1 2
	Icon	"	3 3 3
	Langan's Coq d'Or	"	4 3 3
	Monkeys	"	1 1 2
	Le Suquet	"	2 3 3
	Daphne's	Italian	4 4 2
	La Famiglia	"	3 4 3
	Montpeliano	"	4 3 3
	San Martino	"	4 3 3
	Scalini	"	2 2 2
	The Collection	International	4 5 3
	Conrad Hotel	"	2 2 3
	Pasha	North African	4 3 1
	Mr Wing	Chinese	2 2 1
	Zen	"	2 3 4
	Bombay Brasserie	Indian	2 3 2
	Chutney Mary	"	2 3 3
	Tandoori of Chelsea	"	2 2 4
	Benihana	Japanese	3 3 3
	Blue Elephant	Thai	2 2 1

Price	Name	Cuisine	Ratings
£35+	Arcadia	British, Modern	④④❸
	Bistrot 190	"	④④④
	The Canteen	"	❷❷❷
	Dan's	"	④❸❷
	Goolies	"	❸❷❸
	Kensington Place	"	❸❸❷
	Min's Bar	"	④❸❷
	755	"	❶❷④
	606 Club	"	⑤④❷
	Stratford's	Fish & seafood	❸❸④
	Brasserie St Quentin	French	④❷❷
	Le Colombier	"	❸❸❷
	Lou Pescadou	"	❸❸❸
	Novelli W8	"	④④⑤
	Café Milan	Italian	④④❸
	La Candela	"	④❷④
	Monza	"	❸❷❷
	Il Portico	"	④❷❸
	Sambuca	"	④❷④
	Sandrini	"	❸❸④
	Ziani	"	❸❸❷
	Nikita's	Russian	⑤④④
	PJ's	International	④④❸
	Montana	American	❸❸❷
	Maroush	Lebanese	❷④④
	Ken Lo's Memories	Chinese	❷❷④
	Mao Tai	"	❷❷❷
	Star of India	Indian	❷④❸
	Vama	"	❶❷❸
	Zaika	"	❶❷❸
£30+	Admiral Codrington	British, Modern	❸❸❷
	Charco's	"	④❸④
	Joe's Brasserie	"	④④❸
	The Pen	"	❸❸❸
	Basil St Hotel	British, Traditional	❸❷❸
	Maggie Jones's	"	④❸❶
	Lundum's	Danish	❸❶❸
	Bibendum Oyster Bar	Fish & seafood	❷❷❷
	Ghillies	"	❸❸❸
	The Abingdon	French	❸❸❸
	La Brasserie	"	④④❷
	Chez Gérard	"	④❸❸
	Pelham Street	"	④❸⑤
	Thierry's	"	④④❷
	De Cecco	Italian	❸❷❷
	Formula Veneta	"	❸❷❷
	Leonardo's	"	❸❷❸
	Paparazzi Café	"	④④❸
	Cross Keys	Mediterranean	④❸❷

	Name	Cuisine	Ratings
	Wódka	Polish	④④❸
	Cambio de Tercio	Spanish	❸②②
	Browns	International	④④❸
	The Enterprise	"	④❸②
	Big Easy	American	④❸②
	Shoeless Joe's	"	④④④
	Cactus Blue	South American	④④❷
	Phoenicia	Lebanese	❸②④
	Good Earth	Chinese	❸②④
	Café Lazeez	Indian	❸❸②
	Latitude	Japanese	⑤④❸
	Busabong Too	Thai	❸④④
	Busabong Tree	"	❷❷❸
	S&P	"	❷❸④
	S&P Patara	"	❷❸④
	Thai on the River	"	❸❸②
	Nam Long	Vietnamese	④④❷
£25+	All Bar One	British, Modern	④④④
	At Last	"	❸❸❸
	Brinkley's	"	④❸②
	Café Med	"	④④❸
	The Chelsea Ram	"	❷④②
	The Crown	"	❷❸④
	Le Metro	"	❸❸②
	The Mission	"	❸②❸
	Newton's	"	⑤④④
	Vingt-Quatre	"	❸②④
	Ffiona's	British, Traditional	❸②②
	La Bouchée	French	④⑤❷
	Café Flo	"	⑤⑤④
	Café Rouge	"	⑤⑤⑤
	Francofill	"	④❸④
	Bersagliera	Italian	④❸❸
	Da Mario	"	④❸④
	Elistano	"	❷❷❷
	Il Falconiere	"	❸②④
	Luigi's Delicatessen	"	❷⑤④
	Made in Italy	"	❷④❸
	Olio & Farina	"	④④❸
	Riccardo's	"	❸④❸
	Brompton Bay	Mediterranean	❸②❸
	The Polish Club	Polish	④❷❷
	La Rueda	Spanish	④❸❸
	Balans	International	④❷❷
	Balans West	"	④❷❷
	Deals	"	⑤⑤⑤
	Foxtrot Oscar	"	④④④
	Front Page	"	❸④❸
	The Gasworks	"	⑤④❶

			Ratings
Glaisters	International		④④❸
The Scarsdale	"		④④❷
Windsor Castle	"		❸④❶
Basilico	Pizza		❷❸④
Friends	"		❸④❷
Richoux	Sandwiches, cakes, etc		❸④❸
Troubadour	"		❸④❶
Chicago Rib Shack	American		④④④
La Perla	Mexican/TexMex		❸❷❸
El Gaucho	South American		❸④❸
Havana	"		⑤④❸
Nayab	Indian		❷❸⑤
Noor Jahan	"		❷❷④
Saffron	"		❸④④
Itsu	Japanese		❸❸❸
Sushi Wong	"		❸❶⑤
Jim Thompson's	Pan-Asian		④④❷
Tiger Lil's	"		⑤⑤④
Wok Wok	"		④❸④
Bangkok	Thai		❷④④
The Papaya Tree	"		❸④❸
Thai Break	"		❷❸④
Tui	"		❶❸④
£20+ The Crescent	British, Modern		④❷❷
Deco	"		❸❸❸
Emile's	French		❸❷❸
Aglio e Olio	Italian		❷❸❸
Café Pasta	"		④❸④
Caffè Uno	"		⑤④④
Calzone	"		④④④
King's Road Café	"		④④❸
Picasso	"		④④❸
Spago	"		❸④❸
The Atlas	Mediterranean		❷❷❷
Daquise	Polish		④④❸
Rôtisserie Jules	Steaks & grills		❸❶⑤
Lomo	Spanish		❸❷❷
Coopers Arms	International		❸④❷
Dôme	"		⑤⑤❸
Pitcher & Piano	"		④④❷
Sporting Page	"		④④❷
Wine Gallery	"		④⑤❷
Ed's Easy Diner	Burgers, etc		❸❸❷
Luigi Malones	"		⑤④④
Sticky Fingers	"		④❷❷
Tootsies	"		④❸❸
Geale's	Fish & chips		❸❸④
Ask! Pizza	Pizza		④❸❷
La Delizia	"		❸④④

	Pizza Pomodoro	*Pizza*	④④②
	Pizza the Action	"	④❸④
	Pucci Pizza	"	❸④❶
	Pâtisserie Valerie	*Sandwiches, cakes, etc*	❷❷❷
	Le Shop	"	❸❸❷
	Texas Lone Star	*Mexican/TexMex*	⑤④④
	New Culture Rev'n	*Chinese*	④❸④
	Khan's of Kensington	*Indian*	❷❷❸
	Khyber Pass	"	❷❸⑤
	Malabar	"	❷❷❷
	Memories of India	"	❷❷❸
	Tandoori Lane	"	❷❶❸
	Bar Japan	*Japanese*	❸❸④
	Bonjour Vietnam	*Pan-Asian*	⑤④④
	Mongolian Barbecue	"	⑤⑤⑤
	Krungtap	*Thai*	④❷④
£15+	Chelsea Bun Diner	*International*	❸④❸
	Costa's Fish	*Fish & chips*	❷❶④
	PizzaExpress	*Pizza*	❸❸❸
	Wagamama	*Japanese*	❸❸❸
	Café 209	*Thai*	❸❶❸
	Churchill Arms	"	❷④❸
£10+	Costa's Grill	*Greek*	④❸❸
	Mona Lisa	*Italian*	❸❸④
	Chelsea Kitchen	*International*	④❸④
	Stock Pot	"	④④④
	Caffè Nero	*Sandwiches, cakes, etc*	❷❸❸
£5+	Coffee Republic	*Sandwiches, cakes, etc*	❸❷❷
	Fileric	"	❸❸④
	Pret A Manger	"	❸❶❸
	Starbucks	"	❸❷❷

Notting Hill, Holland Park, Bayswater, North Kensington & Maida Vale (W2, W9, W10, W11)

£80+	I Thai	*East/West*	④⑤❸
£60+	Halcyon Hotel	*British, Modern*	❷❸❸
£40+	Julie's	*British, Modern*	④④❶
	Leith's	"	❷❶❷
	Pharmacy	"	⑤④④
	Bali Sugar	*East/West*	❷❷❸
	Offshore	*Fish & seafood*	❷❸④
	Amandier	*French*	❸❸④
	Chez Moi	"	❸❶❷

	Al San Vincenzo	*Italian*	②②④
	Assaggi	"	①①②
	Orsino	"	④④②
£35+	Alastair Little	*British, Modern*	③③④
	Beach Blanket Babylon	"	⑤④①
	First Floor	"	⑤⑤④
	192	"	④④③
	Rain	*East/West*	④④③
	Jason's	*Fish & seafood*	②②①
	Zucca	*Italian*	④④④
	Dakota	*American*	④④②
	Maroush	*Lebanese*	②④④
£30+	Belgo Zuid	*Belgian*	⑤④③
	The Cow	*British, Modern*	③③③
	Mas Café	"	④④②
	Veronica's	*British, Traditional*	③②②
	6 Clarendon Rd	*French*	③④④
	Halepi	*Greek*	③③②
	The Green Olive	*Italian*	②①②
	Osteria Basilico	"	②③①
	Palio	"	⑤⑤④
	Mediterraneo	*Mediterranean*	②①②
	Julie's Bar	*International*	④②①
	TGI Friday's	*American*	④③③
	Bombay Palace	*Indian*	②②②
£25+	All Bar One	*British, Modern*	④④④
	Café Med	"	④④③
	Raoul's Café	"	③④③
	The Vale	"	②①④
	Brass. du Marché	*French*	③②②
	Café Rouge	"	⑤⑤⑤
	L'Accento Italiano	*Italian*	③②③
	The Red Pepper	"	②④③
	Café Laville	*International*	⑤④②
	Wiz	"	④③②
	Coins	*Sandwiches, cakes, etc*	③④②
	Mandarin Kitchen	*Chinese*	①④⑤
	Royal China	"	①④④
	Inaho	*Japanese*	①③④
£20+	The Good Cook	*British, Modern*	④⑤⑤
	The Ladbroke Arms	"	③③②
	The Prince Bonaparte	"	②③②
	The Westbourne	"	④⑤①
	Kalamaras	*Greek*	③②③
	Caffè Uno	*Italian*	⑤④④
	Calzone	"	④④④

	Rôtisserie Jules	*Steaks & grills*	③①⑤
	Galicia	*Spanish*	③④③
	Café Grove	*International*	④④②
	Tootsies	*Burgers, etc*	④③③
	Ask! Pizza	*Pizza*	④③②
	Tom's	*Sandwiches, cakes, etc*	③④③
	Mandola	*Sudanese*	③④②
	Alounak	*Persian*	①③③
	New Culture Rev'n	*Chinese*	④③④
	Standard Tandoori	*Indian*	③④④
	Japanese Canteen	*Japanese*	⑤⑤⑤
	Southeast	*Pan-Asian*	②③③
	Ben's Thai	*Thai*	③③④
	Tawana	*"*	②④④
£15+	It's	*Pizza*	③②③
	PizzaExpress	*"*	③③③
	Beirut Express	*Lebanese*	②④④
	Ranoush	*"*	①④③
	Mandalay	*Burmese*	②①④
	Khan's	*Indian*	③⑤③
	Street Hawker	*Thai*	③③③
£10+	Caffè Nero	*Sandwiches, cakes, etc*	②③③
£5+	Coffee Republic	*Sandwiches, cakes, etc*	③②②
	Lisboa Patisserie	*"*	①②④
	Starbucks	*"*	③②②

Hammersmith, Shepherd's Bush Chiswick & Olympia (W4, W5, W6, W12, W14)

£50+	The River Café	*Italian*	②③③
£40+	Cibo	*Italian*	②③③
	Grano	*"*	②②③
£35+	Chiswick	*British, Modern*	②③④
	Chinon	*French*	②④④
£30+	Blythe Road	*British, Modern*	③④③
	The Brackenbury	*"*	②③③
	Snows on the Green	*"*	④④④
	Wilson's	*"*	③①③
	Christian's	*French*	③③③
	La Dordogne	*"*	③②②
	Palatino	*Italian*	③③④
	Riso	*"*	— — —
	Springbok Café	*South African*	②①③

£25+	All Bar One	British, Modern	④④④
	The Anglesea Arms	"	❶⑤❸
	Café Med	"	④④❸
	The Havelock Tavern	"	❶④❷
	Stone Mason's Arms	"	❸④❸
	Café Rouge	French	⑤⑤⑤
	Popeseye	Steaks & grills	❷❷⑤
	Rôtisserie	"	❸❷④
	Deals	International	⑤⑤⑤
	Mackintosh's Brasserie	"	④④❸
	The Gate	Vegetarian	❶❷❷
	Paulo's	Brazilian	❸❷④
	Coyote Café	Mexican/TexMex	❸❸❸
	Yas	Persian	❸⑤④
	Nanking	Chinese	❷❷❸
	Anarkali	Indian	❷❸④
	Fat Boy's	Thai	❸❷④
£20+	The Thatched House	British, Modern	❸❷❷
	Café Pasta	Italian	④❸④
	Caffè Uno	"	⑤④④
	Pitcher & Piano	International	④④❷
	Tootsies	Burgers, etc	④❸❸
	Ask! Pizza	Pizza	④❸❷
	Blah! Blah! Blah!	Vegetarian	❷❸❷
	Adams Café	North African	❸❷④
	Alounak	Persian	❶❸❸
	Brilliant	Indian	❷❷④
	Madhu's Brilliant	"	❷❷④
	Mongolian Barbecue	Pan-Asian	⑤⑤⑤
	Esarn Kheaw	Thai	❷⑤④
	Latymers	"	❷❷④
	Sabai Sabai	"	❷❷④
	Silks & Spice	"	❸❸❸
	Thai Bistro	"	❷❷④
	Topsy-Tasty	"	❸④⑤
£15+	Patio	British, Modern	④❸❷
	It's	Pizza	❸❷❸
	PizzaExpress	"	❸❸❸
	Mohsen	Persian	❷④⑤
	Bedlington Café	Thai	❸④⑤
£10+	Caffè Nero	Sandwiches, cakes, etc	❷❸❸
£5+	Coffee Republic	Sandwiches, cakes, etc	❸❷❷
	Pret A Manger	"	❸❶❸

NORTH

**Hampstead, West Hampstead, St John's Wood,
Regent's Park, Kilburn & Camden Town
(NW postcodes)**

£50+	The Landmark Hotel	*International*	(4)(3)(2)
£40+	Bradley's	*British, Modern*	(2)(2)(3)
	Villa Bianca	*Italian*	(4)(3)(2)
	Benihana	*Japanese*	(3)(3)(3)
£35+	Byron's	*British, Modern*	(4)(4)(3)
	The Engineer	*"*	(3)(4)(2)
	Gresslin's	*"*	(4)(4)(5)
	Odette's	*"*	(2)(2)(1)
	L'Aventure	*French*	(1)(2)(1)
	Oslo Court	*"*	(1)(1)(3)
	Artigiano	*Italian*	(4)(4)(4)
	Gaucho Grill	*Steaks & grills*	(2)(4)(3)
	PJ's	*International*	(4)(4)(3)
	Toast	*"*	(4)(3)(3)
	China Blues	*Chinese*	(4)(4)(3)
	ZeNW3	*"*	(2)(2)(3)
	Wakaba	*Japanese*	(2)(3)(5)
£30+	Belgo Noord	*Belgian*	(5)(4)(3)
	Blakes	*British, Modern*	(2)(5)(3)
	Globe Restaurant	*"*	(3)(2)(3)
	Hudson's	*"*	(4)(3)(2)
	Quincy's	*"*	(2)(1)(3)
	The Vine	*"*	(3)(3)(3)
	Mims	*French*	(3)(5)(5)
	Halepi	*Greek*	(3)(3)(2)
	House on Rosslyn Hill	*International*	(4)(4)(2)
	Babe Ruth's	*American*	(4)(4)(3)
	Solly's Exclusive	*Israeli*	(3)(4)(3)
	Cheng Du	*Chinese*	(3)(3)(3)
	Feng Shang	*"*	(2)(3)(3)
	Sushi-Say	*Japanese*	(2)(3)(5)
	Singapore Garden	*Malaysian*	(3)(3)(4)
£25+	All Bar One	*British, Modern*	(4)(4)(4)
	Café Med	*"*	(4)(4)(3)
	The Chapel	*"*	(2)(4)(3)
	Cucina	*"*	(3)(3)(4)
	Ha Ha	*"*	(3)(3)(4)
	Lansdowne	*"*	(3)(4)(2)
	The Queen's	*"*	(3)(4)(2)
	The Salt House	*"*	(2)(2)(3)
	William IV	*"*	(2)(2)(2)

	Café Delancey	*French*	④④④
	Café Flo	*"*	⑤⑤④
	Café Rouge	*"*	⑤⑤⑤
	La Cage Imaginaire	*"*	④❸❸
	Camden Brasserie	*"*	❸②②
	Lemonia	*Greek*	④❶②
	The Black Truffle	*Italian*	– – –
	La Brocca	*"*	❸❸②
	The Park	*"*	❸④②
	Vegia Zena	*"*	❷❷❸
	Sauce	*Organic*	❸❸❸
	Don Pepe	*Spanish*	❸❸❸
	Richoux	*Sandwiches, cakes, etc*	❸④❸
	Manna	*Vegetarian*	❸④④
	Maxwell's	*American*	⑤④④
	Cottons	*Afro-Caribbean*	④❸②
	Mango Room	*"*	❷❸❶
	Gung-Ho	*Chinese*	❷❸❸
	Royal China	*"*	❶④④
£20+	Giraffe	*British, Modern*	❷❷❶
	Daphne	*Greek*	❸❸❸
	Café Pasta	*Italian*	④❸④
	Caffè Uno	*"*	⑤④④
	Calzone	*"*	④④④
	Marine Ices	*"*	④❸❸
	Zamoyski	*Polish*	④④❸
	Troika	*Russian*	④❸❸
	Dôme	*International*	⑤⑤❸
	Ed's Easy Diner	*Burgers, etc*	❸❸②
	Tootsies	*"*	④❸❸
	Nautilus	*Fish & chips*	❶❸④
	Seashell	*"*	❸④⑤
	Ask! Pizza	*Pizza*	④❸②
	Laurent	*Tunisian*	❷❷⑤
	New Culture Revolution	*Chinese*	④❸④
	Weng Wah House	*"*	❸❷❸
	Vijay	*Indian*	❷❷④
	Café Japan	*Japanese*	❷❷④
	Jin Kichi	*"*	❷❷❸
	Noho	*Thai*	④④④
	Silks & Spice	*"*	❸❸❸
£15+	Bar Gansa	*Spanish*	❷④❷
	The Little Bay	*International*	④❸②
	It's	*Pizza*	❸❷❸
	PizzaExpress	*"*	❸❸❸
	Chutneys	*Indian*	❸④④
	Diwana B-P House	*"*	❷❷④
	Geeta	*"*	❷❷④

			Rating
	Great Nepalese	*Indian*	❸❷④
	Wagamama	*Japanese*	❸❸❸
	Oriental City	*Pan-Asian*	④④⑤
	Café de Maya	*Thai*	❸❷④
	Street Hawker	"	❸❸❸
£10+	Retsina	*Greek*	④❸④
	Caffè Nero	*Sandwiches, cakes, etc*	❷❸❸
	Yima	*North African*	❷❸❸
£5+	Pret A Manger	*Sandwiches, cakes, etc*	❸❶❸
	Starbucks	"	❸❷❷

Islington, Highgate, Crouch End, Stoke Newington, Finsbury Park, Muswell Hill & Finchley (N postcodes)

			Rating
£35+	Euphorium	*British, Modern*	❷④❸
	Frederick's	"	❷❷❷
	Lola's	"	❸❷❷
	Village Bistro	*French*	❸❸❷
	San Carlo	*Italian*	❸❷❸
	Idaho	*American*	④④❸
£30+	Granita	*British, Modern*	❷❷④
	Jindivick	"	④❸④
	Kavanagh's	"	❷❷❸
	Chez Liline	*Fish & seafood*	❶❸⑤
	Les Associés	*French*	❸❷④
	The White Onion	"	❶❶❷
	The Real Greek	*Greek*	❷❷❸
	Casale Franco	*Italian*	❸⑤❸
	Maremma	"	❸❷❸
	Anna's Place	*Scandinavian*	④❸④
£25+	All Bar One	*British, Modern*	④④④
	Mesclun	"	❶❶❸
	Café Flo	*French*	⑤⑤④
	Café Rouge	"	⑤⑤⑤
	Le Sacré-Coeur	"	❸❸❷
	Soulard	"	❷❶❶
	Cantina Italia	*Italian*	❷❷❸
	Florians	"	❸❸❷
	San Daniele	"	❸❷❸
	Centuria	*Mediterranean*	❸④④
	Rôtisserie	*Steaks & grills*	❸❷④
	Banners	*International*	④④❷
	Hot John's	"	④④④
	Shoreditch ES	"	④⑤⑤
	Toff's	*Fish & chips*	❶❷⑤

	Restaurant	Cuisine	Ratings
	Cuba Libre	Cuban	⑤④❸
	Tbilisi	Georgian	❷❸④
	Rasa	Indian	❶❷❸
	Tiger Lil's	Pan-Asian	⑤⑤④
	Wok Wok	"	④❸④
£20+	The Lord Palmerston	British, Modern	④④❸
	Le Mercury	French	④④❸
	Paris-London Café	"	④❷❸
	Vrisaki	Greek	❷❷❸
	Café Pasta	Italian	④❸④
	Caffè Uno	"	⑤④④
	Calzone	"	④④④
	The Duke of Cambridge	Organic	❸❸❷
	Angel of the North	International	❸❸❸
	Dôme	"	⑤⑤❸
	The Fox Reformed	"	④❸❷
	Pitcher & Piano	"	④④❷
	Two Brothers	Fish & chips	❷❷④
	Ask! Pizza	Pizza	④❸❷
	Santa Fe	American	❸❷❸
	Gallipoli	Turkish	❷❶❷
	Iznik	"	❷❸❶
	Pasha	"	④❶❷
	New Culture Rev'n	Chinese	④❸④
	Rani	Indian	❸❷④
	Bu San	Korean	❸❸④
	Tuk Tuk	Thai	④④❸
	Yum Yum	"	❷❷❷
£15+	Café Mozart	Hungarian	❸④❸
	La Porchetta Pizzeria	Italian	❷❸❷
	La Finca	Spanish	④④❷
	Upper St Fish Shop	Fish & chips	❷❷❸
	PizzaExpress	Pizza	❸❸❸
	La Piragua	South American	❷④❸
	Istanbul Iskembecisi	Turkish	❷❸❸
	Sarcan	"	❸❷❷
	Anglo Asian Tandoori	Indian	❷❷❷
£10+	Afghan Kitchen	Afghani	❷④❸
£5+	Pret A Manger	Sandwiches, cakes, etc	❸❶❸

SOUTH

South Bank
(SE1)

£60+	Le Pont de la Tour	*British, Modern*	④④❷
£40+	Blue Print Café	*British, Modern*	④④❷
	The County Hall	*"*	⑤④④
	Oxo Tower	*"*	④④❷
	The Butlers Wharf Chop-house	*British, Traditional*	④④❸
	Livebait	*Fish & seafood*	❸④⑤
	Cantina del Ponte	*Italian*	④⑤④
	Tentazioni	*"*	❷❷⑤
£35+	The People's Palace	*British, Modern*	④❸④
	Simply Nico	*French*	❸❸④
	Le Pont de la Tour Bar & Grill	*Steaks & grills*	❷❸❷
	Four Regions	*Chinese*	❷①❸
£30+	Archduke Wine Bar	*British, Modern*	⑤④④
	Laughing Gravy	*"*	❸❷❸
	RSJ	*"*	❷❷❸
	Shakespeare's Globe	*"*	④❸④
	fish!	*Fish & seafood*	❷❷④
	Delfina Studio Café	*International*	❸❸❷
	Bengal Clipper	*Indian*	❷❷❸
£25+	All Bar One	*British, Modern*	④④④
	The Apprentice	*"*	❷⑤⑤
	Cantina Vinopolis	*"*	❷❷❷
	The Honest Cabbage	*"*	❸❷④
	The Lavender	*"*	❷❷❸
	Mezzanine	*"*	④❸④
	Sixty Two	*"*	❸❸❸
	The Waterloo Fire Station	*"*	④④④
	Café Rouge	*French*	⑤⑤⑤
	La Lanterna	*Italian*	❸❷❷
	Gourmet Pizza Co.	*Pizza*	❸④④
	Fina Estampa	*South American*	❸❷④
	Kwan Thai	*Thai*	❸❷④
£20+	Meson don Felipe	*Spanish*	❸❸❶
	Tas	*Turkish*	❷❷❸
£15+	PizzaExpress	*Pizza*	❸❸❸
	Pizzeria Castello	*"*	❷❸❸

**Battersea, Clapham, Wandsworth,
Barnes, Putney, Brixton & Lewisham
(All postcodes south of the river except SE1)**

£50+	Putney Bridge	*French*	③③②
£40+	Belair House	*British, Modern*	③③①
	Lobster Pot	*Fish & seafood*	①②③
£35+	Chez Bruce	*British, Modern*	①①②
	The Glasshouse	"	①③③
	Lawn	"	③④③
	Ransome's Dock	"	②②②
	Redmond's	"	②②④
	Sonny's	"	②②②
	The Stepping Stone	"	②②③
	Prego	*Italian*	④③④
	Riva	"	②②④
	Canyon	*American*	④④③
£30+	Buchan's	*British, Modern*	④③③
	Chapter Two	"	③③④
	The Cook House	"	②②④
	Helter Skelter	"	②②④
	Phoenix	"	②②③
	Time	"	③③③
	Ghillies	*Fish & seafood*	③③③
	Moxon's	"	②②④
	Le Bouchon Bordelais	*French*	⑤⑤④
	Le Gothique	"	④③②
	Monsieur Max	"	①②③
	Le Versailles	"	④④④
	Del Buongustaio	*Italian*	①②②
	Enoteca Turi	"	②①③
	Polygon Bar & Grill	*Steaks & grills*	④②③
	Naked Turtle	*International*	③②②
	La Pampa	*Argentinian*	②③②
	Bombay Bicycle Club	*Indian*	②③②
	Café Spice Namaste	"	②③③
	3 Monkeys	"	②③③
	Thailand	*Thai*	②②④
£25+	All Bar One	*British, Modern*	④④④
	Bah Humbug	"	④④①
	The Blue Pumpkin	"	③②③
	Café Med	"	④④③
	The Depot	"	③④②
	Glaisters	"	④④③
	The Lavender	"	②②③
	The Mason's Arms	"	②④②
	The North Pole	"	④④③

			Rating
	Rapscallion	British, Modern	❸②②
	Scoffers	"	❸❸②
	The Stable	"	❸④❸
	The Sun & Doves	"	❸②❸
	Willie Gunn	"	④②②
	La Bouffe	French	④❸④
	Café Rouge	"	⑤⑤⑤
	Gastro	"	④④②
	Newton's	"	⑤④④
	Le P'tit Normand	"	❸②④
	Antipasto & Pasta	Italian	❸❸❸
	Buona Sera	"	❸④②
	Cantinetta Venegazzú	"	❸④❸
	Metrogusto	"	❷❷❸
	Ost. Antica Bologna	"	❸④②
	Pepe Nero	"	④④④
	Tuba	"	❷❸❸
	Café Portugal	Portuguese	❷❷④
	Popeseye	Steaks & grills	❷❷⑤
	La Mancha	Spanish	❸❸②
	La Rueda	"	④❸❸
	Glaisters	International	④④❸
	Basilico	Pizza	❷❸④
	Eco	"	❷④❸
	Eco Brixton	"	❷④❸
	Pizza Metro	"	❶❷❸
	Royal China	Chinese	❷❷④
	Babur Brasserie	Indian	❶❷❸
	Ma Goa	"	❷❷❸
	Sarkhel's	"	❶❷④
	Nancy Lam's Enak Enak	Indonesian	❸⑤④
	Tiger Lil's	Pan-Asian	⑤⑤④
	Wok Wok	"	④❸④
	Chada	Thai	❷❸④
£20+	The Castle	British, Modern	④④❸
	Café de la Place	French	④❸❸
	Emile's	"	❸❸❸
	Arancia	Italian	❷❸④
	Café Pasta	"	④❸④
	Caffè Uno	"	⑤④④
	Barcelona Tapas	Spanish	❸❸②
	don Fernando's	"	❸❸②
	Rebato's	"	❸❷②
	Alma	International	④⑤②
	Hornimans	"	④④④
	Pitcher & Piano	"	④④②
	The Ship	"	❸④②
	Tootsies	Burgers, etc	④❸❸
	Brady's	Fish & chips	❷❸❸

	Heather's	*Vegetarian*	③③③
	Dixie's Bar & Grill	*Mexican/TexMex*	④⑤❷
	Battersea Rickshaw	*Indian*	❸❷④
	Haweli	*"*	❷❷❸
	Indian Ocean	*"*	❷❸❸
	Pukkabar	*"*	❸❷④
	The Old School Thai	*Thai*	❷❶❸
£15+	White Cross Hotel	*British, Modern*	④⑤❶
	La Finca	*Spanish*	④④❷
	Batt. Barge Bistro	*International*	⑤❸❷
	Bellinis	*Pizza*	④❸❸
	PizzaExpress	*"*	❸❸❸
	Boiled Egg	*Sandwiches, cakes, etc*	④④❸
	Escaped Cafe	*Vegetarian*	❸❸④
	Beyoglu	*Turkish*	❸❷④
	Kastoori	*Indian*	❶❷④
	Shree Krishna	*"*	❶④④
	The Pepper Tree	*Thai*	❷❷❸
	Phuket	*"*	❸❷④
£5+	Fileric	*Sandwiches, cakes, etc*	❸❸④
	Starbucks	*"*	❸❷❷

EAST

Smithfield & Farringdon (EC1)

			Rating
£50+	Maison Novelli	French	③④④
£40+	Bubb's	French	④④④
	Novelli EC1	"	④④⑤
	Smiths of Smithfield	Steaks & grills	– – –
	Gaudi	Spanish	③④③
£35+	St John	British, Modern	③③③
	Café du Marché	French	②②①
	Simply Nico	"	③③④
	Hope & Sir Loin	Steaks & grills	②③④
£30+	Dibbens	British, Modern	③②③
	The Peasant	"	③③④
	The Quality Chop House	"	③③④
	Stephen Bull	"	③③④
	Rudland & Stubbs	Fish & seafood	④③④
	Bleeding Heart	French	②②①
	Chez Gérard	"	④③③
	Club Gascon	"	①②②
	Moro	North African	①②②
	Café City Lazeez	Indian	③③②
	Cicada	Pan-Asian	④④③
£25+	Abbaye	Belgian	④④③
	All Bar One	British, Modern	④④④
	Café Med	"	④④③
	Home	"	③②①
	Vic Naylors	"	④④③
	Alba	Italian	②④④
	Mustards Brasserie	International	④④⑤
	Carnevale	Vegetarian	②③④
	East One	Pan-Asian	④④③
	Pacific Spice	"	④④②
£20+	Al's	British, Modern	④④③
	Fox & Anchor	British, Traditional	②④②
	The Eagle	Mediterranean	②④②
	Dôme	International	⑤⑤③
	Ask! Pizza	Pizza	④③②
	Midi	Middle Eastern	④②②
	Japanese Canteen	Japanese	⑤⑤⑤
£15+	Lunch	International	②②④
£5+	Coffee Republic	Sandwiches, cakes, etc	③②②

	Pret A Manger	*Sandwiches, cakes, etc*	③①③
	Starbucks	*"*	③②②

The City & East End
(All E and EC postcodes, except EC1)

£60+	Tatsuso	*Japanese*	①③④
£50+	City Brasserie	*British, Modern*	④③④
	City Rhodes	*"*	②②③
	Gladwins	*"*	②②③
	City Miyama	*Japanese*	②②④
£40+	The Big Chef	*British, Modern*	④④⑤
	1 Lombard Street	*"*	③③②
	Prism	*"*	②③③
	Whittington's	*"*	③④④
	Gow's	*Fish & seafood*	④③④
	Coq d'Argent	*French*	④④③
	Caravaggio	*Italian*	④④④
	Aykoku-Kaku	*Japanese*	③③⑤
	Pacific Oriental	*Pan-Asian*	④④③
	Suan-Neo	*"*	③④⑤
£35+	Bar Bourse	*British, Modern*	③④③
	Searcy's Brasserie	*"*	③③④
	10	*British, Traditional*	③⑤⑤
	The Grapes	*Fish & seafood*	③③③
	Taberna Etrusca	*Italian*	④⑤④
	Gaucho Grill	*Steaks & grills*	②④③
	Brasserie 24	*International*	③③①
	Brasserie Rocque	*"*	④③③
	Singapura	*Malaysian*	③③④
	Tao	*Pan-Asian*	④⑤③
£30+	The Poet	*British, Modern*	④③④
	George & Vulture	*British, Traditional*	④②②
	Ye Olde Cheshire Cheese	*"*	④③②
	Aquarium	*Fish & seafood*	③④③
	Sweetings	*"*	②②①
	Chez Gérard	*French*	④③③
	Luc's Brasserie	*"*	②②②
	Saigon Times	*"*	③③④
	Gt Eastern Dining Room	*Italian*	②②②
	Babe Ruth's	*American*	④④③
	Imperial City	*Chinese*	③③③
	Café Spice Namaste	*Indian*	②③③
	Sri Siam City	*Thai*	②③④
	Sri Thai	*"*	③③③

Price	Name	Cuisine	Rating
£25+	All Bar One	British, Modern	④④④
	Cantaloupe	"	❷❸❶
	Frocks	"	❸❷❷
	The Bow Wine Vaults	British, Traditional	④④④
	Café Flo	French	⑤⑤④
	Café Rouge	"	⑤⑤⑤
	Fuego	Spanish	④④⑤
	Gourmet Pizza Co.	Pizza	❸④④
	Futures	Vegetarian	❸❸❸
	Shimla Pinks	Indian	❸❶❷
	Thon Buri	Thai	❸❸⑤
£20+	Simpson's of Cornhill	British, Traditional	❸❷❷
	Barcelona Tapas	Spanish	❸❸❷
	Dôme	International	⑤⑤❸
	Pitcher & Piano	"	④④❷
	Pizza Pomodoro	Pizza	④④❷
	The Place Below	Vegetarian	❷④❸
	Shanghai	Chinese	❸❷❷
	Café Indiya	Indian	❷❷❸
	Rupee Room	"	❸❸④
	Noto	Japanese	❸❸④
	Moorgate Oriental	Pan-Asian	④❸④
	Yellow River Café	"	– – –
	Silks & Spice	Thai	❸❸❸
£15+	Reynier	British, Traditional	④❷❶
	Arkansas Café	Steaks & grills	❸❸④
	Faulkner's	Fish & chips	❶❸⑤
	PizzaExpress	Pizza	❸❸❸
	Lahore Kebab House	Indian	❶④⑤
	Moshi Moshi Sushi	Japanese	❷❸❸
£10+	Caffè Nero	Sandwiches, cakes, etc	❷❸❸
	Cranks	Vegetarian	④④④
£5+	Coffee Republic	Sandwiches, cakes, etc	❸❷❷
	Eat	"	❷❸❸
	Pret A Manger	"	❸❶❸
	Starbucks	"	❸❷❷
	Soup Opera	Soup	❷❷❸
	Futures	Vegetarian	❷❸ –
£1+	Brick Lane Beigel Bake	Sandwiches, cakes, etc	❷❷④

MAPS

MAP I – LONDON OVERVIEW

A

Oriental City
Food Court

Rani • Solly's
B
Two Brothers
Toff

Mims

M1

_A41_

NORTH

• Café Japan

_A5_

• Laurent

Map 8

I

Quincy's •
Nautilus •

West
Hampstead

• Gung-Ho

Brocca •

Street
Hawker •

Brent

Wembley

Sushi Say •

North Circular Road _A406_

Geeta • Vijay

Kilburn

The Park •

Little Bay •

Regent
Park

2

William IV •

Southeast
• Vale

_A40_

Map 6

Acton

Notting Hill

_M_

WEST

Map 5

← Madhu's Brilliant
← Brilliant

Map 7

Chelsea

3 _M4_

Chiswick

Glasshouse

• Grano

Map 10

Topsy-Tasty •

Christian's •

Kew

Battersea

• Prego

Fulham

• don Fernando's

Putney

4

← White Cross Hotel

• Canyon

Wandsworth

Monsieur Max

Richmond
Park

MAP 1 – LONDON OVERVIEW

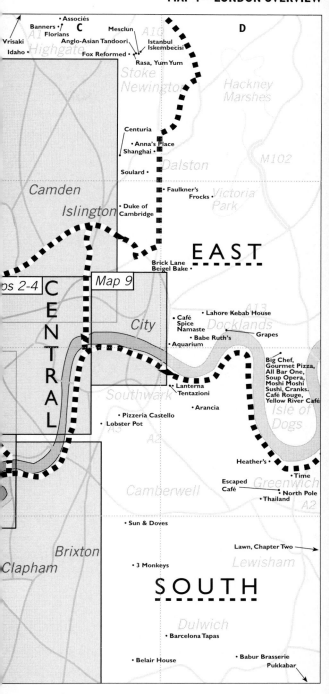

Vrisaki
Idaho •
Banners •
Florians
• Associés
C
Anglo-Asian Tandoori
Fox Reformed •
Mesclun
Istanbul
Iskembecisi
Rasa, Yum Yum
A10
D
Highgate
Stoke
Newington
Hackney
Marshes
M102
Centuria
• Anna's Place
Shanghai •
Soulard •
Dalston
Camden
Islington
• Faulkner's
Frocks •
Victoria
Park
• Duke of
Cambridge
os 2-4
C
Map 9
EAST
Brick Lane
Beigel Bake •
CENTRAL
City
• Lahore Kebab House
• Café
Spice
Namaste
• Babe Ruth's
• Aquarium
A13
Docklands
Grapes
Big Chef,
Gourmet Pizza,
All Bar One,
Soup Opera,
Moshi Moshi
Sushi, Cranks,
Café Rouge,
Yellow River Café
Southwark
•• Lanterna
Tentazioni
• Arancia
Isle of
Dogs
• Pizzeria Castello
• Lobster Pot
Heather's •
• Time
Escaped
Café
• North Pole
• Thailand
Greenwich
A2
Camberwell
• Sun & Doves
Lawn, Chapter Two →
Brixton
Clapham
• 3 Monkeys
Lewisham
SOUTH
Dulwich
• Barcelona Tapas
• Belair House
• Babur Brasserie
Pukkabar

MAP 2 – WEST END OVERVIEW

MAP 2 – WEST END OVERVIEW

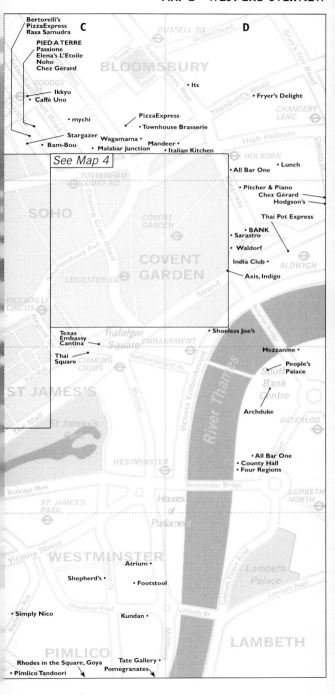

Bertorelli's
PizzaExpress
Rasa Samudra
PIED A TERRE
Passione
Elena's L'Etoile
Noho
Chez Gérard

C

RUSSELL SQ. Guilford Street

Russell Square

Southampton Row

Bernard Street

D

Gray's Inn Road

BLOOMSBURY

Theobald's Road

• Its

• Fryer's Delight

CHANCERY LANE

GOODGE

• Ikkyu
• Caffè Uno

Charlotte Street

Tottenham Court Road

• mychi

PizzaExpress

• Townhouse Brasserie

High Holborn

• Stargazer

Wagamama •

Mandeer •

HOLBORN

• Bam-Bou

• Malabar Junction

• Italian Kitchen

• All Bar One

• Lunch

See Map 4

TOTTENHAM COURT RD.

Charing Cross Road

• Pitcher & Piano
Chez Gérard
Hodgson's

SOHO

COVENT GARDEN

Thai Pot Express

• BANK
• Sarastro

• Waldorf

India Club •

ALDWYCH

COVENT GARDEN

LEICESTER SQ.

Strand

Axis, Indigo

PICCADILLY CIRCUS

Regent Street

Haymarket

Shaftesbury Avenue

• Shoeless Joe's

Texas Embassy Cantina

Trafalgar Square

EMBANKMENT

Mezzanine •

Thai Square

CHARING CROSS

Northumberland Av.

Victoria Embankment

People's Palace

South Bank Centre

ST JAMES'S

The Mall

Pall Mall

Archduke

WATERLOO

St James's Park

River Thames

WESTMINSTER

Whitehall

• All Bar One
• County Hall
• Four Regions

Westminster Bridge

LAMBETH NORTH

Birdcage Walk

ST. JAMES'S PARK

Houses of Parliament

Victoria Street

WESTMINSTER

Atrium •

Shepherd's •

• Footstool

Lambeth Palace

Rochester Row

Horseferry Road

Kundan

Lambeth Palace Road

• Simply Nico

Millbank

Lambeth Br.

LAMBETH

PIMLICO

Tate Gallery •

Rhodes in the Square, Goya

Pomegranates

• Pimlico Tandoori

MAP 3 – MAYFAIR, ST JAMES'S & WEST SOHO

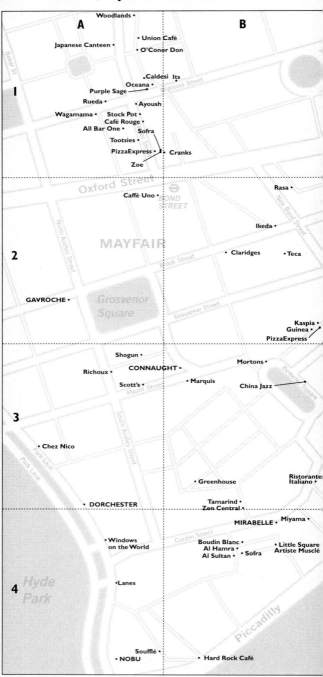

Woodlands •

A   **B**

• Union Café

Japanese Canteen •   • O'Conor Don

•Caldesi Its

1   Oceana •

Purple Sage •

Rueda •   • Ayoush

Wagamama •   Stock Pot •

Café Rouge •

All Bar One •   **Sofra**

Tootsies •

PizzaExpress • • Cranks

Zoe •

Oxford Street

Caffè Uno •   BOND STREET

Rasa •

Ikeda •

MAYFAIR

2   • Claridges   • Teca

GAVROCHE •

Kaspia •
Guinea •
PizzaExpress •

Shogun •

Mortons •

Richoux •   **CONNAUGHT** •

China Jazz

Scott's •   • Marquis

3

• Chez Nico

Ristorante
Italiano •

• Greenhouse

Tamarind •
Zen Central •

MIRABELLE • • Miyama •

• DORCHESTER

Boudin Blanc •
Al Hamra • • Sofra   • Little Square
Artiste Musclé
Al Sultan •

• Windows
on the World

4   •Lanes

**Hyde
Park**

Soufflé •
• NOBU   • Hard Rock Café

MAP 3 – MAYFAIR, ST JAMES'S & WEST SOHO

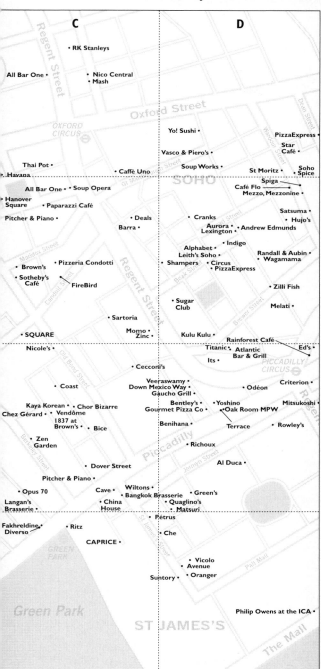

C

D

RK Stanleys

All Bar One

Nico Central
Mash

Oxford Street

Yo! Sushi

PizzaExpress

Star Café

Vasco & Piero's

Thai Pot

Soup Works

St Moritz

Soho Spice

Havana

Caffè Uno

Spiga

SOHO

All Bar One

Soup Opera

Café Flo

Mezzo, Mezzonine

Hanover Square

Paparazzi Café

Satsuma

Pitcher & Piano

Deals

Cranks

Hujo's

Barra

Aurora

Andrew Edmunds

Lexington

Indigo

Alphabet

Leith's Soho

Randall & Aubin

Shampers

Circus

Wagamama

Brown's

Pizzeria Condotti

PizzaExpress

Sotheby's Café

FireBird

Zilli Fish

Sugar Club

Melati

Sartoria

SQUARE

Momo

Zinc

Kulu Kulu

Rainforest Café

Nicole's

Titanic

Atlantic Bar & Grill

Ed's

Its

PICCADILLY CIRCUS

Cecconi's

Coast

Veeraswamy

Down Mexico Way

Gaucho Grill

Odéon

Criterion

Kaya Korean

Chor Bizarre

Bentley's

Yoshino

Mitsukoshi

Chez Gérard

Vendôme

Gourmet Pizza Co

Oak Room MPW

1837 at Brown's

Bice

Benihana

Terrace

Rowley's

Zen Garden

Richoux

Dover Street

Al Duca

Pitcher & Piano

Opus 70

Cave

Wiltons

Green's

Langan's Brasserie

Bangkok Brasserie

Quaglino's

China House

Matsuri

Fakhreldine

Pétrus

Diverso

Ritz

Che

CAPRICE

GREEN PARK

Vicolo

Avenue

Suntory

Oranger

Green Park

ST JAMES'S

Philip Owens at the ICA

The Mall

MAP 4 – EAST SOHO, CHINATOWN & COVENT GARDEN

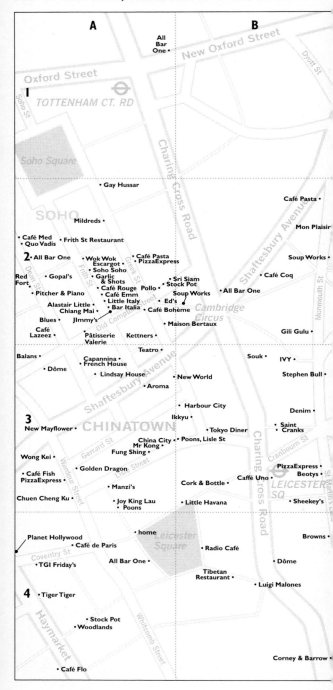

A

B

All Bar One •

New Oxford Street

Oxford Street

Dyott St

TOTTENHAM CT. RD

Soho St

Charing Cross Road

Soho Square

• Gay Hussar

Café Pasta •

SOHO

Mon Plaisir

Mildreds •

• Café Med
• Quo Vadis • Frith St Restaurant

Shaftesbury Avenue

Soup Works •

2 • All Bar One

Frith St

• Wok Wok • Café Pasta
Escargot • PizzaExpress
• Soho Soho

• Café Coq

Red
Fort • Gopal's

• Garlic
& Shots
• Café Rouge Pollo
• Café Emm

• Sri Siam
Stock Pot
Soup Works • • All Bar One

Monmouth St

• Pitcher & Piano

• Little Italy
• Bar Italia

• Ed's

Cambridge
Circus

Alastair Little •
Chiang Mai •

Old Compton St

• Café Bohème

Blues • JImmy's

• Maison Bertaux

Gili Gulu •

Café
Lazeez •

Pâtisserie
Valerie

Kettners •

Teatro •

Balans •

Capannina •
• French House

Souk • IVY •

• Dôme

• Lindsay House

Shaftesbury Avenue

• New World

Stephen Bull •

• Aroma

• Harbour City

Denim •

3

Ikkyu •

• Saint
• Cranks

New Mayflower • CHINATOWN

China City
Mr Kong •

• Tokyo Diner
Poons, Lisle St

Charing Cross Road

Gerrard St

Fung Shing •

Cranbourn St

PizzaExpress •

Wong Kei •

Wardour Street

• Golden Dragon

Caffè Uno •

Beotys •
LEICESTER

• Café Fish
PizzaExpress •

• Manzi's

Cork & Bottle •

SQ

St Martins La

Chuen Cheng Ku •

• Joy King Lau
• Poons

• Little Havana

• Sheekey's

• home

Leicester
Square

Browns •

Planet Hollywood

• Café de Paris

• Radio Café

Coventry St

• All Bar One

• Dôme

• TGI Friday's

Tibetan
Restaurant •

• Luigi Malones

4 • Tiger Tiger

Haymarket

• Stock Pot
• Woodlands

Whitcomb Street

• Café Flo

Corney & Barrow •

MAP 4 – EAST SOHO, CHINATOWN & COVENT GARDEN

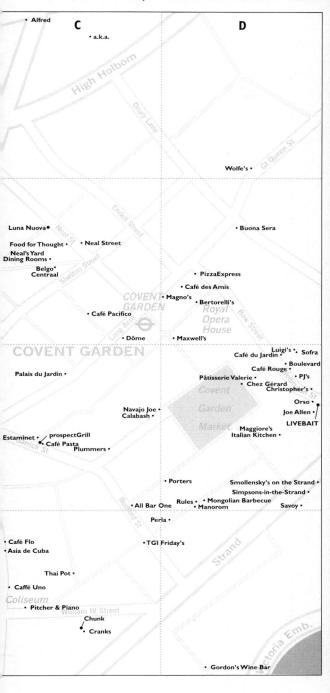

• Alfred

C

D

• a.k.a.

High Holborn

Drury Lane

Gt Queen St

Wolfe's •

Endell Street

Luna Nuova•

• Buona Sera

Neal St

• Food for Thought •   • Neal Street

Neal's Yard
Dining Rooms •

Shelton Street

Belgo•
Centraal

• PizzaExpress

COVENT
GARDEN

• Café des Amis

• Magno's

• Bertorelli's

Royal
Opera
House

• Café Pacifico

Long Acre

Bow Street

• Dôme

• Maxwell's

COVENT GARDEN

Luigi's • • Sofra

Café du Jardin •

• Boulevard

Café Rouge •

Palais du Jardin •

Pâtisserie Valerie •   • PJ's

• Chez Gérard

Christopher's •

Covent

Orso •

Navajo Joe •
Calabash •

Garden

Joe Allen •

LIVEBAIT

Market

Maggiore's
Italian Kitchen •

Estaminet • • prospectGrill

Garrick St

• Café Pasta

Plummers •

• Porters

Smollensky's on the Strand •

Simpsons-in-the-Strand •

Bedford St

Rules • • Mongolian Barbecue

• All Bar One

Savoy •

• Manorom

Perla •

Strand

• Café Flo

•Asia de Cuba

• TGI Friday's

Thai Pot •

• Caffé Uno

Coliseum

• Pitcher & Piano

William IV Street

Chunk

Victoria Emb.

• Cranks

• Gordon's Wine Bar

MAP 5 – KNIGHTSBRIDGE, CHELSEA & SOUTH KENSINGTON

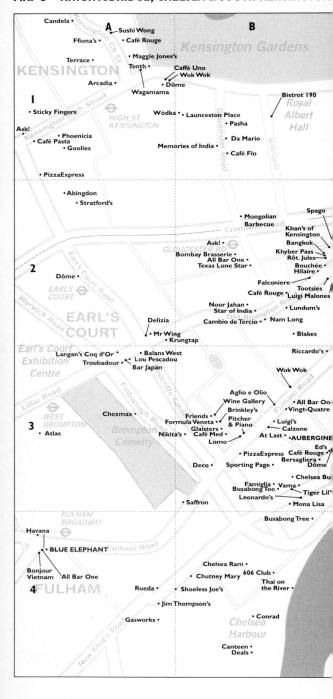

Candela •

A — Sushi Wong

Ffiona's •

Café Rouge

Kensington Gardens

B

• Maggie Jones's

Terrace •

Tenth •

Caffè Uno

KENSINGTON

Wok Wok

Arcadia •

• Dôme

Wagamama

Bistrot 190

Royal Albert Hall

1

• Sticky Fingers

HIGH ST. KENSINGTON

Wódka • • Launceston Place

• Pasha

• Ask!

• Da Mario

• Phoenicia

• Café Pasta

Memories of India •

• Café Flo

• Goolies

• PizzaExpress

• Abingdon

• Stratford's

Cromwell Road

• Mongolian Barbecue

Spago

Khan's of Kensington

GLOUCESTER RD.

Ask! •

Bangkok

Bombay Brasserie •

Khyber Pass

All Bar One •

Rôt. Jules •

Texas Lone Star •

Bouchée Hilaire •

2

Dôme •

Falconiere •

Tootsies

Café Rouge • Luigi Malones •

EARL'S COURT

Noor Jahan •

Star of India •

• Lundum's

EARL'S COURT

Cambio de Tercio •

• Nam Long

Delizia •

• Blakes

• Mr Wing

Krungtap •

'Earl's Court' Exhibition Centre

Langan's Coq d'Or •

• Balans West

Riccardo's •

Troubadour •

Lou Pescadou

Bar Japan •

Wok Wok

Aglio e Olio •

Wine Gallery •

• All Bar One

Brinkley's •

• Vingt-Quatre

Chezmax •

Friends •

Pitcher & Piano •

Formula Veneta •

• Luigi's

Calzone

3

WEST BROMPTON

Glaisters •

• Atlas

Nikita's •

Café Med •

At Last •

• AUBERGINE

Lomo •

Ed's •

Café Rouge •

• PizzaExpress

Bersagliera •

Deco •

Sporting Page •

Dôme •

• Chelsea Bu

Famiglia •

Vama •

Busabong Too •

Tiger Lil'

Leonardo's •

• Mona Lisa

• Saffron

Busabong Tree •

FULHAM BROADWAY

Havana •

• BLUE ELEPHANT Fulham Road

Bonjour Vietnam •

Chelsea Ram •

606 Club •

All Bar One

Chutney Mary •

4

FULHAM

Thai on the River •

Rueda •

• Shoeless Joe's

• Jim Thompson's

• Conrad

Gasworks •

Chelsea Harbour

Canteen •

Deals •

MAP 5 – KNIGHTSBRIDGE, CHELSEA & SOUTH KENSINGTON

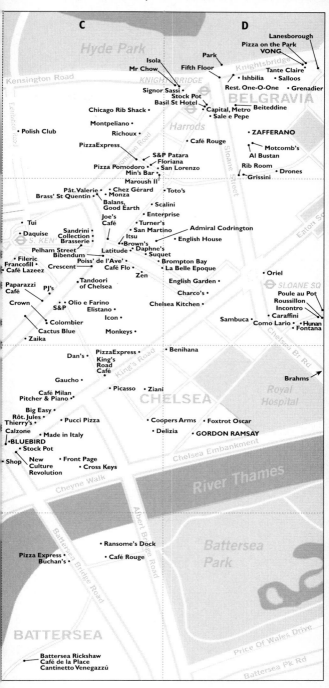

C

D

Hyde Park

Kensington Road

Lanesborough
Pizza on the Park
VONG

Park
Fifth Floor
Isola
Mr Chow
KNIGHTSBRIDGE
Knightsbridge
Tante Claire
• Ishbilia   • Salloos
Rest. One-O-One   • Grenadier
BELGRAVIA

Signor Sassi •
Stock Pot
Basil St Hotel •
• Capital, Metro   Beiteddine
• Sale e Pepe

Chicago Rib Shack •

Harrods

Montpeliano •
Richoux •
• Café Rouge

• ZAFFERANO

• Polish Club
PizzaExpress •
Motcomb's •
Al Bustan
S&P Patara
Floriana
Pizza Pomodoro •   • San Lorenzo
Min's Bar •
Rib Room •
• Drones
• Grissini

Pât.Valerie •   • Chez Gérard   • Toto's
Brass' St Quentin • • Monza
Balans,
Good Earth •
Joe's
Café •
• Enterprise
• Scalini

• Tui
• Turner's
Sandrini
Collection •   • San Martino
Admiral Codrington

• Daquise
Brasserie
Itsu
• English House

Pelham Street
Latitude •   • Daphne's
Bibendum
Poiss' de l'Ave' •   • Suquet
• Fileric
Francofill •   Crescent •   • Café Flo
• Café Lazeez
Zen
• Brompton Bay
• La Belle Epoque
• Oriel

Paparazzi
Café •
Tandoori
of Chelsea •
English Garden •

PJ's •
SLOANE SQ
Poule au Pot
Olio e Farino •
Charco's •
Roussillon •
Crown •
S&P •
Elistano •
Chelsea Kitchen •
Incontro
• Caraffini
• Colombier
Icon •
Sambuca •
Como Lario •   • Hunan
Cactus Blue •
Monkeys •
• Fontana
• Zaika

• Benihana

Dan's •
PizzaExpress •
King's
Road
Café
Brahms

Gaucho •
• Picasso   • Ziani
Royal
Hospital

Café Milan
Pitcher & Piano •
CHELSEA

Big Easy •
Rôt. Jules •
Thierry's •   • Pucci Pizza
• Coopers Arms   • Foxtrot Oscar
Calzone •
• Delizia   • GORDON RAMSAY
•BLUEBIRD   • Made in Italy
• Stock Pot
Shop •
New
Culture
Revolution
• Front Page
• Cross Keys

Chelsea Embankment

Cheyne Walk

River Thames

Battersea
Park
• Ransome's Dock

Pizza Express •
• Café Rouge
Buchan's •

BATTERSEA

Price Of Wales Drive

Battersea Rickshaw
Café de la Place
Cantinetto Venegazzú •

Battersea Pk Rd

MAP 6 – NOTTING HILL & BAYSWATER

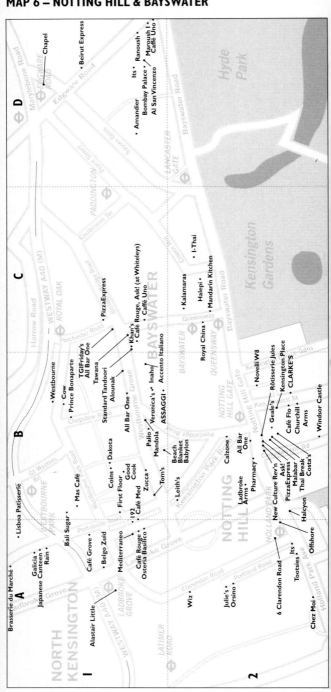

MAP 7 – HAMMERSMITH & CHISWICK

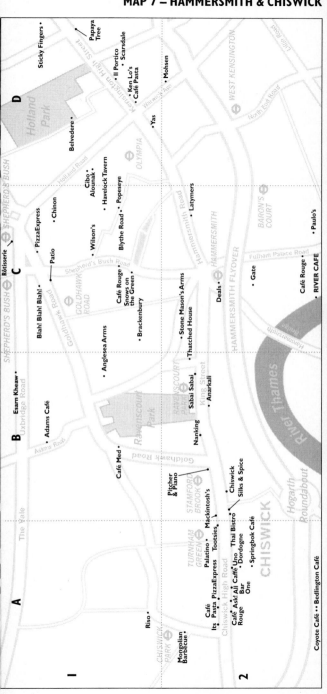

SHEPHERD'S BUSH ⊖ · Rôtisserie · ⊖ SHEPHERD'S BUSH

Sticky Fingers ·

· Papaya Tree

Il Portico · · Scarsdale
Ken Lo's · Café Pasta

· Mohsen

WEST KENSINGTON

Holland Park

Belvedere ·

· Yas

Cibo · Alounak ·
· Havelock Tavern

PizzaExpress ·
Chinon ·

Wilson's · Blythe Road · · Popeseye

Patio ·

OLYMPIA

HAMMERSMITH ROAD

GOLDHAWK ROAD

Blah! Blah! Blah! ·

Café Rouge · Snows on the Green ·
· Brackenbury

Anglesea Arms ·

· Stone Mason's Arms
· Thatched House

Latymers

BARON'S COURT ⊖

· Paulo's

Deals ⊖

Gate ·

Café Rouge · · RIVER CAFE

Fulham Palace Road

HAMMERSMITH FLYOVER

HAMMERSMITH ⊖

RAVENSCOURT ⊖

Ravenscourt Park

Sabai Sabai ·
· Anarkali

King Street

Nanking ·

Café Med ·

River Thames

Askew Road

Goldhawk Road

Esarn Kheaw ·

Adams Café ·

Uxbridge Road

STAMFORD BROOK ⊖

Pitcher & Piano ·

The Vale

Hogarth Roundabout

Mackintosh's ·

Chiswick · · Silks & Spice

TURNHAM GREEN ⊖

Palatino · · Tootsies

Café · PizzaExpress
Its Pasta

Chiswick High Road

Café Aski Ali · Caffé Uno · Thai Bistro
Rouge Bar · Dordogne
One

· Springbok Café

CHISWICK

CHISWICK PARK ⊖

Riso ·

Mongolian Barbecue ·

Coyote Café · · Bedlington Café

MAP 8 – HAMPSTEAD, CAMDEN TOWN & ISLINGTON

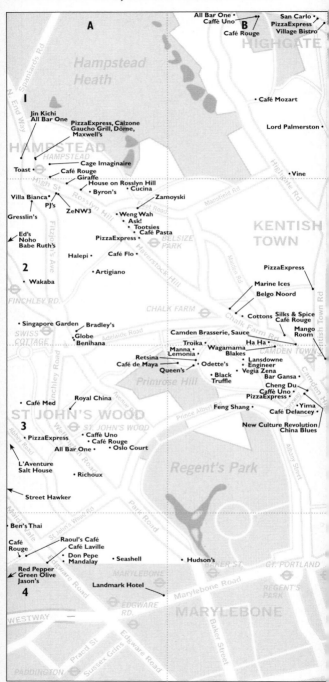

A

HIGHGATE

All Bar One •
Caffè Uno •
Café Rouge

B

San Carlo •
PizzaExpress •
Village Bistro •

Hampstead Heath

• Café Mozart

Lord Palmerston •

I

Jin Kichi •
All Bar One •
PizzaExpress, Calzone
Gaucho Grill, Dôme,
Maxwell's

HAMPSTEAD

Toast •

Cage Imaginaire

Café Rouge

Giraffe

House on Rosslyn Hill

• Byron's • Cucina

Zamoyski •

• Vine

Villa Bianca •

PJ's

ZeNW3

Weng Wah •

• Ask!

Tootsies •

• Café Pasta

KENTISH
TOWN

Gresslin's •

Ed's •
Noho •
Babe Ruth's

PizzaExpress •

Halepi •

• Café Flo

PizzaExpress •

2

• Wakaba

• Artigiano

Marine Ices

Belgo Noord

FINCHLEY RD.

CHALK FARM

Cottons •

Silks & Spice
Café Rouge

• Singapore Garden

Bradley's

SWISS
COTTAGE

Globe
Benihana

Camden Brasserie, Sauce

Troika •

Mango
Room

Manna •
Lemonia •

Wagamama •
Blakes •

Ha Ha •

CAMDEN TOWN

Retsina •

Café de Maya •

Queen's •

• Odette's

Lansdowne •
Engineer •
Vegia Zena •

Bar Gansa •

• Black
Truffle

Cheng Du •

Primrose Hill

Caffè Uno •
PizzaExpress •

ST JOHN'S WOOD

Royal China •

• Café Med

3

Feng Shang •

• Yima
Café Delancey •

New Culture Revolution
China Blues

• PizzaExpress

• Caffè Uno

• Café Rouge

All Bar One •

• Oslo Court

ST. JOHN'S WOOD

L'Aventure •
Salt House •

• Richoux

Regent's Park

→ Street Hawker

• Ben's Thai

Café •
Rouge

Raoul's Café •
Café Laville •

• Don Pepe
• Mandalay

• Seashell

• Hudson's

GT. PORTLAND

Red Pepper •
Green Olive •
Jason's

MARYLEBONE

Landmark Hotel •

REGENT'S
PARK

4

EDGWARE
RD.

Marylebone Road

MARYLEBONE

WESTWAY

PADDINGTON

MAP 8 – HAMPSTEAD, CAMDEN TOWN & ISLINGTON

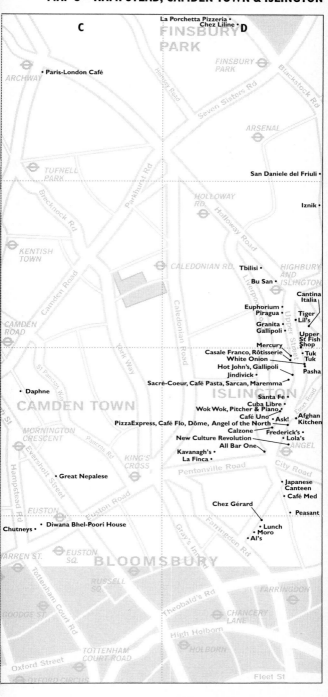

C

D

La Porchetta Pizzeria •
Chez Liline •

FINSBURY PARK

FINSBURY PARK

ARCHWAY

• Paris-London Café

Hornsey Road

Blackstock Rd

Seven Sisters Rd

ARSENAL

TUFNELL PARK

Parkhurst Rd

HOLLOWAY RD.

San Daniele del Friuli •

Brecknock Rd

KENTISH TOWN

Holloway Road

Iznik •

Camden Road

CALEDONIAN RD.

HIGHBURY AND ISLINGTON

Tbilisi •

Bu San •

Caledonian Road

York Way

Liverpool Rd

Cantina Italia

Euphorium •
Piragua •

Tiger •
Lil's •

St Pancras Way

Granita •
Gallipoli •

Upper St Fish Shop

CAMDEN ROAD

Mercury •

Casale Franco, Rôtisserie •
White Onion

• Tuk Tuk

• Daphne

Hot John's, Gallipoli •

Upper Street

Pasha

Jindivick •

Sacré-Coeur, Café Pasta, Sarcan, Maremma •

ISLINGTON

CAMDEN TOWN

Santa Fe •

Essex Road

Cuba Libre •

MORNINGTON CRESCENT

Wok Wok, Pitcher & Piano •

Café Uno • Ask!

Afghan Kitchen

Pancras Rd

PizzaExpress, Café Flo, Dôme, Angel of the North •

Hampstead Rd

Eversholt Street

Calzone •
Frederick's •

• Lola's

New Culture Revolution •

ANGEL

All Bar One •

KING'S CROSS

Kavanagh's •
La Finca •

Pentonville Road

City Road

• Great Nepalese

EUSTON

Japanese Canteen •

• Café Med

Chez Gérard •

• Peasant

• Diwana Bhel-Poori House

Euston Road

Chutneys •

Gray's Inn Rd

Farringdon Road

• Lunch
• Moro
• Al's

WARREN ST.

EUSTON SQ.

BLOOMSBURY

RUSSELL SQ.

FARRINGDON

Tottenham Court Rd

GOODGE ST.

Theobald's Rd

CHANCERY LANE

High Holborn

TOTTENHAM COURT ROAD

HOLBORN

Oxford Street

OXFORD CIRCUS

Fleet St

MAP 9 – THE CITY

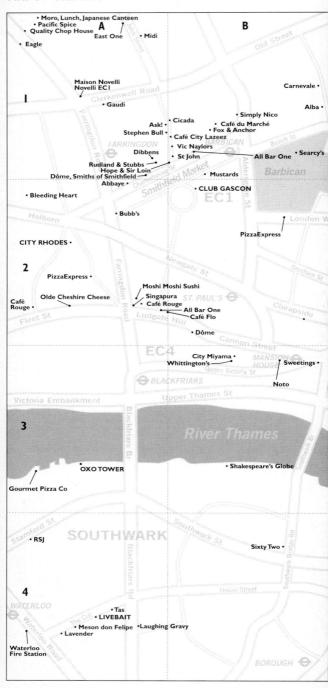

- Moro, Lunch, Japanese Canteen
- Pacific Spice
- Quality Chop House
  East One • Midi
- Eagle

A   **B**

Old Street

Maison Novelli
Novelli EC1

Carnevale •

Alba •

Clerkenwell Road

I

• Gaudi

• Simply Nico

Ask! • • Cicada   • Café du Marché
Stephen Bull   • Fox & Anchor
        • Café City Lazeez
Dibbens   • Vic Naylors
FARRINGDON   • St John   All Bar One • Searcy's
Rudland & Stubbs
Hope & Sir Loin
Dôme, Smiths of Smithfield
Abbaye •   • Mustards

Beech St

Barbican

Aldersgate St

• Bleeding Heart

Holborn

• **CLUB GASCON**

EC1

London W

• Bubb's

PizzaExpress •

CITY RHODES •

2

PizzaExpress •

Newgate St

Gresham St

Olde Cheshire Cheese

Moshi Moshi Sushi
Singapura   ST. PAUL'S
• Café Rouge   Cheapside

Café
Rouge •
Fleet St   All Bar One •
        Café Flo

Ludgate Hill

Farringdon Road

• Dôme

Cannon Street

EC4

Mansion House

City Miyama •
Whittington's •
    Queen Victoria St
BLACKFRIARS

• Sweetings •

Noto

Victoria Embankment

Blackfriars Br

Upper Thames St

3

River Thames

OXO TOWER

• Shakespeare's Globe

Southwark Br

Gourmet Pizza Co

Stamford St

SOUTHWARK

Southwark St

• RSJ

Sixty Two •

Southwark Bridge Rd

Union Street

4

WATERLOO

The Cut
• Tas
• **LIVEBAIT**
• Meson don Felipe • Laughing Gravy
• Lavender

Waterloo Road

Waterloo
Fire Station

BOROUGH

MAP 9 – THE CITY

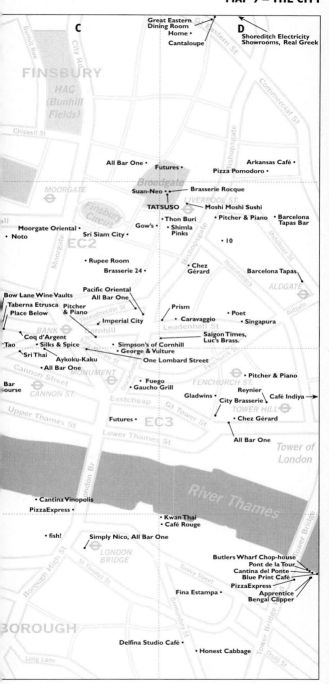

C

D

Great Eastern
Dining Room •
Home •
Cantaloupe •

Shoreditch Electricity
Showrooms, Real Greek

FINSBURY

HAC
(Bunhill
Fields)

Chiswell St

All Bar One •   Futures •

Arkansas Café •
Pizza Pomodoro •

Broadgate

MOORGATE

Brasserie Rocque

Suan-Neo •   LIVERPOOL ST.
TATSUSO •   • Moshi Moshi Sushi

Finsbury
Circus

• Thon Buri   • Pitcher & Piano   • Barcelona
Gow's •   Tapas Bar

Moorgate Oriental •
• Noto

Sri Siam City •

• Shimla
Pinks

EC2

• 10

• Rupee Room

Brasserie 24 •

• Chez
Gérard

Barcelona Tapas •

ALDGATE

Pacific Oriental
Bow Lane Wine Vaults   All Bar One
Taberna Etrusca   Pitcher
Place Below   & Piano

• Prism

Imperial City   • Caravaggio

• Poet
• Singapura

• Coq d'Argent

Saigon Times,
Luc's Brass.

Tao •   • Silks & Spice   • Simpson's of Cornhill
Sri Thai •   Aykoku-Kaku   • George & Vulture
• All Bar One   One Lombard Street

Cannon Street
BANK

MONUMENT

• Pitcher & Piano

Bar
:ourse   CANNON ST.

• Fuego
• Gaucho Grill

FENCHURCH ST.

Reynier   Café Indiya →

Eastcheap   Gt Tower St   Gladwins •   City Brasserie   TOWER HILL

Upper Thames St

Lower Thames St

Futures •   EC3

• Chez Gérard

All Bar One

Tower of
London

River Thames

• Cantina Vinopolis
PizzaExpress •

• Kwan Thai
• Café Rouge

• fish!   Simply Nico, All Bar One

LONDON
BRIDGE

Butlers Wharf Chop-house
Pont de la Tour
Cantina del Ponte
Blue Print Café
PizzaExpress
Apprentice
Bengal Clipper

Fina Estampa •

BOROUGH

Delfina Studio Café •

• Honest Cabbage

Long Lane

MAP 10 – SOUTH LONDON (AND FULHAM)

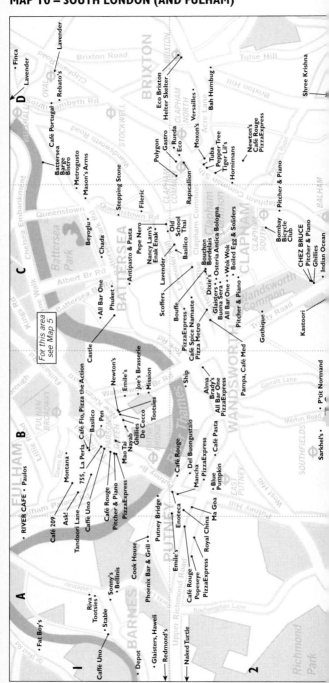